T0374646

Catherine of Aragon

Catherine of Aragon

Infanta of Spain, Queen of England

THERESA EARENFIGHT

The Pennsylvania State University Press
University Park, Pennsylvania

Library of Congress Cataloging-in-Publication Data

Names: Earenfight, Theresa, 1954– author.
Title: Catherine of Aragon : infanta of Spain, queen of England / Theresa Earenfight.
Description: University Park, Pennsylvania : The Pennsylvania State University Press, [2021] | Includes bibliographical references and index.
Summary: "Examines the life of Catherine of Aragon, focusing on her personal possessions and the items she bequeathed to those she left behind, to better understand her as a daughter, wife, widow, mother, and friend; a collector of art and books; a devout Catholic; and a patron of writers and universities"—Provided by publisher.
Identifiers: LCCN 2021027721 | ISBN 9780271091648 (cloth)
Subjects: LCSH: Catherine, of Aragon, Queen, consort of Henry VIII, King of England, 1485–1536. | Queens—England—Biography. | Great Britain—History—Henry VIII, 1509–1547.
Classification: LCC DA333.A6 E27 2021 | DDC 942.05/2092 [B]—dc23
LC record available at https://lccn.loc.gov /2021027721

Parts of chapter 2 are based on "The Shoes of an *Infanta*: Bringing the Sensuous, Not Sensible, 'Spanish Style' of Catherine of Aragon to Tudor England," in *Moving Women Moving Objects (400–1500)*, ed. Tracy Chapman Hamilton and Mariah Proctor-Tiffany (Leiden: Brill, 2019), 293–317; parts of chapter 4 are based on "Two Bodies, One Spirit: Isabel and Fernando's Construction of Monarchical Partnership," in *Queen Isabel I of Castile: Power, Patronage, Persona*, ed. Barbara Weissberger (Woodbridge, UK: Boydell and Brewer, 2008), 3–18; parts of chapter 5 are based on "Regarding Catherine of Aragon," in *Scholars and Poets Talk About Queens*, ed. Carole Levin and Christine Stewart-Nuñez (New York: Palgrave Macmillan, 2015), 137–57; parts of chapter 7 are based on "A Lifetime of Power: Beyond Binaries of Gender," in *Medieval Elite Women and the Exercise of Power, 1100–1400: Moving Beyond the Exceptionalist Debate*, ed. Heather J. Tanner (Cham, Switzerland: Palgrave Macmillan, 2019), 271–93.

Copyright © 2021 Theresa Earenfight
All rights reserved
Printed in the United States of America
Published by The Pennsylvania State University Press, University Park, PA 16802–1003

The Pennsylvania State University Press is a member of the Association of University Presses.

It is the policy of The Pennsylvania State University Press to use acid-free paper. Publications on uncoated stock satisfy the minimum requirements of American National Standard for Information Sciences—Permanence of Paper for Printed Library Material, ANSI Z39.48–1992.

CONTENTS

Where to begin?

With Nicki Vedo, because it all began with her independent study project over a decade ago. Our frustration at Catherine's neglect by scholars led to her paper and to this book.

Countless colleagues at conferences heard this book take shape and generously critiqued my ideas in the Q&A, at the conference banquet, and in many pubs, bars, and coffee shops—Michelle Armstrong-Partida, Charles Beem, Janna Bianchini, Simon Doubleday, Irina Dumistrescu, and colleagues at the workshop on charisma at the University of Bonn, Christine Merie Fox, Tracy Chapman Hamilton, Marie Kelleher, Beth Kunz, Carole Levin, Amy Livingstone, Sara McDougall, Susan McDonough, Allison Machlis Meyer, Lucy Pick, Mariah Proctor-Tiffany, Miriam Shadis, Núria Silleras-Fernández, Zita Rohr, and Ellie Woodacre. Many thanks to my colleagues at Seattle University and the University of Puget Sound. All of chapter 2 owes a debt to the NEH Mediterranean Seminar in 2008 organized by Brian Catlos and Sharon Kinoshita, and the section on Catherine's pregnancies in chapter 4 could not have been written without Monica Green, Rachel Scott, and my colleagues at the NEH summer seminar at the Wellcome Institute in London in 2012. Thank you, Gordon Thompson, for creating beautiful maps of the places Catherine inhabited. Dev McCauley's careful reading of the still rough but nearly final draft and her superb design talents helped me sort out the images and inspired the final stages of this project. And thanks to Ellie Goodman, editor at Penn State University Press, and the two anonymous readers for the Press, whose sharp eyes and intellect guided final revisions and made the book so much stronger.

To family and friends, you listened as I brainstormed and were my first audience for all the ideas in this book. To Warren Wilkins, who has been part of this project since Catherine first took hold of my imagination, boundless love for sharing the journey.

Key research took place beyond libraries, archives, and museums. Heartfelt thanks go to Chiyo Ishikawa, former Susan Brotman Deputy Director for Art and Curator of European Painting and Sculpture at the Seattle Art Museum, for her keen eye and insights into art at the courts of Isabel of Castile and Marguerite of Austria. Ana Cabrera LaFuente of the Museo del Traje in Madrid and the curators at the Clothworkers Centre of the Victoria and Albert Museum in London generously shared their expertise on early modern Spanish blackstitch embroidery. I am indebted to countless other museum curators and conservators who have tended carefully and expertly the objects and portraits of Catherine in the United Kingdom at British Library, the National Portrait Gallery in London, the Museum of London, Shropshire Museums, and the National Trust; and in Madrid at the Prado Museum, the Thyssen-Bornemisza, and the Museo Arqueológico Nacional.

My travels in England and Spain for this book were enlivened and enriched by two sisters, Anne and Susan Webb, dear friends and fellow travelers with a sense of adventure and a love of laughter. Like Catherine of Aragon, they bear traces of both Spain and England. Both were born and raised in Barcelona. Anne now lives in England, and with her keen eye on the road, we drove across England and Wales, to some of the most beautiful landscapes imaginable, in search of traces of Catherine. It was Anne who said, when we were in Ludlow, "Look, that local museum is only a pound. Let's pop in." That spontaneous, casual act led me to an important remnant of Catherine. Susan, in Barcelona, has been my guide to life in Spain since 1981. This book began to take shape from her flat up near Tibidabo over hundreds of wide-ranging and often raucous conversations over dinner on a balcony with a view of the city. Their mother, Joan Webb, sheltered me when I came to Barcelona for an undergraduate study abroad trip and welcomed me into her life like an adopted child. She was my other mother, who taught me more than I can possibly recount. An Englishwoman who grew up in France and spent part of World War II in England, she moved to Spain just because she wanted to learn Spanish. She stayed, of course, and the expansive worldview of her and her children is not unlike that of Catherine—shaped by landscapes and language, culturally rich, and emotionally resonant. Without Joan, Susan, and Anne this book could not have been possible, and it is to them that it is dedicated.

Map 1 | Locations in Spain. © Gordon Thompson 2020.

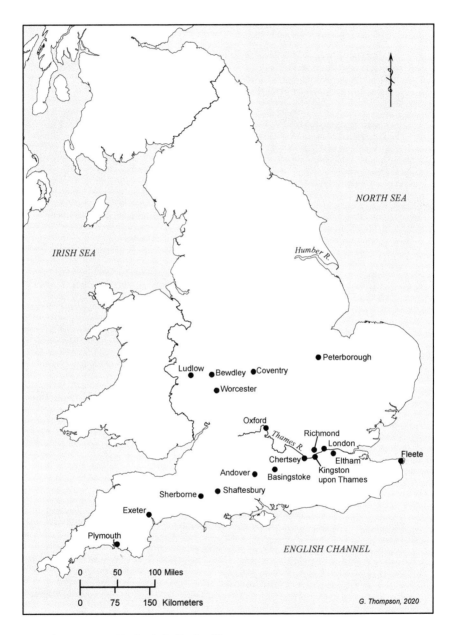

NORTH SEA

IRISH SEA

Humber R.

● Peterborough

Ludlow ● ● Bewdley ● Coventry

● Worcester

Oxford ●

Richmond ●

Thames R. London ●

Chertsey ● ● Eltham ● Fleete

Andover ● Kingston upon Thames

Basingstoke ●

Sherborne ● ● Shaftesbury

Exeter ●

Plymouth ●

ENGLISH CHANNEL

0   50   100 Miles

0   75   150 Kilometers

G. Thompson, 2020

Map 2 | Locations in England. © Gordon Thompson 2020.

CHAPTER 1

Who's That Girl?

Well, that's how it is, can you tell what goes on
within by looking at what happens without? There
may be a great fire in our soul, but no one ever
comes to warm himself by it, all that passers-by can
see is a little smoke coming out of the chimney, and
they walk on.

—Vincent van Gogh, July 1880

This book began with a pair of shoes (fig. 1). I found them by accident. I
was looking for information on the women in Catherine of Aragon's entourage who traveled with her to England in 1501 when she went to marry
Arthur, the eldest son of King Henry VII of England (1457, r. 1485–1509)
and his wife, Elizabeth of York (1466–1503). I turned to the records of
payments to Catherine's servants and attendants that were kept by Gonzalo
de Baeza, treasurer to Catherine's mother, Queen Isabel of Castile (b. 1451, r.
1474–1504). This record book, edited and published as *Cuentas de Gonzalo
Baeza: Tesorero de Isabel la Católica*, is more than just a ledger. It is a trea-
sure trove of life at the Spanish court from 1477 to 1504. Along with the
names and salaries of Catherine's attendants, Baeza recorded payments
to her shoemakers, Diego de Valencia and Diego de Madrid. They had
been making her shoes since she was two years old and continued until

she left for England. In 1501, they were very busy. They crafted fifty-one pairs of *borçeguies* (leather shoes that come up over the ankles), sixty-eight pairs of *xervillas* (slippers), and dozens of lavishly embellished cork-soled shoes called *chapines*. It is likely that these were not all for Catherine, that she gave them as gifts to her *ama* (governess), Inés Vanegas, or one of her maids-in-waiting, María de Rojas or María de Guevara, or another governess, Elvira Manuel. I began to imagine Catherine giving black velvet slippers as gifts at New Year's festivities and wearing the leather shoes of Diego de Valencia while dancing at court, strolling through gardens in Granada, and boarding the ships that took her to England. Shoes are just a sliver of what Baeza paid for—hundreds of yards of silk, linen, and velvet for everything from fancy skirts to nightshirts; sateen bonnets and embroidered shawls; leather jackets and gloves. Baeza's careful accounting reveals a young girl dressed in a black velvet *verdugado* (hooped skirt, known in England as a farthingale), her hair braided with pink grosgrain silk ribbons, and wearing embroidered velvet *chapines*.[1]

I was intrigued. What do Catherine's shoes tell us about her and her world? Do clothes make the woman? Who was that girl in those shoes? Why should we care about her shoes?

Catherine was one of the great queens consort of England. The outlines of her life are well documented in both scholarly and popular biographies. She was born in 1485, daughter of the powerful Spanish sovereigns Isabel of Castile and Fernando II of Aragon (b. 1452, r. Castile 1475–1504, r. Aragon 1479–1516). Her names reveal her blended cultural identity. She was christened Catalina, the Castilian version of the name of her grandmother, Catherine, the daughter of Constanza of Castile and John of Gaunt, the Duke of Lancaster. In early childhood, she was betrothed to Arthur, the Prince of Wales, and afterwards in Castile she was called *la princessa de Gales*, and in England, the Princess of Wales. They were married in November 1501, but five months later she was a widow. Seven years later, she married his brother Henry, later King Henry VIII (b. 1491, r. 1509–47), and became Queen Catherine of Aragon. Catherine was fluent in Spanish, Latin, French, and English and was patron of humanist luminaries such as Erasmus, Juan Luis Vives, and Thomas More. She was one of Henry's closest advisers on international diplomacy, she supervised a complex household at half a dozen royal courts, and she

FIG. 1 | Unknown artisan, chapine, 1550–1650. Silk, metal; Italian. Brooklyn Museum Costume Collection at the Metropolitan Museum of Art, New York, gift of the Brooklyn Museum, 2009. Gift of Herman Delman, 1955 (2009.300.1449a,b). Image © The Metropolitan Museum of Art. Image source: Art Resource, New York.

managed the operations of her reginal properties. She served as regent of England during a war with Scotland and was the mother of the queen regnant of England, Mary I (b. 1516, r. 1553–58). Her power diminished as it became apparent that she would not bear a son for Henry, but she remained faithful to him as his attentions turned to other women and when he ultimately sought a divorce to marry Anne Boleyn. In January 1536, at age fifty, she died nearly alone in a castle in Cambridgeshire and was buried in a simple tomb in Peterborough Cathedral.

To her English subjects she was Kateryne of Spayne, a foreign-born bride who brought to England her Castilian accent and entourage and seemingly exotic customs. For her symbol as queen, she adopted the pomegranate. This fruit, not native to England, is the "apple of Granada" and the symbol of the Muslim Nasrid kingdom of Granada, which had been recently conquered by her parents. For the members of her household, the pomegranate was a symbol of belonging, an affiliation with the queen, and a mark of social status. For Catherine, it was a memento of a childhood spent in a warmer climate eating figs and oranges and growing up in a society inhabited by Christians, Jews, and Muslims while witnessing the inquisition and expulsion of Jews. But a pomegranate was a doubly ironic choice, symbolizing fertility yet a poignant reminder of Persephone's annual season in the underworld.

For a royal woman who lived her entire life in public, she is surprisingly difficult to get to know. Very little of the copious bibliography on the Tudor era is devoted solely to Catherine. Biographers for the last century and a half have relied on the same set of narrative sources: mostly the English Calendars of State Papers (Spain and Venice), official letters and papers that are concerned with government, and a few letters to, from, or about Catherine, edited and published well over a century ago. Reading narrative sources in search of Catherine the woman is like looking through a telescope with a poor lens. Faint traces remain. We know she's there, but we see mostly outlines or shadows. Contemporaneous writers see Catherine at public events and at court, but, until she gives birth to a child, she is incidental to their story of politics and war. To Tudor chronicler Edward Hall, Catherine was the king's bedfellow, who wore "the straugne fashion of the Spanyshe nacion," had two children, and then was divorced.[2] Scholarly biographers, until recently most of them men, devote most of their books to Henry VIII, Anne Boleyn, and the King's Great Matter, otherwise known as the divorce.[3] Conventional biographies outline the contours of her life, and studies on her actions as a regent and landlord reveal her as a powerful woman, but these books are oddly one-dimensional, repetitive, poorly theorized, and, frankly, a little dull. Without relying on even a trace of feminist or gender theory, many biographers regard Catherine through Henry's actions. They uncritically portray Catherine as someone to whom things were done—Arthur married her; Henry married her; her father neglected her; Henry loved her and then rejected her; Henry divorced her, sent her away to languish at Ampthill and Kimbolton Castle, and then had her buried far from London. Catherine is depicted as passive, without effective agency, almost a bystander to her life. When she is pregnant, Henry's fears and concerns are front and center. When she is regent for Henry in 1513, her role in the defeat of the Scots at the Battle of Flodden gets lost in the story of Henry's unsuccessful military adventures in France. Her diplomatic efforts with her father, Fernando, and her nephew, Emperor Charles V, are downplayed as minor compared to those of Thomas Cardinal Wolsey and Thomas Cromwell. The only time Catherine comes alive is in June 1529, when she appears before the papal legatine court at Blackfriars and publicly defies Henry's efforts to divorce her. After that, she literally disappears from view, shoved aside by Henry in secluded castles in order to muffle her voice and diminish her power. The overall impression from reading these books is that Catherine rarely did things and almost never did anything of consequence. Popular novels and biographies follow a similar narrative and use the same sources, but they focus on personal details to the point of sentimentalizing her life. These authors rely on the teleological trope of a tragic queen and portray her as the cast-off, long-suffering widow of the Tudor prince Arthur and the dowdy, pious wife of Arthur's brother, Henry VIII, who rejected her in favor of the more elegant Anne Boleyn.[4] The drama of Anne's swift death at the hands of an executioner before a crowd at the Tower of London is hard to beat. Catherine's slow, pitiful death in the countryside suffers by comparison.

SIFTING THROUGH ARCHIVES AND LIBRARIES IN SEARCH OF CATHERINE

Catherine may have died quietly, but her life was eventful. It was a long (by sixteenth-century standards), significant, and emotionally rich one. As I began to dig deeply into the materials for her life, my first reaction was frustration. Documents have not survived for various reasons—and not just the routine loss of archival material due to bugs, worms, and fire. I had a devil of a time locating sources beyond the Calendars of State Papers, which are often fragmentary, incomplete translations or transcriptions of letters and papers that may be lost, seriously damaged, or quietly stored in an unnoticed private collection.[5] Many of the original letters from the Spanish Calendar, located in the archives of Simancas in Spain and the Habsburg archives in Vienna, some in cipher, have not been fully translated. The Spanish chronicle sources for Catherine's life outline her life until her marriage to Arthur, but the English chroniclers ignore her between Arthur's death in 1502 and her marriage to Henry in 1509. She is busy as a close adviser to Henry for the first few years of their marriage, especially during her regency of 1513, but soon after that Thomas Cardinal Wolsey steps in as Henry's adviser and she is largely absent from governmental records. A few dozen letters exchanged between her and her Spanish family are vital and often vivid, but they tell only fragments of Catherine's story. Many of the narrative sources that are often available for noteworthy people at that time are intermingled with the kings' records in the archives. Papers relevant to Catherine were lost or simply neglected in favor of Henry's other wives, notably Katherine Parr.[6] Most often when we do hear Catherine, it is an act of ventriloquism, her words filtered through men's voices in letters, official documents, diplomatic reports, memoranda, and legal proceedings.

Making matters worse, after her death, Henry VIII's animosity toward her led to attempts to erase her memory. There are everyday acts of erasure, such as Anne Boleyn's refashioning of many of Catherine's material possessions after her death. Sometimes, however, the erasure was more disturbingly deliberate, politically or religiously motivated. An ardent Protestant or at least an ally of Henry scratched out the names "Prynses" and "Quene Kateryne hys wife" from a lavish book of hours that belonged originally to one of Catherine's ladies at court.[7] Another unknown knife-wielding soul cut Catherine's pomegranate badge from the cover of a book owned by both Catherine and Henry and had it replaced with a cock, one of Henry's badges.[8] What prompted this violent erasure? Was it just religious zeal that caused an anonymous reader to violently scrape her name from the text of a book? Was it animus? Fear? Why did they hate her so much that they wanted to obliterate all traces of her? If she was a person to whom things were done, why did Henry and his allies try to destroy her and erase her memory? Were they afraid of her erudition, her deep Catholicism? But how do we explain the scholarly neglect? The answer, partly, is that writers of history in early modern England emphasized the deeds of men and downplayed the acts of women. In his chronicle *The Union of the Two Noble and Illustre Families of Lancastre and Yorke* (published in 1548), Edward Hall, an eyewitness to the reign of Henry, mentions Catherine only when her presence is utterly unavoidable, such as when he writes about the divorce.[9] After the death of Mary I in 1558, tempers cooled a bit, and England grew more secular; during

Elizabeth I's disputes with Philip II of Spain in the 1680s, Catherine was deemed dangerously Spanish, linked to a Black Legend that regarded Spain as religiously intolerant and exceptionally evil.[10] The memory of her faded.

Since 2009, as part of an increased interest in queens and queenship, Catherine has begun to emerge from the shadows. Literary scholars look at Catherine's patronage of humanist writers and literary depictions of her. They consider Catherine as a subject of chronicle histories that use her as a device to convey a point about queenly virtues in the hotly contested confessional age of the Reformation. After her death, and especially during the reign of her daughter, Mary I (r. 1553–58), literary representations transformed Catherine from a Spanish Catholic to a more palatable English one, or depicted her as a very real queen in politically charged plays that take up thorny issues of legitimacy, tyranny, and religion, or used her life story to promote wifely virtues of patience and duty. During the reign of Elizabeth I (b. 1533, r. 1558–1603), Catherine's life was used as a model for the Catholics in England and on the continent, but she disappeared from the English sources. The Victorians, seeking a different model of queenship based on personal character and public persona, revived her story but downplayed Catherine's vexing Catholicism and emphasized instead her steadfast loyalty and devotion to the realm.[11]

Historians of late tend to focus on selected themes, rather than taking on the full sweep of her life. For example, Timothy Elston considers Catherine's erudition, her patronage of humanist scholars at court, and her role as the dedicatee of Juan Luis Vives's *Education of a Christian Woman* (1527).[12] The best new work on Catherine, by Michelle L. Beer, uses a fresh set of sources to shed important light on her as royal adviser to Henry VIII, diplomat for her father, and manager of her estates.[13] Beer works primarily with archival sources and uses with great caution the letters and state papers that appear in calendar form. A calendared document sometimes includes fully transcribed copies of letters and memoranda, but often calendars are abbreviated and fragmentary. Most, but hardly all, of the documents for the period have been calendared; few have been printed in full, and even then, some are filled with errors. Complicating things further, calendars include in detail only what the nineteenth-century archivists compiling the calendar of documents decided to include and to describe. Catherine may be mentioned, but her voice, the fullness of expression, and the tone and color of her phrasing have been lost.[14] And unarchived letters in private collections pop up at auction. For example, in 1920, an autograph letter by Catherine owned by a manuscript collector, Alfred Morrison (d. 1897), was sold at auction at Sotheby's in New York. The letter, dated 22 February 1531 and written in Spanish, is addressed to her nephew, the emperor Charles V, regarding the divorce.[15] An item in the calendared letters at around this date provides this context: a letter written in French, dated 21 February 1531, from imperial ambassador Eustace Chapuys to Charles, mentions Catherine but says nothing about her intention to write to Charles (see chapter 6 for more on this letter). The calendar notes that this transcript of Chapuys's letter is based on the original in the Vienna Archives (presumably the Haus-hof und Stadt Archiv), but no archival reference is noted. It appears that the letter currently in the collection of the Morgan Library was not known to the archivist who prepared the calendar.[16]

SEEING CATHERINE, OR MAYBE NOT, IN PAINTINGS

To try to dispel some of the shadows, I turned to portraits of her, thinking that an artist would be able to help. Yet even portraits can be unreliable. Take, for instance, an image that has long been considered to be a portrait of Catherine by the Estonian artist Michel Sittow (1469–1525), now in Vienna (fig. 2). Sittow, court painter for Queen Isabel from 1492 to 1502, knew Catherine.[17] The painting depicts a young woman with golden-blonde hair dressed in a deep-brown velvet dress embellished with scallop shells over a delicately embroidered shift. This fits contemporary descriptions, which complimented Catherine on her lush, thick, golden hair. The scallop shells are associated with Saint James, known to the Spanish as Santiago, the patron saint of pilgrims to the city of Santiago de Compostela, whose emblem was the scallop shell. Her pensive and serene demeanor as she faces the viewer with modest, downcast eyes also suits descriptions of Catherine. The halo is a mark of her well-known piety. The headdress, a velvet hood trimmed with gold and red, is typical of fashion in early sixteenth-century England. Her jewelry, a thin

FIG. 2 | Michel Sittow, *Catherine of Aragon*, ca. 1514 (or Mary Rose Tudor, date uncertain). Oil on panel, 29 × 20.5 cm. Kunsthistorisches Museum, Vienna, inv. no. 5612. Photo: Erich Lessing / Art Resource, New York.

cord that drops down beneath the neckline and two splendid, heavy gold chain necklaces, matches her status as elite, probably royal. The smaller one is made of linked squares of filigreed gold interlaced with the initials C and K alternating with the Tudor rose emblem. In 1915, art historian Max Friedländer argued this was a portrait of Catherine, and since then this painting has appeared on the cover of almost every biography of her.[18]

It is a beautiful painting, but it may not be a portrait of Catherine. Sittow's paintings pose a riddle for scholars; only a few are verified to be his, and there is little agreement as to the dates of creation. This portrait may have been painted in 1503 or 1504, when some scholars think Sittow may have been sent to England by Queen Isabel to paint a portrait of Catherine,[19] or after 1506, when Sittow left Spain to work in the service of Marguerite of Austria, Catherine's sister-in-law, but before 1515. If it was painted around 1507, she would have been twenty-two years old; in 1515, Catherine would have been thirty. It is hard to believe that this is an image of a thirty-year-old woman, but appearances can be deceiving, because Tudor-era painters did not aim to record a true likeness as much as an ideal one. Portraits were valued because they recorded the physical presence of a person and signified their status and value as a noteworthy person. They were used for very specific political purposes—as a pictorial statement of dynasty, as part of marriage negotiations, as a gift to cement a relationship and represent the donor's loyalty to a king, queen, or patron. It was common for an artist's original portrait to be copied by other artists in the workshop, making it difficult to know if an image is a likeness or simply an idealized reimagining of the original. The problem is that no contemporary records exist that document whether any of the portraits of Catherine successfully captured her likeness.[20] It makes just as much sense that the portrait was painted around 1507, when Catherine was a young, marriageable widow, as that it was commissioned as a possible betrothal painting.

In 2008, Paul Matthews argued that this was a betrothal portrait of Henry VIII's sister Mary Rose, a potential bride for Charles, Catherine's nephew and the future Habsburg emperor.[21] His argument hinges on the dating and the details: the K on the necklace is not a reference to Catherine, but rather to Karolus (Charles), and the necklace may be based on one she received as a gift from him. The marriage did not take place, and Matthews hypothesizes that the Habsburg diplomats at London had the portrait made at the request of Marguerite of Austria to please Henry.[22] His hypothesis is not entirely convincing. He argues that the scallop shells were not Catherine's emblem, but there is no reason why she would not wear a gown with a scallop-shell border. Matthews argues that she should have been painted with a pomegranate, but in no substantiated portrait of her does she appear with a pomegranate—not in the embroidery or weave pattern, not in the jewelry, not as a button or a decorative element. Sittow painted secular and other religious images without specifying the name of the living subject, and Frederick Hepburn argues that the painting may simply be a representation of Saint Katherine of Alexandria, which would help explain the presence of the halo.[23]

Even more problematic is another work by Michel Sittow that is also considered to be a painting of Catherine (fig. 3), based on facial features that are nearly identical to those in the portrait in Vienna. The subject has reddish-blonde hair and her eyes are modestly downcast, but the similarities end there. This painting is redolent with allusions to skin and fragrance. Shimmery, wavy golden hair lies loose on her shoulders, while a stray wisp falls across her forehead. The neckline of her luxurious scarlet dress over a linen shift discreetly reveals bare skin at her neck, but her shoulders are covered with a rich blue shawl. Sittow has painted an audible stillness in her breath and her gaze. Touches of gold and blue, and a scarlet dress, signal luxury, wealth, security. The painting is alive with imagination. It is a portrait, but it is unlikely that it is a portrait of Catherine, especially when compared with known portraits of her (see chapters 4, 5, and 6). It is more likely a picture of Mary Magdalene painted for a patron whose identity is not yet known. Mary Magdalene was the patron saint of penitential sinners, people ridiculed for their piety, and, significantly, people who work in the sensual and fleshly world: pharmacists, glovemakers, tanners, and perfumers. Our eyes are drawn to the softly rounded face and lips and to her hands, which cradle an unguent jar with a lid embellished with roses, the emblem of the Tudor dynasty. There are twenty-seven bones in the human hand and more nerve endings in the fingertips than in almost any other sensory area of the body. Hands express love, desire, longing, artistry, abandon, protection, vulnerability, poise. Fingertips are one of the most sensory parts of the body.[24] Here, as they lightly pry open and are about to touch the oily contents of the unguent jar, they suggest

FIG. 3 | Michel Sittow, *Catherine of Aragon as the Magdalene*, ca. 1500. Oil on panel, 32.1 × 25.1 cm. Detroit Institute of Arts, Detroit. Founders Society purchase, General Membership Fund. Photo: Bridgeman Images.

touching and feeling, a physical closeness, an intimacy, a sensuality, and a desire that borders on sexual. Touch is also ethereal, as Mario Equicola, in his 1525 treatise *De natura d'amore*, suggests when he equates touch to the "celestial parts that Plato called 'aether' and Aristotle called 'the fifth element.'"[25]

The idea that Catherine, wife of Henry VIII and a pious and decorous mother, would allow herself to be depicted as Mary Magdalene, the patron saint of sexual temptation, is difficult to take seriously. If this is so, then what are we to make of the similarities with the subject of the Vienna portrait? Sittow's depictions of women tend to have similar features, and the facial features in both this painting and the Vienna portrait are strikingly similar. They may form a type, an ideal or an idea of a person rather than an actual person.[26]

Both of Sittow's paintings convey important details about fashion and symbolism through details of dress, jewelry, pose, hairstyle, headdresses, inscriptions, or objects in the background. They may be telling us something about Catherine, but, taken alone, they are not enough. There is, fortunately, more. To get to know Catherine, to get a glimpse of her mental world, and to fill out the world around her, we need to turn to the stuff of her material world.

Tucked away in regional museums in Spain and England are fragments of Catherine's life, the scattered bits of clothing and shoes that she wore or books she read, the tapestries and little stools that furnished her rooms, and the amulets and votives of saints that were part of her devotional life. These things were saved for centuries because they mattered to her and to those she held dear—the gifts she gave loved ones at New Year's celebrations, the hooped skirts and gabled headpieces she wore, the jewelry that adorned her neck and fingers, and her shoes. Enameled miniatures worn close to the body were emotional links between Catherine and the people closest to her. Objects owned by Catherine or connected to her in some way can be found in the collections of the Victoria and Albert Museum, the National Portrait Gallery, the Museum of London, and regional archives in the English hinterlands. But the work demands patience and persistence. Modern curatorial practices at, for example, the Victoria and Albert Museum group objects related to Catherine by function (World Ceramics), geography (British Galleries), or material (Textiles).

This makes sense from a formal typological or iconographic standpoint, but in practice it erases Catherine from the history of British art. Yet her late medieval Spanish sensibility and taste had a profound influence on the Tudor style, from her *chapines* and her *verdugados* to a taste for exotic tooled-leather book covers and the demand for Spanish silks, Spanish embroidery, and jewelry. Catherine links them, even though the catalog does not specifically refer to them as relating to her. A connection to Catherine is made explicit only for a lavish wooden writing box and an intricately carved boxwood rosary, and only then because the arms of her second husband, Henry VIII, also decorate both the box and the rosary.

WHY DO CATHERINE'S SHOES MATTER?

Her shoes matter to us because they mattered to Catherine, and because through them she comes to life. A decorous wife and mother, she continued to wear her richly embellished luxurious *chapines* until late in her life. An inventory of her possessions at Baynard's Castle, the queen's official residence in London, taken by Sir Edward Baynton, on orders from King Henry on 14 February 1536, just a few weeks after her death, noted seven pairs of shoes "of the Spanysshe fashion, corked and garnysshid with golde."[27] These shoes, covered in a luxurious fabric and garnished with gold trim, are visual symbols of a sumptuous Spanishness that was shaped during her childhood in Medina del Campo and Granada, crafted in Valencia and Madrid, and brought with her to London. Her shoes remind us of the potent link to Spanish opulence that she carried with her to the end of her life. They were also a clear expression of her femininity. Men in the sixteenth century wore flat-heeled shoes, such as soft leather boots and sandals, or clogs to stay out of the mud, or the extravagantly pointy-toed *poulaines*,[28] but never platform shoes. And they reveal an almost defiant independence, as though she is demanding that we look at her as the subject of her life, not the object of men's desires and dynastic ambitions.

It pains me to say that not a single pair of Catherine's actual shoes has survived. The shoes depicted in figure 1 fit the description of her shoes in the inventory of 1536, but they are not Spanish, or even English; they are

Italian and were probably crafted after her death. All that remains of Catherine's shoes is the thin description in Baynton's "viewe" of her possessions. This is a long list written in the dry language of someone solely interested in counting things. He did not care to note the color of the fabric or the curve of the cork sole. If the object appeared to be a precious art object, he mentioned that it was made of gold or was studded with gems. He moved from room to room and listed the things she owned, in no particular order—from costly things such as tapestries, ivory chess pieces, and liturgical objects to commonplace things such as a bed and bedsheets, little stools, cushions, tables both plain and fancy, needle cases, ladles and a brass skillet, a looking glass, a cradle, and a pair of balances.

The objects in this inventory reveal the everyday life of an exceptional woman surrounded by material things kept in cupboards and closets, hung on the walls, and worn on her feet. A postmortem inventory such as this was not exceptional and was not limited to noble and royal families. Much of what we know about merchant families and the rise of a consumer culture in the later Middle Ages comes from inventories of their possessions.[29] Art historians have plumbed the details of inventories of medieval queens as makers, patrons, and collectors of art to study the physical, artistic, familial, and personal relationships and communities of a queen's life.[30] We know, for example, that fourteenth-century Clémence of Hungary, Queen of France, was an avid patron and collector of exquisite objects, books, and jewelry, and from this, Mariah Proctor-Tiffany has tracked the movement of art across fourteenth-century Europe, including objects given by Clémence as gifts to people who mattered to her.[31] The richly detailed inventory of Clémence's possessions tells part of the story of her life. In a dramatically different way, so does the parsimonious inventory of Catherine's possessions. There are few art objects sought after by collectors and museums in Baynton's inventory of Catherine's possessions because, by the time of her death, her jewelry and genuinely precious objects had been seized by Henry. Because she was no longer a queen, there was precious little left for Baynton to tally up.

This inventory of what remained brings us closer to the day-to-day life of Catherine, yet, in truth, we are still two steps removed from her. We have Baynton's words, not hers. The language of the inventory retains, however, a fragmentary glimpse of the language Catherine would have used to describe the things she touched, things that surrounded her and filled her senses. Yet an inventory is more than a written record that lists possessions. It is a form of documentary archaeology, and to make sense of it, we read each object in that room and listen to what they say to us.[32] The list of objects allows us to imagine her in a room with her attendants and friends, where we believe we are entering for just a moment into her mental world. We get a clear sense of her personal identity though the value, memory, and meaning in a type of shoe she had worn since childhood. The tapestries on the walls, the skillet, small stool, gold cup, and frayed blanket give personality and texture to the day-to-day rhythm of her life.[33] Reading the material objects—a heraldic emblem, a few paintings, a livery badge, embroidered cushions, baby blankets, a bit of silk tunic, a pillow, a rosary, illuminated manuscripts and printed books, tapestries, an embroidered napkin, yards of fabric and ribbons—alongside chronicles, official reports, and inventories reveals a lost world of her personality, desires, intentions, and personal relationships. She looked at them daily, touched them, and wore them out. Even seemingly worthless objects mattered to her. In the margins of the inventory, Baynton noted a broken branch of coral as one of the "necessaries" for Catherine while she was in childbed. That bit of coral, believed to possess the power to protect a pregnant woman from harm and ensure a safe delivery of a healthy baby, reminds us of her painful struggles to have a child.

This inventory is also a statement of value, but not as a quantification of the resale value of kitchenware, pin cases, and curtains, even when the items were noted to be broken or in poor condition. A few of the items went straight to Henry and his new wife, Anne Boleyn: some wool and linen cloth; a case of wooden trenchers; two hand towels of fine Holland cloth with embroidery of Venice gold and silk fringe; a rich cloth of fine linen with a picture of Christ baptized by Saint John embroidered in Venice gold; a desk covered with black leather trimmed with gilt nails; and a coffer covered in crimson velvet, trimmed with gilt nails and with four tiles inside, each of them gilded. This is an odd assortment of objects; some are mundane, like the trenchers, and others, like the desk and coffer, are more regal. Items like these appear in museum collections, but is doubtful that they belonged to Catherine, Henry, or Anne.[34]

Through this inventory we can see, if not the actual object, then an image of what Catherine valued personally and what mattered to her. We can see how she regarded herself in both the very public court and the intimate space of her chamber. When examined closely, these objects are the expressive marks of her personal and political identity, her physical and intellectual worlds. They are a link between present and past that reveals fresh insights about her as a girl at home in Spain, a young bride and widow seemingly adrift in a foreign land, a wife (again) and mother, a loyal and devoted friend, a defiant queen, and an almost-but-not-quite-forgotten queen.[35] They tell the story of Catherine's personal and political identity as she transitioned from Catalina de Aragón, a Spanish *infanta* (royal daughter), to Catherine of Aragon, Queen of England. Through the simple listing of her possessions, she begins to come to life through the power of imagination.

Taken together, an inventory and objects create a rich, multilayered source that bears complex messages and demands a close reading. For example, on exhibit at a regional museum in Ludlow, near the border with Wales, where Catherine lived during her brief marriage to Arthur, is a chasuble, a full-length garment worn by a Catholic priest while saying Mass. This garment, made of cloth of gold, contains an embroidery of a pomegranate decoration, cut from another garment. This embroidery was applied to the velvet background to form a cross on the back and a single strip on the front. The pomegranate motif that appears on the cloth was Catherine's own personal emblem, and as she was known to embroider the design herself, it seems likely that this material and the embroidered pieces were taken from Catherine's own gowns. Just before her death, she made a "supplication," not a will, because making a will was not allowed for a wife whose husband outlived her. Among her wishes—that her debts be paid, small sums be given to her servants, and donations be made to the Franciscans—"she bequeathed her robes and dresses to be used as Church ornaments. The furs she had, she reserved for the princess, her daughter, to whom she likewise bequeathed a necklace with a cross, which she herself had brought from Spain." Henry's chancellor, Thomas Cromwell, tried to prevent this gift of her gowns, asserting "that the bequest of her robes to the Church was superfluous, considering the great abundance of ecclesiastical vestments in England, and that although the Queen's will was not accomplished in this respect, something would be done in the abbey where she should be interred that would be more notable and worthy of her memory."[36]

Catherine's servants ignored Cromwell. Curators at the museum in Ludlow trace the dress and chasuble to the Throckmorton family of Coughton Court and then the Blounts of Mawley Hall, where it remained for over four hundred years until passing from their chapel to the church at Cleobury Mortimer in 1959. This chasuble is a testimony to someone's affection for Catherine and their Catholic religious piety, which led them to risk the wrath of a Protestant king or queen. It is a sly, quiet gesture by recusants who kept faith with both their Catholicism and the memory of her.

Later, in the final inventory of Catherine's possessions taken after her death, the scribe noted that she bequeathed four small, frayed quilts to her daughter, Mary. These quilts were used by Catherine during the lying-in period of Mary's birth and were willed to Mary as swaddling for her own children. Catherine does not say why she kept these quilts or what they meant to her. She doesn't need to. These quilts are deeply emotional objects that convey love and affection and ultimately, sadness, because we know, from our vantage point centuries later, that Mary never had a chance to use them because she never gave birth to a child.

SO, WHO IS THAT GIRL?

This book is about Catherine, but it is neither a conventional biography nor an event-based history. I follow her life cycle—childhood, marriage, widowhood, marriage again, motherhood, and the last years of her life in isolation—rather than political events. But context is vital, so each chapter is accompanied by a thumbnail list of events that affected her life. I surround Catherine with the people who mattered to her and situate them in physical locations—her childhood homes in Spain, and then her homes in England at Ludlow Castle, Durham House, Richmond, Eltham, Baynard's Castle, and the Palace of Placencia at Greenwich.

The portrait of her in chapter 2 depicts her as a child surrounded by the women at the Isabelline royal court of her childhood in Spain—in Arévalo, Seville, Granada, and Barcelona—who shaped her identity. Her taste, sensibility, judgment, and wide-ranging interests were formed by this extraordinary childhood immersed in the sunshine of the countryside of Castile and cities rich with Christian and Muslim art and architecture. Chapter 3 is a group portrait of Catherine and the people who mattered to her from her arrival in England in 1501 until her marriage in 1509. She is surrounded by her extensive family and friends in the Tudor court and the network of her sisters and sisters-in-law in Spain, Portugal, and the Netherlands who sustain her after a tragic early widowhood. These personal relationships form four concentric circles: the inner circle of her Spanish family; the next circle of her English family and her sisters-in-law Margaret and Mary; at a slight remove are her closest friends, María de Salinas, María de Rojas, and Margaret Pole; and finally, her loyally devoted Spanish and English attendants and household officers. These relationships sustained her through a wedding and four funerals—her husband, mother, mother-in-law, and father-in-law.[37] Chapter 4 is a portrait of the early, happy, busy years of her second marriage. From 1509 until 1520 she was deeply engaged in both the political and personal life of an English queen consort who balanced her work as adviser to the king, regent, and ambassador with pregnancies, miscarriages, stillbirths, the painful death of her two-month-old son, and finally the birth of a daughter, Mary, who survived to rule as the first queen regnant of England since Matilda (1102–1167, r. 1141–48). Chapter 5 portrays Catherine during the 1520s as an attentive mother who supervised the education of her daughter to prepare her for a life that held the possibility of ruling as a sovereign queen. She complemented this with her active patronage of writers, artists, universities, and members of religious orders. This decade that started so promisingly at the Field of the Cloth of Gold ended in a tumultuous court case when her world was upended by Henry's pursuit of a divorce. Chapter 6 is a portrait of a tragic end to a life that began so auspiciously but ended with her dying alone, save for only the dearest and most valiant friends. She was buried at Peterborough Cathedral in 1536, then unburied during the English Civil War in 1643, and a memorial slab was installed at Peterborough in 1895 that is carefully tended to this day by a volunteer group, "the Katherines of England." Her memory is preserved in the traces of her that remain despite all efforts to erase her and, finally, in a liturgical garment made from one of her gowns. The resonant objects of this last period of her life are among the most poignant and personal remnants of her that we have. The final portrait in chapter 7 is the representation of a lifetime of power, embodied in a Spanish *infanta* who became an English queen consort and whose defiant resistance to her husband's efforts to divorce her is proof of her enduring legacy.

PUTTING IT ALL TOGETHER: A NOTE ON METHODS

In writing this book, I have deliberately turned away from a form of research, analysis, and writing that is very familiar to me and to many people who write and read scholarly books. In order to see Catherine as a person, I had to step back and take a look at the world around her, at the places she saw and the things she touched, wore, slept in, and looked at. I started with one source, a record of royal accounts of the purchases for her when she was a child. The words on the page filled out a world around her, one where words signified things, and those things—shoes, for example—thickened my description of her, revealing bits of her world that remained obscure in the royal accounts. I came across things we don't see anymore, things that a dictionary didn't describe well enough to make sense of the term. When I began to research a *chapine*, and I realized it was a platform shoe, and that shoes like that were in museums, I shifted the location of my research.

Taken together, the narrative accounts, the museum catalog descriptions, and the objects themselves form a multilayered set of analogous sources that brings to light more than just the cost of silk ribbon. They tell a story of the exuberance of braided hair, the measurement of a girl's height and waist, and the experience of wearing those silk ribbons. A notation in an account that describes something as being as commonplace as a hair ribbon conveys a quality of feeling that opened up for me the sensibility, judgment, taste, and interest of Catherine.

To give primacy to the objects is to look closely at an array of objects—portraits, fashion, textiles, jewelry, books, domestic architecture, household goods. To understand those objects, I rely on methods and theories from a range of fields—feminist and gender theory, anthropology, history of art, culture, politics, and emotions. I draw on a variety of methods to understand the specific history and material culture of Catherine's world. There is no simple definition of what material culture entails, but most often the focus is on everyday objects such as tools, pottery, textiles, and furniture, with an eye to how things empower people. Studies on material culture go beyond the question of what individuals do with objects, and this has led to some innovative ways of rethinking medieval artworks.[38] The term "material culture" also suggests that the widest variety of objects can be studied, rejecting a hierarchy that emphasizes painting and sculpture.[39] Objects have been studied in terms of their social value by taking into account what they are made of, their size, and their "biography."[40] Recent studies on medieval women have demonstrated that material culture is a fruitful way of exploring objects as an important nexus between women, dynasty, and power.[41] Anthropologist Annette Weiner noted that all personal possessions, both modest and lavish, invoke intimately a connection with their owners. Seen in this way, objects owned by Catherine, whether in public or private, symbolize her personal experience and identity. Objects she gave as gifts are "inalienable possessions" that succeed her through time. The accumulated significance of gifts given and received "make[s] their economic and aesthetic values *absolute* and transcendent above all similar things. Each object differs in value even from other objects of the same class that in some instances may circulate as common currency in exchange. In this way, certain possessions become subjectively unique."[42] Seen in this way, even a humble bit of embroidery takes on a personal value that far exceeds the cost of the materials.

With all this in mind, in this book I chose to trace Catherine's life along the arc of her personal life and to use a range of materials to better understand her as a daughter, wife, widow, and mother from her perspective, from the things and the people that mattered most to her, that constituted her world.[43] The point of this book is to explore the ephemeral and ineffable material traces of Catherine that remain, hidden in plain sight along the edges of England, in places like Ludlow, Peterborough, and Worcester. It is both looking at her and looking at her world through her eyes, what she saw when she looked at what mattered to her.

It is here—amid descriptions of fraying quilts and ragged little chairs, the mementos of the people who mattered most to her—that Catherine's personal and emotional world comes to life. Jewelry was more than just a gemstone and a bit of embroidery more than an adornment. They were gifts to a trusted and loved companion that assumed an identity and association as they were turned to more personal and intimate uses. Gifts of shoes and miniature portraits take on new meaning as sensory experiences that solidified the relationship between Catherine and her family and friends. Ritual events such as weddings, christenings, and coronations were deeply entwined with objects such as rings, veils, and crowns that are a representation of the person. A rosary given as a wedding gift is both a precious object of beauty and a devotional object that connects earthbound humans with heavenly spirits. When the giver is a queen, the objects are charismatic; they are able to cast a spell on individuals. The thing represents the person, a loved one, and has the power to invoke memory. It is a kind of visual metaphor for identity. To observe relationships revealed through everyday objects like shoes, clothing, textiles, and pottery is to be made aware of "the fascinating presence of absences."[44] No matter where Catherine was—in another room, another palace, another town, or buried at Peterborough—her essence remained present and alive through the things she touched that made meaningful her memory. When touched, as a rosary in prayer, or transformed, as a woman's dress into a priest's liturgical garment, they gain an abstract but powerful value. In other words, an inventory is a "kind of personal geography of the queen's immediate surroundings."[45] The objects in that inventory define the contours of Catherine's life and form bridges across five centuries that allow us to see her a little better, to get to know who she was.[46]

Some of the objects I found now reside in museums and archives, but that is not where they would have been found during Catherine's life. Place matters; it informs our education and shapes our worldview. I wanted to put the objects I found into the landscape she knew as a child and the one that she saw as a sixteen-year-old new bride in a new country that was strikingly different from Castile. So I followed her around from the intense sunshine and golden hills of Castile to a greener, cooler, cloudier, rainier place, not dry and dusty, with different trees, shrubs, and flowers, different vistas from the roads. I have traveled to most, and lived in some, of the places she lived in when she was a child in Spain. On research trips to England, I made a point of getting out of the archives and tracing her steps through London, Winchester, Richmond, Greenwich, Windsor, Hereford, Worcester, Gloucester, and Peterborough, through East Anglia, Hampshire, Cambridgeshire, and Shropshire, where I visited Ludlow Castle, where Catherine spent her honeymoon during one cold, wet winter.

On that trip to Ludlow, I was with a friend who grew up in Spain and has lived her adult life in England. We poked around the castle, built in the late eleventh century by Walter de Lacy after the conquest of England by Duke William of Normandy. What remains of Ludlow reveals a stout, compact castle situated on a fairly low hill (350-foot elevation) nestled at the confluence of the rivers Teme and Corve and guarding a valley between Clee Hill and Mortimer Forest. The castle was more functional than comfortable, designed for knights and soldiers guarding the border with Wales. That winter of 1502, the rooms would have been dark and cold, with tapestries and carpets to warm the walls.

After we mucked around the castle and had tea in the gift shop, we headed into the town. It's a small town, and we poked our heads into St. Laurence's Church and small shops, got lost in the tangle of streets, and lamented that the Castle Lodge, where Catherine lived briefly while in Ludlow, was closed for repairs. While we were trying to sort out where to have lunch, Anne stopped in front of the Buttercross, a grand building that once housed a butter market. She saw a sign pointing to the local museum and said, "Look, that local museum is only a pound. Let's pop in." We climbed the stairs, and when we got to the front desk to pay the pound, I asked if there was anything special we should see. The kind woman at the desk said, "Well, we just installed the Catherine of Aragon chasuble."

I nearly fell over. I had been expecting to see vintage photos and objects that told the story of Ludlow, not this. The curators at the Shropshire Museum generously shared their detailed documentation of the chasuble, with a shaggy-dog story of provenance that is recounted in chapter 6. For a historian, a place like Ludlow is where the intellect and historical memory collide, where analysis and emotion combine to create an understanding of a person that is not possible from simply reading words on a page.

This anecdote sums up my methods for this project: a combination of archival research (paleography, codicology, transcription), textual analysis (linguistics and literary studies), some art-historical analysis of the objects and artworks (aesthetics, technique, material culture, analysis of the materials), archaeology and bioarchaelogy (castle architecture, evidence from burials), environmental studies (topography, spatial mapping), and finally, the simple but powerful impressionistic research that comes from personally standing on the ruins of Ludlow Castle to get the lay of the land. To gain even the most modest expertise in these methods took a lifetime of studying medical technology, English literature, art history, and medieval and early modern history.

The organization of this book finally came together after a conversation with Chiyo Ishikawa, an art historian and former Susan Brotman Deputy Director for Art and Curator of European Painting and Sculpture at the Seattle Art Museum. I was trying to decode the paintings of Michel Sittow (discussed in chapter 2). As we talked about material culture and art, she mentioned two exhibitions curated by Wanda Corn on Gertrude Stein and Georgia O'Keeffe, and one on Frida Kahlo organized by Claire Wilcox and Circe Henestrosa. She suggested that I take a close look at how they organized the materials to use objects as a way to study these women's lives. The Frida Kahlo show was still up at the Brooklyn Museum, and I was on sabbatical, so I booked a flight to New York and spent two days watching people look at an extraordinary exhibition. It was a revelation. And it became the organizing principle of this book: Don't get lost in the conventional arc of biographical narrative that follows political events; focus on what mattered to Catherine, spend time looking at it and describing it, contextualize the art or dress or shoes, and let those objects tell her story.

One consistent image in the story of Catherine's life is the pomegranate, her personal emblem, the touchstone around which everything in her life swirls. The geometry of the seeds and pith captivated artists, and the sweetness of the juice inspired cooks in the Mediterranean and ancient mythologies. A quick tour of places Catherine visited in England turns up pomegranates everywhere. They adorn cornices, lintels, tombs, and wall carvings in cathedrals and are woven into household textiles and liturgical garments. On livery badges and hand-tooled book covers, her pomegranates pierce or are pierced by Tudor roses. The pomegranate is a vivid representation of Catherine's personal geography, and it reveals a woman whose childhood was spent amid a complex mix of Christian, Jewish, and Muslim histories and cultures. When she landed in England in 1501, she brought more than just a dowry of silver and gold plate and dozens of shoes. She brought a culture, a sensibility, and a way of living in the world that still resonates beyond the museum walls.

CHAPTER 2

An *Infanta* at the Court of Castile, 1485–1501

❧

En cada provincial donde llegaba, se acomodaba a
los usos y costumbres de ella y vestía sus trajes; hoy
parecía en Galicia gallega y mañana vizcaína en
Vizcaya. Sabía quiénes eran las mujeres principales
del lugar y enviábales a pedir prestados tocados y
vestidos de la tierra.

In each province they arrived at, they adapted to the
uses and customs and dressed in that dress: today
they looked Galician in Galicia, and tomorrow like
a Viscaína in Viscaya. They knew who the ranking
women were in each place and asked them about the
headdresses and clothing of the region.

—F. Bermúdez de Pedraza, 1638

AT HOME AT A COURT ALWAYS ON THE MOVE

Catalina's personality, sensibility, and outlook were shaped by the people,
places, and cultures she encountered as part of her life at the itinerant
royal court of Castile and that she took with her to England. This was,
in some ways, typical for women who were expected to move to another
man's home to marry. Along with a trousseau and a dowry, all foreign

brides brought with them their language and literature, culture and rituals, ceremonies, styles of dress, art, and habits of living.[1] Catalina's experience was distinctive because she was raised in realms with a rich variety of languages, cultures, landscapes, and religions that she encountered and absorbed as she traveled with her family across the peninsula. For fifteen years she traveled throughout the Spanish countryside, sometimes in her father's realms of the Crown of Aragon, but most of the time she was with her mother's court in Castile. Because these courts were not located in fixed capital cities, the family was often on the road, staying in royal towns and military camps, moving in formal processions into Medina del Campo, Alcalá de Henares, Barcelona, Córdoba, small towns and villages, and religious sites.

As she traveled, she came into contact with an array of cultural influences—Mudéjar and Gothic, Christian and Muslim—in the towns she visited and at the court of her parents, who relished the mix of styles even as they conquered the Nasrid kingdom of Granada. Some places mattered to her more than others: Arévalo, where her grandmother lived; Guadalupe, her spiritual home; Seville, site of many family gatherings; and Granada, where she soaked up both the sun and Islamicate culture. The act of travel shaped Catalina's aesthetic taste and created meaningful social practices. But the royal processions promoted more than just Isabel and Fernando's ambitions. Catalina received an important education in queenship as she watched her parents interact with their subjects and convoke the regional assemblies of nobles and townspeople. Her identity was shaped by the geography of the Iberian Peninsula—from the mountains of the north to those of the south, and inland and coastal cities. She spoke several languages and could read even more, a cultural fluency she gained during a childhood spent literally on the move.

Written descriptions tell us where she went, what she saw, and what she wore amid the royal festivities of entries. But even more revealing than brief descriptions of what was in the mule packs are the remains of the actual places and things Catalina saw as she traveled. She absorbed the complex culture of late medieval Spain and then brought to England not only tangible objects but also an array of cosmopolitan customs and viewpoints that complicate notions of Spanish nation and identity.[2] These experiences shaped her identity and were part of her social, intellectual, and cultural baggage when she left Spain in 1501 for England to marry Arthur Tudor (1486–1502), eldest son of Henry VII (1457, r. 1485–1509) and his wife, Elizabeth of York (1466–1503), and heir to the English crown.

WHERE SHE WENT, WHAT SHE SAW, WHAT SHE WORE

Catalina's travels began shortly after her birth on 15 December 1485 at Alcalá de Henares.[3] Since she was the fifth child and a girl, the political importance of her birth was not as momentous as that of her brother, Juan. Still, it was the Christmas season, and the family stayed at court and celebrated her birth with banquets and gift-giving. She was swaddled in Breton linen and dressed in green-and-white velvet dresses with gold lace for her baptism, and her maid, Elena de Carmona, was paid 11,100 *maravedíes* for her service (for comparison, the bishop of Palencia, who baptized Catalina, received 3,650 *maravedíes*).[4] Fernando left soon after to wage war against the Nasrid leader of Granada while the family spent the winter of 1486 in the north. Isabel took the children to her birthplace, Madrigal, where the royal residences blended Romanesque, Gothic, and Mudéjar styles. They then moved on to Arévalo, a small town of tremendous symbolic importance. Steeped in the legends of ancient Iberians, the Visigoths, and the Christian victory at Las Navas de Tolosa during the Reconquest, it was also where her mother, Isabel of Portugal, was born. This gave the queen a moment to spend time with her mother, show off her new baby daughter, and use the occasion to show her children how to serve their parents personally. It was a brief sojourn, however. In the spring, Isabel went to the royal monastery of Guadalupe with all the children, but because they arrived during Lent, there were no royal entry festivities. After Easter, they turned southward to be closer to Fernando. On 11 June, they were in Córdoba to celebrate Fernando's victory over Boabdil with a solemn procession in which Queen Isabel and *infanta* Isabel processed on foot from the Great Mosque-Cathedral to the parish church of Santiago. The chroniclers do not say exactly where Catalina would have been in all this, but at six months of age it is doubtful that she would have been active in the ceremonies.[5] The queen then moved on to Illora, Granada, and Moclín, but again the chronicles are silent on the whereabouts of the young children until late June, when Isabel and the children stopped at Córdoba. She dropped off Juan, María, and Catalina at Jaén while she and Fernando went north to Santiago de Compostela. In late fall, the family was reunited in Salamanca and Ávila and spent the winter at Alcalá de Henares.[6]

In late medieval Spain, the celebratory play of ceremonies and banquets at theatrically staged dramas welcomed the royal family as they moved about the realm. This powerful blend of personality and art was a public display that celebrated celebrity, charisma, and political power. On these road trips through Spain, the king brought his wife, and a few steps behind them rode their children.[7] The baby of the family in this entourage was *infanta* Catalina. She spent her entire childhood traveling with her siblings and her mother (and sometimes father) along with dozens of women and men who fed, clothed, educated, and pampered her. An attentive child, she learned vital lessons from her mother as the family moved with Spanish armies who fought the Muslim ruler of Granada. She grew up in towns near battlefields, listening to news reports of her mother at the head of armies, and was only seven years old in 1492 when her parents captured Granada. After the city was captured, she spent long periods of time in Granada surrounded by art, architecture, fabrics, food, and fashion that would come to be deeply embedded in everything she did.

As the family moved around, Catalina and her four siblings—Juan, Isabel, Juana, and María—formed an essential part of a tradition of ostentatious processions that solidified royal political authority. Catalina was closest emotionally to her next-oldest sister, María, only three years her senior. María's own birth was fraught with sadness because her twin died at birth (or was stillborn). The relationship of these two sisters was closer than that with the eldest, Isabel, who was fifteen years older and married to the King of Portugal before Catalina even knew her, or even Juana, six years older. Isabel and Fernando publicly displayed their children, like the spectacle of gems, rich brocades, and military weapons at the festivities of a royal entry, as the physical embodiment of the wealth of the realm. But the royal children were more than glittery objects—they were an extension of kingly hegemony. They were the future; they were symbolic promises of dynastic stability and prosperity.

Amid all the commotion, it is not easy to spot Catalina, however. Whereas sixteenth-century chroniclers gave rich and vivid details of a royal entry, most of the chronicles for the period 1485–1501 are thin on ceremony and thick with details on wars and regional unrest. Chroniclers Fernando de Pulgar, Diego de Valera, and Andrés Bernáldez reveal the interplay of personality at court, but they rarely mention the *infantas* by name.[8] Catalina's eldest sister, Isabel, and brother, Juan, are often named, but the other *infantas* are identified only when they get betrothed, married, or widowed. This was not willful neglect. Catalina was very young and spent much of her time in the nursery. With four siblings ahead of her in the successions, she was a distant witness to the momentous events of the wars against Granada, the onset of the Inquisition, the westward sea voyages of Christopher Columbus. Most often, we see her and her sister María watch their siblings leave home to marry, start families, and, in the case of Isabel and Juan, die young. Catalina is mentioned only twice: at the celebrations for her betrothal to Prince Arthur in 1489 and when she left Spain to marry him in 1501. But even that trip did not generate much comment, at least not in the royal records (more research into local records may well reveal more substantial details). These records can only provide a glimpse, a *visteza*, but they tell an important story of what an *infanta* might learn about queenship by paying attention to the landscape, the culture of the towns, and the people of late medieval Spain.

Moving a household was immensely complex, a political act in itself. Records of the household document the movements of the king, queen, and their children as they govern their subjects and wage war with the kingdom of Granada. Chroniclers reveal a court constantly on the move, a "traveling city" that attracted great lords, diplomats, bureaucrats, warriors, lawyers, church officials, and the whole infrastructure of people who cooked, cleaned, served, dressed, undressed, tutored, and tended to the royal family.[9] The war against Granada until 1492 placed extraordinary demands on the family. Fernando and Isabel sometimes had to leave their children at another court with their governesses, tutors, confessors, and attendants. It was an exhausting way to live. Catalina celebrated sixteen birthdays in Spain in at least ten different places: Alcalá de Henares, Aranjuez, Barcelona, Baza, Córdoba, Granada, Madrid, Seville, Tortosa, and Zaragoza. As the family moved around, they dressed in local styles, asking the high-ranking women in each place for information about the headdresses, clothing, and customs of the region.[10] From the household accounts of Isabel's treasurer, Gonzalo de Baeza, we can calculate the economic costs of daily life on the road. We can tally up the costs of the public display in yards of velvet and silk, lengths of silk grosgrain hair ribbons, hundreds of rabbit pelts, precious gems, and the salaries of the attendants who accompanied the royal family: a procession of sweaty mules slowly making their way from Murcia to Valladolid in 1488 cost a hefty 90,226 *maravedíes*.[11]

COSSETED BY DEVOTED WOMEN AT COURT

The royal household Catalina inhabited was not simply a domestic space. Her home was a building and a palace, a royal residence and a fortress, with gardens and chapels as well as private chambers. It was the site of familiarity, friendship, nurturing, political intimacy, and sexual intimacy within a stone structure that housed a group of people who lived and worked under the same roof. It was a private space where the relationships among the residents, especially routine activities such as sleeping and eating, touched on a public space that involved impersonal elements of governance. The royal household was a site of political, economic, and cultural production and consumption for power brokers, diplomats, prominent writers, artists, architects, musicians, and dramatists and their patrons, where social interaction combined with conspicuous displays of power and influence. Dynastic ambition and patriarchal institutions shaped the organization and ethos of the elite and royal household, but everyone in the royal household, from the king and queen to the people who made the beds, was bound, or ought to have been bound, by real affection for the royal children who spent much of their young lives traveling around Spain.[12]

Isabel was a devoted mother who kept her daughters close to hand, supervising their education and preparing them for marriage to a foreign prince or king and for life in a foreign court. Women had an important place in Catherine's privy chamber and court, and household accounts reveal gift exchange as a powerful means of expressing rank and importance. Royal majesty needed to be surrounded by richly dressed courtiers, and women received gifts of cloth from the king and queen. Many of the women at court, from nurses to governesses, often came from the same family and were shared by all of Isabel's daughters, providing continuity and stability in the household. Some of the women were part of Catalina's entourage from infancy—her governess (*ama*), Inés Vanegas, and her two daughters, Inés and Teresa; her personal attendants, María de Salinas and María de Rojas; and Elvira Manuel, her guardian (*guarda de las damas*) in Spain and her main attendant (*camarera mayor*) in England. These women were vital to Catalina. As she moved from Spain to England, as she was transformed from *infanta* to princess to queen, her Spanish friends and attendants in her household at court who had served her since childhood were the mainstay of her life. They were with her at her parents' court and moved with her to London; a dozen or so stayed with her during her widowhood; and one very faithful friend, María de Salinas, was with Catalina in the last days before her death.

To educate Catalina and her sisters Isabel, Juana, and María in the customs and practices of life in a royal court, Isabel selected women of her own itinerant court who were trained in Latin, religious conduct, and decorous behavior. When Catalina was an infant and toddler, there was considerable overlap of the households of the three *infantas*, which can complicate sorting out who was who at court. The earliest records, from 1486 to 1491, include Elena de Carmona, her *criada* (maid), but there are several payments made to an unnamed *ama*. The accounts note three women who serve as *criada de las infantes*: Elvira Mendes (who also appears often in the payment records as *criada* for Juana), Aldonça Suares (*criada* for María), and Elvira de Torres.[13] Beginning in 1491, however, when Catalina was six, newly betrothed to Arthur and styled as the *princessa de Gales* (Princess of Wales), the accounts record payments to women in Catalina's household who are named. These women served only Catalina and remained part of her household for the next decade; some served Catalina beyond her childhood and as queen after her marriage to Henry VIII.

Catalina was also served by prominent noblewomen, bound to the queen and her daughters by ties of service and friendship, who shaped the social and cultural education of the *infantas*.[14] They were expected to be clever, cultivated, and sophisticated but not learned, to be friends and servants and guides to the cultural norms of life at court and to protect her by controlling access to her.[15] They combined sewing, embroidery, spinning, and weaving with intellectual and cultural pursuits.[16] This relationship is not easily defined, with fluid boundaries dependent on personality and experience. Over the course of a lifetime, a noblewoman serving at court could be tutor, mentor, casual friend, close confidante, and as intimate as a favorite sister. The relationship was reciprocal, and not just in terms of monetary compensation. Both sides gained much: the royal family received vital loyal service from noblewomen who, in return, met their future husbands from the pool of noblemen in service to the king and *infante* Juan.

When viewed over time, the household accounts for Catalina increase in both number and the richness of detail in both who was paid and for what service. There were as many as 92 women at Isabel's court, 61 of whom served the queen, with 13 in the household of the *infanta* María and 6 for the *infanta* Catalina. The Isabelline court appears to be typical of the age but much smaller than that of later queens Isabel of Valois (178 women) and Mariana of Austria (more than 300 women).[17] Typical also of royal households is a significant number of noblewomen, many of whom were daughters of or married to the highest-ranking nobles at court. There is evidence of a loyal group of noblewomen at court whose annuities suggest that they are part and parcel of the royal entourage but not as intimate. Their social status meant that they did not have an official position such as *ama* or *criada*, a nurse or wet nurse, and many of them are members of prominent noble families resident at the court of Isabel and Fernando: Isabel de Ribadeneyra, Inés Enríquez (daughter of the count of Buendía), Constança de Bazan, María Pimentel, Mayor de Figueroa, and Mençia Manuel.[18] These women do not appear in the accounts often, suggesting that they were not particularly close to Catalina and that their presence at her court was part of a congenial kinship alliance, the sort of service noblewomen were expected to perform for a queen. They were paid in a combination of annuity payments and gifts, a common practice among elite and royal households, where the public and private, personal and political were blended smoothly.[19] The personal intimacy that these gifts symbolize is evident in the routine gifts of clothing, shoes, and jewelry worn by the *infantas*.

Amid the faces at court, one group of women stands out. Inés de Vanegas and her daughters, Inés and Teresa, are the women most often cited in the accounts. Inés, the mother, first appears in the household accounts on 23 March 1495, when she is called *ama de la ynfante Catalina*, and for her service to the queen she was paid in clothing—yards of black cloth for a habit, cape, and apron ("18 varas de paño negro, de que le fizo merçed para vn abito e vn manto e vn tabardo para su vistuario, que costo 6,075 mrs").[20] The mention of a gift of black fabric perhaps suggests that Inés, the mother, was a widow, but black was a fashionable color. Little at present is known about her, her family background, or even her husband, who presumably was part of the royal court. Her increasing importance to Catalina is clearly shown in the substantial rise in the amount of her annuity payments. On 12 October 1498, she was paid an annuity of 10,185 *maravedíes*; a year later that annuity was significantly increased to 50,000. In 1501, her annuity was 66,000 *maravedíes*. This considerable sum would remain consistent until her death in 1504. She is clearly someone who mattered greatly to Catalina as *princessa de Gales*, even after the death of Arthur and Catalina's dramatic change in status.[21]

Slightly lower on the social scale are noble or gentlewomen who were occasional members of Catalina's intimate household. Beatriz de Torres, noted as maid ("criada de la ynfante doña Catalina"), was paid 40,000 *maravedíes* for service ("le fiso merçed para su vistuario").[22] Ana de Pliego, daughter of one of the guards in her chambers ("hija de Fernando de Pliego, moço de camara de la ynfante Catalina"), received payments for materials for clothing for María and Catalina,[23] and Inés de Jaén, a maid ("criada de al ynfante doña Catalina"), was given the substantial sum of 50,000 *maravedíes* as a wedding gift ("de que le fiso merçed para ayuda de su casamiento").[24] These women had specific, very intimate, tasks to perform and were paid for them, but wedding gifts were not bestowed on all the women at court. The generous gift to Inés de Jaén at her wedding implies a relationship based on more than just employment. But the gift could have been motivated by the need to create a binding political alliance. In the absence of other sources, it is not possible to know for sure what sort of relationship it was.

The question of compensation for royal service is complicated because it is situated at the intersection of class and gender and has as much to do with the future status of the child—heir to the realms or potential bride of an archduke or a king. The salaries and compensation for noblemen and male household officials who served Juan, heir to the realms, were higher than for most of the women in Isabel's court who served the daughters. Bernardino Fernández de Velasco, her chief chamberlain (*camarero mayor*) after 1492, was paid 67,600 *maravedíes* annually, but his duties encompassed the entire household. Personal status and the importance of the work sometimes mattered more than one's sex. Juana Manuel, Isabel's principal *ama* (also called *guarda de las damas*), supervised the women at court and was paid the considerable sum of 250,000 *maravedíes*, but this may have been a one-time lump-sum payment. This exceeds that for the *primo aya* for *infante* Juan; he was paid 200,000 *maravedíes*, but he had only one child, not four, to worry about. Juan was the heir, but it is significant that the salaries are even roughly comparable. This is far from a notion of equal pay for equal work in the fifteenth century, but it is a marker of the importance of caring personally for the royal children and the lofty social rank of the person in charge.

Men and women of less lofty rank did work, no matter how important, that was clearly valued less. Isabel's court physicians received annuities of 60,000 *maravedíes*, while other medical staff received 35,000. Musicians at court received annuities between 25,000 and 30,000. Catalina's tutors Andrés Miranda (a Dominican from the monastery of Santo Domingo, near Burgos) and Alessandro Geraldino were each paid an annuity of 50,000. The status of the *infanta* mattered in the case of Miranda, whose salary was increased in 1495 because the *infanta* Juana became engaged to Philip, Archduke of Austria (and of Burgundy), and Catalina was betrothed to Arthur Tudor, making Juana an archduchess and Catalina the *princessa de Gales*. This salary is less than the 60,000 paid to *infante* Juan's tutors, but it was still among the highest of the members of the household. It is striking, then, to find that Beatriz Galindo, who had served Isabel for years and married one of Isabel's secretaries (Francisco de Madrid), was paid far less than the Geraldino brothers, only 15,000 *maravedíes* annually.[25] Galindo, the author of commentaries on Aristotle and a book of Latin verse, was educated at one of the colleges at the University of Salamanca and may have been one of Antonio Nebrija's students, so it was likely her sex, not the quality of her education, that explains the discrepancy in her salary.

More lowly were Catalina's attendants—both men and women—who cared for clothing, shoes, jewelry, and personal objects (such as books and toys), who were paid between 6,000 and 10,000 *maravedíes* annually. What these sums do not show, however, are the marriage gifts (often monetary, but also valuable objects) bestowed by Isabel, which could be substantial and which men at court did not receive. Gentlewomen of modest rank, such as Francisca de Torres, Juana de Porras (called Porricas), and Nieta, were paid 10,000, 6,000, and 8,000 *maravedíes* on 20 October 1500. Little is known about these women beyond the fact that they were permanent members of the household. They were paid for expenses they incurred to move Catalina's household from Écija to Seville, and the same three were paid the same amounts again on 10 March 1501. Nieta may be a nickname, suggesting that she was part of the intimate circle around Catalina but probably not a noblewoman.[26] At the bottom of the social hierarchy were a few slaves and a female dwarf who was first part of *infanta* María's court at Lisbon, then came to Catalina's court in Spain, and moved with her to England, where she was known as the "Spanish fool."[27] But these women at court were valued highly and respected. After Queen Isabel's death, King Fernando ordered a final set of annuity payments to be paid to the women who had served in Isabel's court, among them some of the loftiest and lowliest. On 10 June 1504, Blanca Manrique, Aldara de Portugal, Francisca de Ayala, Isabel (daughter of Constança), Marina Ruiz, and Inés (a slave) received payments of an unspecified amount.[28]

Women at court were also involved in the physically intimate rituals of eating, dressing, fixing hairstyles, and adorning Catalina's body with jewelry. This calls to mind another instance of the importance of touch, in the myth of the famed royal touch of the king to heal the sick. In this case, however, it is not the royal person who does the touching; it is a trusted attendant who has proximity to the charisma of royalty. Women serving at court formed concentric circles of power that surrounded the royal bodies of the king and queen. The personal attendants formed outer layers of human touch, from the breast that fed the infant to the hands that tied the ribbons in a dress. They tutored, trained, and advised the *infanta* while adding a layer of insulation from other people at court. Attendants at court, both men and women, physically represented the power of proximity to the royal person. Royal attendants were a human cordon that functioned like public great rooms leading through antechambers to the personal intimacy of the privy chamber and, finally, the bedroom.

As Inés de Vanegas prepared for the next move with the children, she must have thought, What does a royal toddler need for a road trip? Amid records of the expenses for red silk, green wool, and black sateen for smocks, tunics, shifts, and shirts, Baeza includes payment for three rods of navy blue (*naval*) for napkins (*pañizuelos de cuchillos*).[29] Small napkins such as these, and there are many of them noted in Baeza's accounts, would have been tucked in the luggage packs, used perhaps on the road, or placed on the tables at the royal castles along the route.

The next few years were slightly more settled. In March 1487, Isabel was with all the children in Córdoba while Fernando waged war in Málaga. In early April, the queen left Catalina and María nestled safely in Montoro while she and *infanta* Isabel went to Málaga for a siege that lasted until 18 August. In mid-November, Fernando, Isabel, and *infante* Juan went to Zaragoza to convene the Corts. The entire family celebrated the Christmas holidays there and stayed until mid-February 1488. In March, Fernando and Isabel received word from English diplomats that Henry VII of England was seeking Catalina as bride for his son, Arthur.[30] The family was in Murcia by May and in Valladolid at Christmas. From Baeza's accounts of the purchases for Catalina that year, we can imagine her learning how to walk using a small cart for guidance ("mostrarse anda la ynfante"). Royal tailors fashioned her clothing into a mixture of styles: a green satin dress in the Morisco style ("sayo morisco"), a purple velvet Portuguese-style skirt, and an ermine-lined red silk *mantilla*.[31]

PRINCESSA DE GALES

In March 1489, Isabel, the children, and the entourage of the household traveled to Arévalo and Guadalupe on their way to Valladolid for meetings with the pope and an embassy of French nobles. But all these dignitaries mattered little to Catalina, then aged three. The main event for her was her first public ceremony on 30 March to celebrate the Treaty of Medina del Campo, her formal betrothal to two-year-old Prince Arthur, son of King Henry VII of England.[32] Festivities to celebrate betrothals were vital to the ceremony of the dynastic continuity of monarchy, as revealed in the letters sent to Henry VII discussing the suitability of the match. The ambassadors, awed by the wealth and sophistication, described Queen Isabel as "a thing so rich no man has ever seen the equal."[33] The chroniclers tell us that Valladolid was filled for days with large, sumptuous banquets ("fiestas de grandes e sumtuosos gastos"). The English ambassadors, Thomas Salvage and Richard Nanfan, reported to Henry VII that "on the 22nd and 25th jousts and bullfights were held in their honour."[34] The display worked in favor of Isabel and Fernando. The English agreed to the Castilian marriage and a decrease in the dowry, and they stipulated that if Arthur were to die before Catherine, she would inherit one-third of the revenues of Chester, Cornwall, and Wales.[35]

This all may sound romantic, but it is difficult to know how much Catalina realized what was happening. She may not have realized yet that she was the future Princess of Wales. All she knew was that she was opulently dressed and that her mother held her up for all to see.[36] Catalina was not only a child; she was a diplomatic prize who had little choice in the matter—she was duty-bound to obey her parents, who negotiated the marriage and prepared her for life in a foreign court. Her betrothal to Arthur was first negotiated the year before, and Fernando and Isabel were ready to send her to England, presumably to learn English customs and practices, but the negotiations dragged on for years.

By April 1489, after the parties were over, Isabel and the children went to Arévalo and Guadalupe on the way to Córdoba, the former site of the Islamic Caliphate. She was just old enough to begin to absorb the strikingly different architecture of the city, even if all she saw was the exterior of the Great Mosque with its delicate carvings on the walls. In May, the queen and the children were in Jaén and Úbeda, and from mid-June to December, she and *infanta* Isabel went to the camp at Baza, leaving behind the rest of the children. Catalina spent her fourth birthday at Baza and, with the rest of family, went to Seville on 30 December, where they would have resided at the magnificent palace, the Reales Alcázares, near the cathedral.[37] Built in the twelfth century, this palace, originally the fortified residence of the Almohad caliphs, was converted into a Christian royal residence by King Pedro IV in the fourteenth century with much of the original Muslim structure left intact. Catalina would have wandered around the gardens, fountains, pools, and dazzlingly colorful painted tiles on the floors, walls, and ceilings.[38] In 1490, the entire family stayed mostly in Seville, with forays into Ejica, from at least Easter to December.

There were no immediate plans to send her to the Tudor court, so she had to learn about both England and English queenship from a distance. How did a foreign-born bride learn to be a queen consort? What did she need to know to negotiate the complex rituals and ceremonies of court? Who taught her how to supervise household officials? When did she learn this? Catalina had a long betrothal, at least a decade. How did her family prepare her? First, Isabel made certain that her daughter was well educated. By 1492, Catalina began her formal studies, and her tutors would have schooled her and her siblings on the history of the Muslim conquest of Spain and the reconquest by their Christian ancestors. This was vital preparation for the practice of queenship. Isabel and Fernando's children received a rigorous education in an intellectual milieu where literacy was expected and cultural patronage the norm.[39] Household accounts show that Isabel carefully selected and compensated her children's tutors, the brothers Antonio and Alessandro Geraldino.[40] Isabel's servants, Andrés Miranda, a Dominican at the monastery of Santo Domingo (Burgos), and Beatriz Galindo (*la Latina*, "the Latinist"), were also important in educating the children and worked closely with the Geraldino brothers. Alessandro accompanied Catalina to England in 1501, served as her confessor, and wrote *De eruditione nobelium puellarum* (On the education of noble girls, 1501) at Isabel's request (Isabel continued to pay annuities to Alessandro Geraldino until her death in 1504). At age eleven, Catalina owned a breviary.[41] Her conventional religious studies were complemented by close contact with theological writings on the Inquisition, which was particularly active during the 1490s, and could not have avoided news of the inquisitors' actions. When the family stayed at the Real Monasterio de Santo Tomás in Ávila, Catalina would have noticed Pedro Berruguete working on the retablo (ca. 1493–99) depicting Saint Dominic de Guzmán and the Albigensians and presiding over an auto-da-fé.[42] At age twelve she was expected to exercise some discretion and had learned to supervise servants. Her studies included philosophy, literature, and religion as well as music (she could play the clavichord and harp).[43] She studied late medieval ideas on virtue, justice, and proper queenly behavior and Christianized versions of classical philosophy and natural science concerning medical understandings of the differences between the sexes.[44] She would have read, or known of, works that dealt with the education of women, such as Juan Rodriquez de la Camara's *El triunfo de las donas* (The triumph of women, 1443), Alvaro de Luna's *El libro de las virtuosas y claras mugeres* (The book of virtuous and famous women, 1446), Fray Martín Alonso de Córdoba's *Jardín de la nobles doncellas* (The garden of noble maidens, 1468), and Francesc Eiximenis's manual for female instruction, the *Carro de las donas* (The carriage of women, fifteenth century), which may have been brought to court by Beatriz Galindo.[45] It is also likely that she read or knew of Juan de Flores's *Grisel and Mirabella*, *The Slander Against Women*, and *The Defense of Ladies Against Slanderers*, works in the *querelle des femmes* genre that were dedicated to an unnamed female reader who may well have been Isabel.[46]

The English wanted to be sure that Catalina would adjust smoothly to her new home, and Queen Elizabeth of York wrote to Isabel, wishing to hear about Catalina's health, and also wrote to both Isabel and Catalina.[47] News circulated between the ambassadors at both courts, but the first step was to master a language that they all had in common. She could speak French, English, and German in addition to Castilian and Latin, prompting Beatriz Galindo to note that Catalina surpassed her mother in Latin learning.[48] Latin gave her the ability to converse with royal advisers and read official documents. Beyond languages, Catalina would have to rely on the example of her mother. Isabel was a superb tutor. For the next ten years, Catalina watched her mother act in public and in private, govern as a queen regnant, wage war and make peace, work closely with religious leaders, and negotiate with her husband on the nuances of a royal partnership. These, her first lessons in queenship, guided her throughout her life.[49]

LOOKING UP FROM HER BOOKS TO SEE NEW LANDSCAPES AND CULTURES

In 1490, while the family was in Seville, for five-year-old Catalina the highlight would have been two weeks of public festivities in May to celebrate the upcoming wedding of *infanta* Isabel and Afonso of Portugal. Bernáldez briefly comments on the lavish and expensive banquets ("muy grandes fiestas e torneos e grandes alegrías . . . muy grandes gastos"), which lasted fifteen days, at which Catalina may have worn her first hooped skirt (a *verdugado*), made of green silk with a green brocaded underskirt.[50] On at least two occasions, in July and September, Fernando and Isabel left the children in Seville with their attendants (not named) to attend to business in Córdoba.[51] The family stayed in the south in 1491, mostly in Seville (until April), Zubia, and Baza.

Catalina, now six, traveled with a small court of her own, women who were bound to her by ties of service and friendship. She would have noted the somber tone of life at court as they sadly welcomed the return of *infanta* Isabel, widowed only six months after her wedding. As war with Granada accelerated, the children were once again left in a safe place when Fernando and Isabel set up camp at Santa Fé, outside Granada, in September. During the final push to win the war, the *infantas* stayed in nearby Zubia, but they knew that danger was nearby. A candle in their mother's bedchamber started a fire that engulfed the entire camp and sent the queen and her *infanta* Isabel outside in their nightgowns. By November, the war was over, and the victory celebrations began in January 1492. Catalina missed the official public surrender (witnessed by Juan and either *infanta* Isabel or Juana) but probably took part in the solemn entry into the city. She was in Granada (or Santa Fé) until May, but chroniclers do not note her presence in the fortified palatine city of luxury and wealth known as the Alhambra. This magnificent and enormous hilltop fortress-palace complex, with its cluster of barracks, gardens, bathhouses, a mosque, a dungeon, and a cemetery, was constructed under a succession of rulers from 1232 to 1492. The exterior of the Alhambra is sparely decorated, but the interior mimics and references natural elements in a grand fashion with gardens, fountains, beautiful vistas, sculpted porticos, and lavish rooms meant to display wealth and power. The labyrinthine city was her first taste of Muslim art and architecture unmediated by Christian influence. She would have heard the Muslim call to prayers and seen veiled women and the sophisticated beauty of the Alhambra palaces' pools, baths, intricate ceilings, and patios with fountains.[52]

Fernando and Isabel converted the Mexuar, a chamber used by the Nasrid kings for the meetings with the council and to grant audiences, into a royal chapel. They and their children lived in the royal residence,

FIG. 4 | Alhambra, Mirador de Lindaraja, interior, view from Salon de Lindaraja, looking north-northeast, ca. 1360s. Photo © Bildarchiv Foto Marburg / Art Resource, New York.

the Cuarto Dorado (Gilded Room), with its richly painted Mudéjar-style coffered ceiling. They wandered about rooms such as the *mirador* (lookout) of Lindaraja with its hybrid styles and multilayered surfaces, covered with wood, ceramic, and low-relief carved plaster ornament known as *ataurique*, gazing out windows that look out onto a garden (fig. 4). The eye-catching receding arches, arabesques of vine scrolls and ribbons, and stucco *muqarnas*, ornamented vaulting sliced into geometric and foliated patterns interwoven with Arabic inscriptions that form a cupola or corbel, created a glittering honeycomb of color, pattern, and texture.[53] Catalina probably read or spoke no Arabic, so the inscriptions at the Alhambra would have been unintelligible, but the art transported her into another culture, another way of seeing and imagining the world.

   Amid the richness of her shoes, clothing, food, and cosmetics, one object stands out—the pomegranate. It is a significant sign of her identity

FIG. 5 | Unknown artisan, livery badge, Tudor rose and pomegranate (Catherine of Aragon), early sixteenth century. Museum of London Picture Library, 82.255/5. Photo © Museum of London.

that after having lived in Granada for over two years she adopted the pomegranate as her personal emblem. This ancient symbol of fertility and regeneration, which in the Christian church is a sign of Christ's resurrection, symbolized the promise of heirs. After her marriage to Henry, she merged it with the Tudor rose, as in, for example, a small cast-pewter badge, no more than 1 1/2 inches high (fig. 5). This badge probably dates either to the time of her marriage to Arthur (1501) or to her subsequent marriage to Henry (1509). It shows both the Tudor rose and Catalina's pomegranate emblem and was worn by members of Catalina's household in England as a marker of identity and of affiliation with her personally.[54] It was a vivid, constant reminder to those closest to her that she was, and always would be, a child of Spain.

In March 1492, the family settled in Barcelona, but chroniclers do not include Catalina among those of the royal family who attended the public reception on 21 April 1493 of Columbus after his return to Spain. She was there, part of the noisy, fragrant, vibrant, public festivities at court, but not significant enough yet to catch the chroniclers' eyes.[55] Catalina was, however, quietly paying attention. The knowledge, if not the sight, of her mother waging war must have been an impressive lesson in queenship for Catalina, more vivid than anything her tutor, Alessandro Geraldino, could assign. Queen Isabel was praised widely by chroniclers and ambassadors for her work organizing provisions, supervising the supply lines, and staying so close to Fernando throughout the fighting. It was not a surprise to Bernáldez that Catalina, as Queen of England in 1513, followed her mother's example by organizing and provisioning the English troops who defeated the Scots and killed the Scottish king at the Battle of Flodden.[56]

While living in Barcelona and traveling in eastern Spain throughout 1493 and 1494, Catalina began to absorb more of the blended cultures of late medieval Iberia. In Valencia, Catalina would have seen, or at least known of, the emotive portraits of Christ and the Virgin Mary by the Italian painter Paolo de San Leocadio.[57] When the family stopped in Córdoba, she could not have missed seeing the Great Mosque and worshipping in the chapel built by King Enrique II in the fourteenth century. In Toledo, she would have been part of the religious festivals at the magnificent cathedral, filled with an astounding array of altarpieces (*retablos*), stone sculptures, tomb effigies, and illuminated manuscripts.[58] While in León, she would have worshipped at the Real Basilica Colegiata of San Isidoro, a site of royal religious patronage, and could have seen Visigothic king Recceswinth's crown over the altar, the crucifix of Fernando I and Sancha, and in the treasury, the *arqueta de las Bienavenutranazas*, with Kufic characters on one side.[59]

Fernando and Isabel were avid patrons of artists, and an itinerary of their travels can also be read as a tour of artworks-in-progress.[60] In 1494 and 1495, the royal family spent time in Valladolid, Medina del Campo, Segovia, Madrid, Tordesillas, Guadalajara, Burgos, Almazan (Soria), Romanos (Aragón), Caspe (Aragón), Xerte (Baix Ebre), and Tortosa (Baix Ebre).[61] At the royal monastery of Santa Clara in Palencia, Juan de Nalda would have been at work in 1493 on a retablo with images of the Virgen de la Misericordia and la Misa de San Gregorio.[62] As she moved across the landscape of almond groves and vineyards, she absorbed a visual culture that reflected centuries of interaction and was inextricably part of her identity, which was more than simply Castilian or Aragonese and might be more aptly termed "Spanish." We get a glimpse of her life in a painting of Isabel and Fernando in the chapel of the royal lodgings at the monastery of Santo Tomás in Ávila, shown kneeling in prayer before the Virgin Mary, with the Christ Child on her lap (fig. 6). Isabel, wearing an ornate red gown with gold embroidery, kneels before Saint Dominic, the founder

FIG. 6 | Master of the Catholic Monarchs, *The Virgin of the Catholic Monarchs*, ca. 1490. Oil on wood, 123 × 112 cm. Museo Nacional del Prado, Madrid, ID# P001260. Photo: Album / Art Resource.

of the Dominican Order, one of her daughters (probably Isabel), and an unidentified man. Behind Fernando is Saint Thomas, the namesake of the monastery; Prince Juan; and the Dominican Inquisitor General, Tomás de Torquemada. Based on the fashion of the clothing, the painting was completed no earlier than 1491, perhaps as late as 1497, which suggests that Catalina was at the monastery while the artist, who may have been Pedro de Salamanca, was finishing this painting.[63] The queen and king are shown as political equals, kneeling on the same visual plane. This imagery depicts Isabel's political theology of Christian unity and persecution and later expulsion of the Jews, which would have been reinforced in Catalina's lessons. The message of this painting—the power of a queen regnant linked to the power of orthodox Christianity—was a powerful lesson in queenship for a young girl preparing to be a Queen of England.

She had firsthand experience as a subject of a painting when, in 1496 or 1497, Isabel and Fernando commissioned the Netherlandish painter Juan de Flandes to paint her. This exquisite painting (fig. 7) is perhaps the earliest depiction of *infanta* Catalina, painted when she was between eleven and thirteen years old.[64] It is quite small (12 × 8 in.) and strikingly intimate. The rosebud she holds in her right hand is tightly closed, barely revealing red petals, signifying that she is a mere bud of a girl, a virgin. The three leaves on the rosebud stem suggest the Trinity and symbolize piety. The painter rendered Catalina with delicate pink lips, a straight long nose, and perfectly clear skin—the sign of an unblemished soul. Her face is solemn and modestly direct; her blue-gray eyes are neither downcast nor evasive. Her golden-red hair is neatly pulled off her face and coiled around silk grosgrain ribbons, a style typical of the Mediterranean.

This portrait was not intended to depict Catalina as she was; its purpose was to convey an idea of her to a very particular audience.[65] On 15 August 1497, a ceremony at Woodstock formalized again the betrothal, and this painting was probably intended to show her off to her future father-in-law, Henry VII.[66] Juan de Flandes used fashion in his portrait of Catalina to convey an alluring Spanishness, knowing this would appeal to the international ambitions of the young Tudor dynasty. Her modest off-white cotton, wool, and linen dress, a *hábito* (shift), has gathers at the sleeves and the neckline and suggests a hint of breasts. The appliquéd borders on the collar and set-in sleeves are decorated with an Islamicate pattern of blackstitch embroidery. This type of dress was most often worn indoors, or if less decorated it might be worn as an undergarment. It suggests home and familial intimacy.[67] King Henry VII would see in this portrait a highly desirable diplomatic prize for two royal families jockeying for political advantage. The painting, redolent of potential power in a fresh, youthful girl, a mere bud, a virgin brimming with fecundity and the promise of children, sent a clear political message: this Spanish princess knows how to be attractive to an English prince.

FIG. 7 | Juan de Flandes, *A Spanish Princess* (possibly Catherine, or Juana), ca. 1496. Oil on panel, 31.5 × 21.2 cm. Museo Thyssen-Bornemisza, Madrid, inv. no. 141. Photo: Album / Art Resource, New York.

Catalina spent the next four years traveling less but saying goodbye to her siblings as, one by one, they left home to marry. At this moment of transition from "medieval practices under fragmented political rule to the early modern period and the nominal rule of one king over the peninsular realms," she found herself left behind in Tortosa, Cavia, Palenzuela (Palencia), Burgos, and Valladolid.[68] In August 1496, the family was in Laredo to bid farewell to *infanta* Juana, who departed Spain for Flanders to marry Philip of Burgundy, and then left for Valencia de Alcantará to bid farewell to her sister Isabel as she departed for Portugal to marry King Manuel. The family gathered again in 1497 in Burgos for Juan's wedding on 18 March to Marguerite of Austria, and in Medina del Campo when he died on 4 October. Marguerite, pregnant at the time of Juan's death, delivered a stillborn child, but rather than return to Burgundy, she stayed in Castile until September 1499. Marguerite was only five years older than Catalina, and during those two years they forged a close bond as Catalina worked on her fluency in French.

In 1497, Isabel's ambassador in London, Rodrigo de Puebla, reported to her that Elizabeth of York and Margaret Beaufort, Henry VII's mother, "wish that the Princess of Wales [Catalina] should always speak French with the Princess Margaret [of Austria], who is now in Spain, in order to learn the language, and to be able to converse in it when she comes to England. This is necessary, because these ladies do not understand Latin, and much less, Spanish. They also wish that the Princess of Wales should accustom herself to drink wine. The water of England is not drinkable, and even if it were, the climate would not allow the drinking of it."[69] Their friendship spanned both time and space, as they shared a love of visual art, music, and literature, confronted shared family tensions, and navigated diplomatic crises.[70]

Most of 1498 was spent in Zaragoza and Alcalá de Henares, and 1499 and 1500 in Seville and Granada, where, in late April, she bid farewell to her sister María—her constant companion since birth—on her departure to marry Manuel of Portugal.[71] On 19 May 1499, years of planning for a wedding finally came to fruition when the final negotiations for her marriage to Arthur were marked with a proxy ceremony in England. The agreement to the details of the betrothal was signed by Catalina, attached by a green silk cord, and carried in a wooden box that the ambassador

Rodrigo de Puebla had brought with him from Spain. With a promise of a dowry of 200,000 *escudos* and a treaty of trade between the two realms, Catalina and Arthur began to correspond in Latin.[72] In one letter, dated 5 October 1499, Arthur replied to a letter from Catalina that he appreciates her "most entire love" that led her to write to him and express her "ardent love."[73] This letter is sentimental, more aspiration than fact, as they had never set eyes on each other, but it set a promising tone for a future together. Catalina may not have known Arthur beyond a few letters and reports from the Spanish ambassadors, but she knew a little bit about England. Her parents named her Catalina in honor of her grandmother, the daughter of *infanta* Constanza of Castile and John of Gaunt, the Duke of Lancaster. And the English royal family knew a little bit about her, too. Queen Elizabeth of York and her mother-in-law Margaret Beaufort advised Queen Isabel to be sure that Catalina learned to speak English a little. To the English who greeted her in November, she was Ladie Kateryne of Espayn, a foreign-born bride who brought her household, possessions, culinary tastes, and exotic customs with her.[74] Modern English speakers call her Catherine of Aragon (sometimes spelled Katherine), but to her Spanish family she was always Catalina. This transformation affected her profoundly. Her change of name marked a very personal change of identity. It is something that kings never (or rarely) experience. When a man inherits a realm from his father, he does not need to learn a new language or change his name. Only rarely, when a man gains a realm by conquest and it is the only one he rules directly, does he have to consider moving, learning a new language, and consider his foreignness to his subjects.[75] But the English in 1501 took note of the foreignness of Catalina, her accent and the "straunge diversitie of rayment of the countreth of Hispayne." During the long voyage across the Bay of Biscay to Plymouth, and then over land to London, *infanta* Catalina was transformed into Catherine, Princess of Wales, bride of an English prince.

TIME LINE: AN *INFANTA* AT THE COURT OF CASTILE, 1485–1501

1485

| 16 December | Catalina is born at Alcalá de Henares, the fifth child of Queen Isabel of Castile and King Fernando of Aragón. |
| Winter | The queen and the children spend the winter at Arévalo and Guadalupe, then travel southward via Ávila and Salamanca and join Fernando in Jaén. |

1486

18 January	Henry VII of England marries Elizabeth of York.
11 June	The family arrives in Córdoba to celebrate Fernando's victory over Boabdil in Granada.
20 September	Arthur Tudor born at Saint Swithun's Priory.

1487

| March | At Valladolid, Catalina and her parents celebrate the betrothal agreement with Henry VII of England for her to marry Arthur. |
| 6 or 7 July | Fernando and Isabel sign the memorandum of agreement for the formal betrothal. |

1489

| March | At Medina del Campo, Catalina is officially betrothed to Arthur, eldest son of King Henry VII of England and Elizabeth of York. |

1490

| May | In Seville, Catherine attends the public celebrations for the proxy wedding of her sister Isabel to Prince Afonso of Portugal. |

1491

Spring	Siege of Granada begins.
28 June	Birth of Prince Henry, later King Henry VIII.
November	Perkin Warbeck claims to be heir to the throne of England, upsetting marriage negotiations for the marriage of Arthur and Catalina.

1492

2 January	Triumphal royal entry into Granada.
31 March	Alhambra Decree orders the expulsion of Jews from the kingdom of Castile and Crown of Aragon.
3 August	Christopher Columbus begins his voyage westward.
12 October	Royal entry into Barcelona.

1493

15 March	Catalina is in Barcelona when Christopher Columbus meets formally with Isabel and Fernando after his return from the Americas.
21 April	Catalina travels in the north and northeast and spends most of her time in Barcelona, Valladolid, Segovia, Tordesillas, and Guadalajara with her mother, brother, and sisters.

1495

15 August	A ceremony at Woodstock, with Spanish ambassadors standing proxy for Catalina, formalizes her betrothal to Arthur.

1496

August	Catalina, in Laredo, is at the formal farewell to her sister Juana, who leaves Spain for Flanders to marry Archduke Philip of Burgundy.
September–October	Catalina, with Isabel and Fernando, stays in Oña and Tortosa; Valencia de Alcantará prepares to send *infanta* Isabel to Portugal to marry Manuel.
October	Henry VII, Fernando, and Isabel sign a new treaty of marriage between Arthur and Catalina.

1497

February	Pope Alexander VI grants a dispensation for the marriage of Catalina and Arthur.
18 March	Catalina attends the wedding in Burgos of her brother Juan to Marguerite of Austria, daughter of Emperor Maximilian and Mary of Burgundy.
25 August	Formal betrothal of Catalina and Arthur.
September	Catalina's sister Isabel marries King Manuel of Portugal.
4 October	Catalina's brother Juan dies, and his sister *infanta* Juana becomes the presumptive heir to the throne of Castile.
15 August	Proxy wedding of Catalina and Arthur at Woodstock.

1498

February	Reratification of the marriage treaty of Catalina and Arthur.
23 August	Catalina's sister Isabel dies. Her son, Miguel, is recognized as heir to the kingdom of Castile.
2 April	Marguerite of Austria gives birth to a stillborn daughter.

1499

19 May	Catalina marries Arthur by proxy at Tickenhill Manor.

23 November	Execution of Perkin Warbeck, pretender to the English throne, smoothing diplomatic relations between England and Spain and setting in motion final plans for Catalina's wedding to Arthur.

1500

24 February	Catalina's sister Juana gives birth to a son, Charles (later King Carlos I of Spain, Habsburg Emperor Charles V). Marguerite of Austria returns to the Netherlands and is godmother to Charles.
19 July	Death of Prince Miguel. Catalina's sister Juana named heir presumptive to the kingdom of Castile.
October	*Infanta* María leaves the court of Castile to marry Manuel of Portugal.
Autumn	Catalina and Arthur celebrate another proxy wedding.

1501

May 21	Catalina leaves Granada for England, traveling across Spain to the Bay of Biscay, stopping in Toledo, Guadalupe, Medina del Campo, Valladolid, and Santiago de Compostela.
17 August	Catalina sets sail from La Coruña to England on 17 August but turns back due to severe storms.
27 September	Catalina's royal entourage departs Laredo.
2 October	Catalina lands at Plymouth.

CHAPTER 3

One Wedding and Four Funerals

The Princes [Catalina] was ordred to hir dyner, and
this day, where as she ever tofore was servyd aftir the
guyse and maner Hispayne, now unto hir was used
the accustomed service of the Realme of England.

—*Receyt*, 49

CROSSING BORDERS AND THRESHOLDS

Catalina was already a seasoned traveler on 1 May when she began to make
her way northwest from Granada to La Coruña, then across the Bay of
Biscay, and finally to the southern coast of England in November 1501 for
her marriage to Arthur. Over the course of the five-month journey, she
crossed political, linguistic, cultural, sartorial, and culinary boundaries
as she transformed from Catalina, a Spanish *infanta*, to Catherine, the
English Princess of Wales. The first border was a deeply personal one that
marked her farewell to Spain and her childhood. The second border crossing took place when she landed at Plymouth and processed into London
and into Englishness. The third border was the legal one that she crossed
when she married Arthur and crossed the marital threshold from bride to
wife to widow. As she crossed each border, each threshold, she gradually
shed some of her Spanish identity. Observers both in Spain and England

marked this transition in their comments on her physical appearance, demeanor, manners, language, and clothing. These three thresholds reveal not only that Catherine was a vital conduit of transnational culture that internationalized England, but also that for her, unlike for kings, who rarely moved when they married, this profound shift in location and identity was part and parcel of the lived experience of a foreign-born bride.

BORDER CROSSING I: THE JOURNEY ACROSS CASTILE

Catalina spent her last year in Spain in Granada with her mother until 1 May getting ready for her departure on 21 May. That spring, both Catalina and her mother had been ill with a fever, and Isabel was so ill she was unable to travel with Catalina.[1] But the queen entrusted her daughter to the care of Gutierre de Cárdenas, one of the oldest and most trusted members of her council.[2] Workers at court were busy packing her possessions. The accounts note payment for one small chest (*cofre*) that cost 1 ducat. They do not tell us how big this *cofre* was, but perhaps it resembled a small chest (*arqueta*) in the Museo Arqueológico Nacional in Madrid that measures 15.25 × 30.5 cm, made of hammered iron with delicate tracery and elaborate locks. Or it could have been larger, roughly 30.5 × 63.5 cm, made of iron and wood, covered in leather.[3] The record does not specify whether the *cofre* was intended to be used as a *cofre de boda*, a decorated box to keep betrothal gifts exchanged between the couple.[4] Nor is there any mention of an *arca de esponsales*, a wedding chest that was used to carry a bride's wedding attire and personal items, such as her undergarments, stockings, shirts made of fine Holland linen, napkins, bedsheets, and table cloths.[5] But if she had one, it may have looked like those in the collection of the Victoria and Albert Museum, walnut and rosewood *cassoni* inlaid with bone and colored woods, made around 1500 in Spain.[6] She had several large carved and decorated wooden storage chests covered in red velvet equipped for cartage on a mule (*arcas ensayaladas*) made for her in 1499 to carry her wardrobe.[7]

The cost of moving Catalina across Castile was considerable. For example, in January 1501 it cost 8,470 *maravedíes* to pay for thirty-one mules to move Catalina, referred to as the *princesa de Galis*, from Écija to Seville, along with her household attendants Francisca de Torres, Porras, Nieta, and Juana de Murcia. The mules carried not only the clothing, shoes, and personal items but also silver for her chapel. They may been carrying household objects, some utilitarian and some lavish, such as a luster-ware bowl emblazoned with the heraldic arms of her great-aunt, María of Castile. This large (51 cm in diameter) tin-glazed earthenware basin, currently in the Victoria and Albert Museum, was created in Manises, Spain, sometime before 1458 (the queen's death). This was not a piece of export pottery, and the connection to the Aragonese royal family makes it likely that Catherine brought it with her.[8] At every stop along the way, the expenses included fees for settling Catalina and her attendants into their accommodations, paid to the lady (*dueña*) who was in charge of closing the doors and to the woman who lit the lamps.[9] These expenses and the complex work of moving were repeated at every stop.

The inventories of what was carefully packed into Catalina's baggage reveal that she dressed very well. The household accounts are thick with descriptions of luxurious fabrics for clothing for Catalina and as payment to the women and men at court. Page after page lists an astounding array of clothing that reveals a distinctive Spanish fashion; the *verdugado*, or hooped skirt, was the most famous. In the relaxed comfort of the private chamber, she would wear a less ornate and more comfortable *basquiña*.[10] Her wardrobe included skirts made of black, turquoise, red, or purple velvet; red silk waistbands; leather gloves; linen shirts and black velvet shifts (*abitos*); hundreds of yards of hair ribbons, dozens of velvet stockings, lengths of velvet and silk from Spain and Italy; a cloak; and sateen bonnets and hats in black velvet with Florentine gold and black and white silk embroidery and buttons.[11] Black silk and velvet may have seemed sober and severe in appearance, but they were luxury fabrics. It was costly to achieve a rich black color (a complex dyeing process), and it took three times as much thread to shear silk or wool to create a plush velvet.[12] Red silk (*carmesí*) and taffeta (*tafetán*, supposedly named for the rustling "tif-taf" sound it makes when the wearer walks) enhanced the luxurious effect of the cut of Spanish clothes that had evolved to show off expensive brocades: hooped skirts (*verdugados*, later called *guardainfantes*; the English called them farthingales), circular capes, thick rows of braiding, fringe, embroidered trim, lace cuffs and ruffs (*golillas*).[13]

Amid this ordinary excess of a royal wardrobe is an extraordinary number of shoes. In preparation for her departure, royal shoemakers Diego de Madrid and Diego de Valencia crafted for her fifty-one pairs of *borçe-guies* (soft leather buskins that were very close fitting to the leg, wide at the heel and narrow at the toes, made in a myriad of colors, and sometimes adorned with bands of color) and sixty-eight pairs of black *xervillas* (lightweight leather slippers). Her baggage also included cork-soled platform mules known as *chapines*, probably covered in velvet and intricate embroidery such as those made for her in 1497: "twelve pairs of *chapines* from Valencia for the *infantas* [María and Catalina], six of them one hand high and the other six three fingers high, at 175 [*maravedíes*] each, some of them more, totaling 1,990 [*maravedíes*]."[14] *Chapines* were a regal variant of shoes that were a staple of Mediterranean societies, sturdy and very handy to keep skirts from dragging through the muck of medieval streets.[15]

What was Catalina planning to do with all those shoes? Well, first of all, she would wear them. She would don brightly colored, perhaps embroidered, hose made from Holland linen. In the privacy of her chamber, Catalina had two options: a sandal, perhaps the flat-soled cork the Muslims in Spain called an *aqraq*, or *xervillas*, made of fine leather with very thin soles and closed backs that could be worn inside a *chapín*. In more public places, she would have worn *borçeguies*. The finest-quality buskins were made of cordovan leather (named for the Spanish city Córdoba, the etymological source of the English words "cordovan" and "cordwainer," a shoemaker), but sheepskin was often used, too. Made with turnsole construction (put together inside out and turned right side out when finished), they could be soled with goatskin, lined with cloth or fur, and could have a modest platform sole.[16]

The *chapín* was by far the most distinctive and complex shoe. These thick-soled platform shoes were the status footwear of discriminating women of all ages.[17] *Chapines* were ubiquitous in Spain, so unremarkable as to be commonplace, worn by women of all ranks. They were made from five layers of cork fragments pegged together with sharp-pointed pieces of cane, wider at the sides, narrow toward the ends, with a rise at the heel. The bits of cork were then covered with leather, frequently goatskin, with an outer sole that was flat and oval. The *chapín* was often

lined with canvas or goatskin, finished along the upper edge with over-
hand stitching, with pierced holes for lacing up the shoe. Finally, it was
decorated with stamped or stitched patterns, gilt trim, and incised tool-
ing in a Hispano-Muslim style with animal or floral designs.[18]

The Spanish passion for *chapines* made by shoemakers in Valencia, a
city famed for the manufacture of gilt leather, fueled regional economies.
Guilds of Valencia, Barcelona, Granada, and Seville strictly regulated the
making of gilded *chapines* to ensure quality. The fashion spread to Portugal when another sister, Isabel, before leaving Spain in 1490 to marry King
Afonso of Portugal, tucked into her baggage two pairs of *chapines* embroidered with gold thread that cost more than three-quarters of the price of a
team of mules.[19] On the most basic level of accounting, the cost of shoes
varied widely, depending on the style, fabric, and decoration. The price
of Catherine's slippers ranged between 31 and 77 *maravedíes*, the buskins
cost 36, and the *chapines* were most expensive of all, at 175 *maravedíes*.[20]
But the number of shoes in her closet is not an indication of feminine
vice; her brother, Juan, ordered new shoes every month.[21]

Was she simply stocking up on favorites, concerned that she might
not find English shoes to her liking? Perhaps, but shoes for an *infanta*
were more than just a practical way to cover her dainty feet. And she was
young and active; her shoes probably wore out quickly. Was she bringing
with her a bit of Spain that brought her physical comfort and nostalgia
for home? Embellished and bejeweled *chapines* were impractical outdoors
and were clearly intended to be worn at home.

Was she vain, frivolous, or prone to excess, like her sister Juana,
who was said to have had more than seventy pairs? The *chapines* worn
by elite women were distinctive.[22] They were excessively high, gilded,
jewel-studded, and often embellished with a metal ring around the base
of the shoe as much for durability as for panache. Each pair of these costly
chapines could consume as much as half a yard of richly colored velvet or
silk to cover the leather, and a dizzying array of embellishment options:
hand-painted designs, several ounces of silver-gilt ornaments, gold thread,
brocade, filigree, and semiprecious stones. It was not only the height of the
sole but also the opulence of many *chapines*—embellished with embroidery and studded with gems—that moved the fashion off the street and
into the royal court as a status symbol.

But beyond the beauty and artisanal expertise, shoes in a royal setting had cultural significance. The practice at court was to wear the shoes a few times and then give them to a favored attendant. This kind of gift-giving was customary at court. The royal family gave personal items such as clothing as gifts to the women and men at court, perhaps at the formal New Year's Day gift-giving, or to mark other events, or as compensation.[23] A gift of shoes is deeply symbolic, reflecting the economics and intimacy of the relationship to Catalina and emphasizing that her ladies at court were extensions of the *infanta*'s physical person. A handmade shoe takes on the shape of the wearer's foot. It captures the way she walked, whether she favored one foot over another, whether she had a limp or a bunion, or was pigeon-toed. An elaborately decorated pair of *chapines* signified the wealth and fashion aesthetic of the wearer. Catalina's gift of shoes symbolized the importance of the recipient as someone who had an intimate relationship to the *infanta*. And yet, even once transferred to another woman and at a remove from Catalina's body and wardrobe, her shoes would always remain markers of her taste and identity.

It is not surprising, then, that the shoes attracted the outrage of moralists like Alfonso Martínez de Toledo, who attacked the wearers for their squandering of cork for what he regarded as a needlessly exaggerated fashion. Chapines were linked to sexual maturity, as in the phrase "to put into *chapines*," to marry off one's daughter. In a familiar critique of women and fashion, some praised the high-soled shoes for making women walk slowly, while others felt that the high-stacked *chapines* were cumbersome and dangerous, designed to keep women at home. It should not surprise us, then, that *xervillas* and *chapines* were common gifts from a Spanish husband to his wife, suggesting sensuality, luxury, and intimacy.[24]

Catalina probably did not fully appreciate the cultural significance of her shoes. In her mind, her cork-soled shoes were part of an Iberian fashion. The fabric and decoration were sensuous, exotic, luxurious—they were what *infantas* wore. But they reveal her taste for some things and disdain for others. They hint at her character, her social rank, and even her sexual preference.[25] On a deeper level, *chapines* signaled the social and cultural differences of her foreignness, and would set her apart when she landed in England.[26] How could she have known that people would talk, that they would take note of her shoes and skirts and intricately braided and beribboned hair covered with delicate *mantillas* and find them strange? Would it have crossed her mind, or even that of the ladies in her entourage, that Spanish fashion could have such a powerful political valence? Catalina may have thought she was just wearing shoes, but she and her Spanish shoes were about to move out and move on to a place with very different customs. She was about to enact a new social script, with new obligations of her as a public person. She would be intensely observed. The act of observation and judgment transformed a pair of Catalina's shoes from a necessity into an item of fashion and style that signified her complex personal and political identity.

And so, in the summer of 1501, as the royal procession moved northward, Catalina, for the sake of practicality, might have kicked off her *chapines* and put on the *borçeguíes* as she journeyed to places both familiar and important to her. On the overland trip to the Cantabrian coast, from 21 May to 17 August, Catalina passed through Écija, Seville, Toledo, the royal monastery at Guadalupe, Madrid, Segovia, Medina del Campo, Valladolid, Zamora, Santiago de Compostela, and finally La Coruña.[27] The sojourn in the Guadalupe monastery was a sentimental farewell to a town she knew well. The monastery was a blend of architectural styles with a fourteenth- to fifteenth-century church and cloister built in the Mudéjar style. She would have stayed at the Hospedería Real and visited the shrine of the Virgin Mary before she continued her journey northward.

Her escort across Spain numbered roughly sixty people, headed by ambassadors Alonzo de Fonseca, the archbishop of Santiago; Antonio de Rojas, the bishop of Mallorca; Pedro de Ayala, the protonotary; and Diego Fernández de Córdoba and his wife, Beatriz Enríquez de Velasco, the Count and Countess of Cabra.[28] Catalina's personal household was managed by Doña Elvira Manuel with her husband, Pedro Gómez Manrique, lord of Valdezcaray, and their son Inigo, the master of Catherine's pages.[29] Ladies-in-waiting who accompanied her from Spain included her longtime governess, Inés de Vanegas, with her daughters Inés, María, and Teresa de Figueroa, who stayed on after the wedding.[30] Her most important ladies-in-waiting who stayed on after the wedding were Francesca de Caceres, Catalina de Montoya, María de Rojas, María de Salinas, and María de Salazar.[31] Her household staff also included her tutor, Alessandro Geraldino; various administrative staff; and familiar members of her chamber since childhood, Francisca de Torres, Porras, Nieta, Juana de Murcia, and Blanca; as well as unnamed stewards, butlers, marshals, laundresses, cooks, and bakers.[32]

BORDER CROSSING 2: *Infanta* CATALINA LANDS IN ENGLAND

The last leg of her trip was a zigzag from La Coruña to the Bay of Biscay and back again. They sailed on 17 August, but thunderstorms and rough seas, the "wiendes and jeopardies," made the voyage perilous and made her ill, so they turned back on 21 August. "It was impossible not to be frightened," wrote one of those on board. King Henry worried that storms would drown her before she had even caught sight of England.[33] They remained there a month while Catalina recovered and the weather improved. With the help of Stephen Brett, an English pilot sent by Henry who knew the route, they tried again, sailing from Laredo on 27 September. Calmer seas prevailed, and they landed not at Southampton, as planned, but farther west, at Plymouth, on 2 October. Plymouth was a prosperous enough port, though not well enough known for her companions to recall its name when questioned about the journey years later.[34]

For the second time in her life, Catalina was front and center in a royal ceremony. But this time she was a young woman, not a toddler, and she was in London, not Valladolid. At Plymouth, she was met by Lord Broke, steward of the king's household, and the Duchess of Norfolk, who brought "a goodly companye with her." She and her entourage made their way across Devon to Exeter, through Dorset to Sherborne and Shaftesbury, to Amesbury Abbey in Salisbury, and finally to Basingstoke in Hampshire. After thirty-three days of travel, on 6 November Catalina arrived at Dogmersfeld. Henry, "not soo intentifly satisfied with the chere, servyce, and diligente attendans" of his subjects, traveled from Richmond to greet her in person. They conversed as best they could, in "mooste goodly words and uttred of the langueges of bothe parties."[35]

This meeting is often recounted as clash of cultures and a display of royal sovereignty over a newly arrived subject. The English chronicler of *The Receyt* dwells on the modesty of Catalina, who, at the command her parents, stood fast in her refusal to meet the king privately before the marriage. The English accounts tell of Henry VII's refusal to respect her privacy, "that if she were in her bed, he wold se and commone with her." Her modest reaction reflects what she would have learned at the court of her decorous mother and was probably much like that of the English women at court. It is difficult to imagine that either of Henry's daughters would have reacted differently, especially in light of the care that Henry VII's mother, Margaret Beaufort, and his wife, Elizabeth of York, took to safeguard the reputations and well-being of Princesses Margaret and Mary. This is not a clash of two differing notions of sovereignty, one personal and the other national, the brash openness of the English king and the zealously guarded reputation of the bride-to-be. It is best read as an expression of Catalina's character—diplomatic in her willingness not to fuss over differences, calm in the face of an unexpected action, and emotionally strong enough to let Henry take the lead without losing her head.

Read through feminist eyes, this has a ring of masculine dominance and female submission, which renders England as boldly masculine and Spain as demurely feminine. It also has a tinge of the now-discredited myth of the "lord's first night," in which a bride is forced to have sex with her lord before her husband in a game of feudal superiority. But there is no suggestion at all that Henry physically threatened her or anyone else in the room. Henry was not impetuous; he acted after giving the situation some thought ("certayn musing of the myend") and decided that it was important to meet her before the wedding to see for himself what she looked like and how she behaved. He first encountered the Count of Cabra, the archbishop of Santiago, and the bishop of Mallorca before entering her chamber, where she, most likely with the Countess of Cabra and other women in the household, welcomed him in an "honorable metyng."[36] What is most striking in this story is Catalina's demeanor. There is no drama, no mention of her as uneasy about meeting a king in her private chamber. The mood described is calm, diplomatic. These traits are the first signs we have of Catalina's personality—the ability to remain steady, reasonable, strong, and gracious under tremendous pressure— which will emerge countless times over three decades of life in England.

Queen Isabel had requested that the reception and celebrations be modest, "more in accordance with my feelings, and with the wishes of my

Lord (King Ferdinand), if the expenses were moderate. We do not wish that our daughter should be the cause of any loss to England, neither in money, nor in any other respect."[37] But Henry VII and Elizabeth of York had other ideas. Nobles and gentry were instructed to be ready upon an hour's warning to greet Catalina. The Privy Council ordered that she should enter London in rich fashion, with a carriage and horses splendidly arrayed for her and nineteen more for her attendants.[38] Henry VII's account books record that he sent a number of musicians and minstrels to accompany the Spanish entourage.[39] At every stop along the way across southern England she was met with a festive banquet, and again the chroniclers emphasize differences: "whereas she ever before was served after the guise and manner of Spain, now unto her was used the accustomed service of the realm of England."[40] The service could have been simply who sat where, which Catalina needed to learn in order to get to know the people at court and their titles, something she had learned to do at banquets with foreign dignitaries at the court of Castile. But in the theater of a royal court, it also meant that she would transform herself, her "guise and manner," by putting on new styles, learning a new language, eating new foods, kicking off her *chapines*, and donning proper English flat-heeled shoes.

Most scholars who study pageants and royal entries focus on men as the creators and producers of these elaborate works of art. They pay close attention to the vast sums of money spent and the theatrical and literary aspects, such as masquing, architecture, and literary devices. Men are considered the makers, while women appear in the accounts as merely passive bystanders who watch from the sidelines.[41] But appearances are deceiving. In the elaborate royal entry of 1501, Catalina may appear passive as she rode across southern England and was welcomed by dignitaries and townspeople. She may not have been an active creator of each entry— that was the task of the townspeople—but she was the focus, the reason for the creation. By her presence, she made visible her dynastic power as bride and potential mother of an heir. Pageantry on this scale involved women at every level, from the women who embroidered the livery to Queen Elizabeth of York herself, who participated actively in planning the celebrations in London.[42] Catalina was the object of everyone's attention. She literally stopped traffic. Her physical presence reminded the English spectators that she was the reason they were there at that time, on that day. Her charisma as a young, foreign, virginal royal princess about to marry the heir to the throne was central to the entire pageant.

She and her companions rested at Chertsey until 6 November, when they began the final leg of the long journey to Lambeth. There, they were met by Edward Stafford, the Duke of Buckingham, and his brother Henry; Richard Gray, the Earl of Kent; the abbot of Bury St. Edmunds; and between three hundred and four hundred people dressed in Buckingham's black-and-red livery. The "retynue of Hispayn" were greeted to the "olde and famous appetitis that thenglisshe people have ever used in the welcomynge of their acceptable and welbiloved straungers."[43] The Spanish strangers were met by multitudes in London, so many people that there were no rooms available to house guests.

Both Margaret Beaufort and her daughter-in-law, Queen Elizabeth of York, were a vital part of the preparations. The request that Catherine learn French before her arrival came from both Margaret and Elizabeth, but it was Margaret who composed the list of Catalina's attendants for the festivities. She hosted a sumptuous feast for Catalina's reception on her way to the wedding, and, to make her Spanish guests feel comfortable among the English, she assigned an English companion for each Spanish lady and lord.[44] Elizabeth of York made arrangements for Catalina to spend the night before her wedding in the queen's lodgings at Baynard's Castle, surrounded only by the queen's household and men of Catalina's entourage.[45] On Saturday, 12 November, Catalina dined at Lambeth Palace, and then she and her retinue mounted their horses, slowly processed eastward toward Southwark, and assembled at St. George's Field along a route that was established in the fifteenth century.[46]

Catalina then began her formal introduction to the city she would call home and the people who would come to adore her. But her "Spanishness" was apparent to the English. The visual elements of her style signified foreignness, an exotic southern sensibility that startled, even shocked, the English. Her attire attracted comment almost immediately. Thomas More, humanist and later chancellor, was particularly harsh in his descriptions of the women in the entourage: "Except for three, or at the most four, of them, they were just too much to look at: hunchbacked, undersized, barefoot pygmies from Ethiopia. If you had been there, you would have thought they were refugees from hell."[47] This is not a comment on attire. It is a denigration of a group of people from a foreign court who do not resemble the fair-haired, fair-skinned elites of England. It is an exceptionally stark racial comment coming from a man widely regarded as one of the most influential humanists of his age. His association of dark-skinned Spaniards with Ethiopians and hellish monsters reflected an English Christian attitude of whiteness as superior that took shape after the expulsion of the Jews from Castile in 1492. Medieval English writers whitewashed their history; the expulsion of Jews from England in 1290 and the island's geographic remoteness from Africa and the East led to cultural insularity. More's comment testifies to the success of that whitewashing of history and reveals his own very limited experience with people other than the white descendants of the Anglo-Saxon and Norman invaders. This prejudice lurked in the corners of society while Catherine was alive and found full expression in a burst of anti-Spanish sentiment after her death and during the reign of Mary.[48]

London was bedecked with images of the castles and lions of Spain with the portcullis and roses of the Tudor family. The observers left a detailed record of her theatrical entry into London. She was feted with a massive outpouring of celebration: six separate pageants, tableaux vivants, mock battles, and masques on themes of the Christian virtue and matrimonial honor of the bride and bridegroom. At the London Bridge pageant in honor of her namesake, Saint Katherine of Alexandria, the herald proclaimed "the trust and affeccion," the performers noted that her marriage, her "honorur temporall," was the dynastic result of the marriage alliance. In order to balance out the two powers, Saint Katherine shared the stage with the British Saint Ursula.[49] As she crossed London Bridge and made her way along Gracechurch Street, Catalina saw a large timber-framed castle, covered in canvas and painted to look like stone, erected in the road. This "Castle with Portcullis" was festooned with English royal imagery: gold crowns, Saint George's crosses, the red roses of Lancaster, a red dragon holding an iron staff, and the king's arms. As she continued on Cheapside to Saint Paul's churchyard, she was greeted by other pageants and *tableaux vivants* depicting the stories of Saints Katherine and Ursula, Hesperus, castles, and many speeches and was showered with ostentatious gifts at the first greeting by the lord mayor and the aldermen of Cheapside.[50]

At the last pageant, they were formally met by Queen Elizabeth of York and Margaret Beaufort, the mayor of London, aldermen, sheriffs, and fellows of guilds and crafts, wearing their livery so that there would be no confusion about who was with whom. Those attached to the royal household wore green-and-white damask jackets embroidered with silver and gilt threads into garlands of vines, with a rose in the middle stitched in gold.[51]

There was also no confusion about which ones the "welbiloved straungers" were. The English who attended the festivities celebrating Catalina's arrival in England noted "the straunge diversitie of raiment of the countreth of Hispayne":

> And aftir theim rode the Princes upon a great mule richely trapped aftir the manour of Spayne, the Duke of Yorke on her right hand and the Legate of Rome on her left hande. She was in riche apparell on her body aftir the manour of her contre, and upon her hed a litill hatte fashounyd like a cardinalles hatte of a praty brede with a lase of golde at this hatt to steye hit, her heere hanging down abowt her shulders, which is faire aburne, and in maner of a coyfe betwene her hede and her hatt of a carnacion colour, and that was fastenyd from the myddis of her hed upwards so as men might weell se all her heere from the myddill parte of her hed downward.[52]

The "riche apparell on her body aftir the manour of her contre" would have been a *saya* or gown with full pleats made of yards and yards of silk satin with a long train. The color of the gown is not noted, but it may have been black silk satin; Spanish women at that time preferred black velvets and satins with double-sided blackstitch embroidery used to decorate the neckline and cuffs of the white linen smock. English women preferred bright, pale colors, and their dress was less complex, less decorative, without the Spanish preference for full sleeves with lavish over- and undersleeves. The English fashion favored a more fitted look, with low-cut, square-necked bodices cut to emphasize a woman's upper body and arms. Catalina chose to wear her hair loosely bound in a coif covered with a little hat with golden laces braided in her hair so that her auburn hair hung down around her shoulders, a sign of her status as an unmarried woman. The English fashion was a gabled hood, a headdress made with a pointed arch in the front that resembled the gable on a house, with linen lappets that draped down the side and hung down back, often studded with gems. Catalina's look was seen by the English onlookers as elegant, and was a clear contrast to their own more severe look, in which their hair was tightly bound under the hood. The novelty went beyond her hair. Shoes in England were mostly flat-soled, with a fabric upper and square toes, not at all like Catalina's lavishly decorated *chapines*.[53] The riding gear of the Spanish women drew attention, especially the stirrups "of marvelous fashion," and while the English ladies rode sidesaddle on the right, the Spanish rode on the left.[54]

This public act of entry into London was the culminating moment of a long, staged journey from Spain to England and from Catalina's natal family to a marital one. The vivid and awestruck descriptions that focus on her body and her clothing, hair, headdress, and shoes highlight the importance of dress and fashion as a way to communicate to everyone not only her status but also the subtle power of her exotic allure.

She then was escorted to a more private reception at the bishop's palace at Saint Paul's, where the Spanish were greeted by the archbishop of Canterbury, the bishop of Durham, and many prelates. Gifts were exchanged at the church door. Basins filled with coins were given in thanks to her, and in return she gave an offering to Saint Erkenwald. Finally, everyone went home. Later that afternoon, with great ceremony, Catalina met with Elizabeth of York at Baynard's Castle, the queen's residence in London, where they spent time in "goodly commynycacion, dauncing, and disportes." That evening, "with torchis light to a great nombre, she was conveyed and brought honorable to her lodging" at the bishop's palace, where she spent one last night as a Spanish *infanta*.[55]

A WEDDING AND A THRESHOLD: *Infanta* CATALINA BECOMES PRINCESS CATHERINE

On the morning of Sunday, 14 November, Catalina entered Saint Paul's through the west door with a "great and goodly number" of attendants, including Prince Henry, the Count of Cabra, and Margaret Pole, the Countess of Salisbury and wife of Sir Richard Pole, Arthur's chamberlain and sheriff of Merioneth. Margaret, twelve years older than Catalina, became her guide to life and customs at court and her steadfast friend.[56] In Saint Paul's she saw a sight both familiar and strange. Manuscript illuminations depict the exterior of Saint Paul's as far simpler in appearance than the flamboyantly decorated Isabelline-style churches of Valladolid, Toledo, and the royal chapel at Granada. Once she stepped inside, she would have felt at home amid the stained glass, vaulted ceiling, and long nave. The altar was covered with silver and gold liturgical objects, relics, and reliquaries; the choir was hung with tapestries made of arras cloth; and all the entries and walls were decked in red cloth. The church was already filled with witnesses, but notably not visible were the king and queen, who stood and watched the wedding through lattice windows of a closet off to the side. To mark his change from single man to husband, Arthur changed clothes at Saint Paul's to the "apparel of weddyng and spousage."[57]

But it was what Catalina wore that aroused the English imagination. Again, the author emphasized her Spanishness:

> she were that tyme and daye of her maryage uppon her hed a coyf of whight silk with a bordre of goold, perle, and precious ston, beyng of an unche and an half of brede, the which covered the great parte of hir visage and also a large quantite of her body toward her wast and myddill; her gown very large, both the slevys and also the body with many plightes, moch litche unto menys clothyng; and aftir the same fourme the remenant of the ladies of Hispayne were arayed; and beneth her wastes certain rownde hopys beryng owte ther gownes from ther bodies aftir their countray maner.[58]

Catalina wore a dress of white sateen, in a style strongly influenced by French, Burgundian, Italian, and Islamicate styles.[59] Her white silk gown had wide pleated sleeves, a Spanish fashion that would quickly catch on in England.[60] The train of her resplendent wedding dress was carried by Cecily of York, the sister of Queen Elizabeth and first lady of the

FIG. 8 | Pere Garcia de Benavarri, *Banquet d'Herodes*, altarpiece of the Iglesia de San Juan del Mercat, Lleída, fifteenth century. Tempera, stucco reliefs, and gold leaf on wood, 197.5 × 125.7 × 6.4 cm. Museu Nacional de d'Art de Catalunya, Barcelona, inv. no. 064060-000. Photo: Album / Art Resource, New York.

bedchamber.[61] Cinched at her "wast and myddill" and beneath her waist were "certain rownde hopys beryng owte ther gownes from ther bodies." This hooped skirt was a distinctive fashion item that Catalina brought from Spain to the Tudor court, the *verdugado*, or farthingale. The skirt was originally designed in fourteenth-century Castile to conceal a queen's unexpected pregnancy and was nearly architectural in its construction.[62] These skirts can be seen in a fifteenth-century Catalan painting (see fig. 8), which depicts women wearing skirts with very circular hard hoops (*aros*), as few as six or as many as fourteen, mounted outside the skirt in a fabric different from that of the skirt itself to cast a shadow that highlights the structure of the skirt. The *verdugado* drew attention to the wearer's hips, especially later, when the hoops were sewn inside the skirt, and caught the eye of social critics who frowned on the fashion. Some skirts were half-hooped, with only half the length of the skirt hooped, or the hoops were placed only in the front. Dresses could be hooped, too, with tucks and pleats added to create a voluminous flounce in all directions.[63] The fashion, intended to emphasize a woman's sexuality by accentuating her hips and highlighting her breasts, spread to the continent and dominated women's fashion for the next two centuries.

As minstrels struck up "such melodies and myrthe as they coude," Catalina and Arthur, hand in hand, he on her right side, processed solemnly through the choir entrance toward the high altar, and turned around in a circle so that everyone could see that they were, in fact, the Spanish *infanta* and the English prince.[64] After the Mass of the Trinity and blessings, they went to the bishop's palace to witness the seventh pageant, a mountain of metals, jewels, and gold flowers that depicted the royal emblems of France, England, and Spain. A feast followed, and at around 5:00 PM the Duchess of Norfolk, Elizabeth Talbot, and the Countess of Cabra, Beatriz Enríquez de Velasco, escorted Catalina to the bedroom. John de Vere, the Earl of Oxford, inspected the bed, and then the couple was left alone. What happened next is the subject of much debate, but one chronicler was optimistic: "The day thus with joye, mirthe, and gladnes, deduced to his ende."[65]

On that day, *infanta* Catalina was officially and forevermore Catherine, Princess of Wales. She had traveled a great distance, across land and sea, to be part of a deeply held custom of women leaving their family, carrying with them their customs, their language, their culture with them and, through the act of marriage, assuming a new identity. Whether or not she was actually wearing a pair of *chapines*, she was a married woman, "in her *chapines*" in the metaphorical sense, old enough to have sexual intercourse.

The story of what happened on their wedding night is often repeated but impossible to verify. Did she have sex with Arthur? Can we trust her when she said no, she did not, that when she married Henry she was a virgin? Can we be certain that she did not have sex with Arthur, at least not the penetrative sort of sex that leads to pregnancy? Men and women at court stated that Catherine and Arthur went to bed together, but that is not proof of sex. Elvira Manuel and Francesca de Caceres, the women in Catherine's chamber who would have had the most intimate knowledge of her, who dressed and undressed her and inspected the bedsheets, were "looking sad and telling the other ladies that nothing had passed between Prince

Arthur and his wife, which surprised everyone and made them laugh at him."[66] We need to be skeptical of information gleaned through a keyhole, based on political motives, or reported three decades later, but women's testimony was deemed to have legal force in cases involving marriage and sexuality.[67] Less reliable are the depositions from four members of Arthur's household who testified about the first night and later sleeping arrangements, which include the story of Arthur's boasts of having spent the night in Spain. Even if the statements are true and accurate, they are just that, boasts recounted two decades later by men who escorted Arthur to bed.[68]

This question will never be answered definitively, but it is worthwhile to consider the point of view of Isabel of Castile, Elizabeth of York, and Margaret Beaufort. Isabel was very careful to protect Catherine from an early marriage, fearing that she would end up dead from either the physical effects of intercourse too often or at too young an age. We may never know exactly how much of her mother's fear Catherine understood, but the lesson was reinforced by Margaret Beaufort's own very real concern for the health of young brides. Childbirth in medieval Europe was risky no matter how old the mother, but far riskier for very young girls, something Margaret knew firsthand. When she married Edmund Tudor, he was twenty-five and she was twelve years old, and thirteen when she gave birth. It was a very difficult childbirth, and she was never pregnant again, leading some to speculate that her sexual relations with Edmund were physically brutal or that childbirth scarred her. The dangers of sex and childbirth at a young age led both Margaret and Elizabeth to oppose the marriage of Henry VII's seven-year-old daughter Margaret to James IV of Scotland, then twenty-four, because she feared that James "would not wait, but injure her and endanger her health until the young princess was suitably old enough to consummate the marriage."[69] The couple waited six years and were married in 1503. Catherine had learned the value of patience. The most likely scenario is that she assessed Arthur's poor health, and they may well have engaged in some form of sexual intimacy, prompting Arthur's boast. But Catherine was not a woman to kiss and tell, so she revealed no details until much later. From Catherine's standpoint, it would have made sense to take it slow, making it unlikely that they consummated the marriage and likely that she did indeed tell the truth at the divorce proceedings in 1529.

We know that Catherine repeatedly asserted that she slept with Arthur for the 139 nights of their marriage, but she asserted that she did not have sex with him. She repeated this when Arthur's brother, Henry, was seeking a papal dispensation to marry her, and later, forcefully, during the divorce trials. Elvira Manuel and all the women in her household swore that Catherine remained a virgin throughout. When Henry VIII married Catherine, everyone accepted her testimony that she was a virgin. I am inclined to trust her to tell the truth of what happened in her four-month marriage to a shy teenager raised by men, a young man who was not a risk-taker in terms of physical acts. He was raised in a homosocial court and had very limited experience of any kind around women except day-to-day interactions with women older than his mother.[70] Catherine, on the other hand, had male tutors and confessors, giving her a social ease with men in a variety of public settings. But it is one thing for her to converse with a tutor at court and another to share a bed with her husband. Both Catherine and Arthur were young and sexually inexperienced. They would have known that they were expected to have children quickly, but they were cautious and confident they had plenty of time.

The next day Catherine stayed in with two English attendants, Mary Blount, the countess of Essex, and Agnes Tilney, the widow of Thomas Howard, the Earl of Surrey. On Tuesday, the king made an offering of grace and met with an array of nobles and prelates, both English and Spanish. Then the newlyweds met with the king: "The Princes was ordred to hir dyner, and this day, where as she ever tofore was servyd aftir the guyse and maner Hispayne, now unto hir was used the accustomed service of the Realme of England."[71] To mark this moment of profound personal, political, and cultural transformation, Elizabeth of York and Henry VII presided over a week of pageants, jousts, banquets, dancing, masques ("disguising"), hunting, games, sports, and Spanish musicians.[72]

Catherine got lost in the crowd in the descriptions of this week of merriment until the following Monday, when "the Hispaynyardes" departed, taking with them letters and messages to Queen Isabel and King Fernando along with books, pictures, and souvenirs of the wedding. Catherine was, of course, sad to see them go, "with great hevynes to bere and suffer the departing of frenship and company." In a gesture of generosity, Henry, showing great sensitivity to both her mood and her personality, took her aside and showed her his library at Richmond Palace, filled with "many pleasaunt bokes" in both Latin and English.[73] Here in England's first royal library, amid some of the finest illuminated manuscripts and printed books by authors familiar to her, she was in an intellectual home. Henry gave her and her attendants jewels, too, and his recognition of the emotionally charged relationship of Catherine and her attendants is striking. Henry saw the "hevynes" of her heart and took pleasure in helping her regain her sunny disposition. This moment marks another packing up and moving. Catherine may have learned to do this while growing up, but she was no longer in Spain with her mother. She was in a cold and damp climate, with people she had only just met who spoke a language she was still learning, and about to move to a new home with a husband she barely knew. But she did what she was trained to do. She "drew herself into the maner, guyse, and usages of Englond" and set out to be a pleasing wife to "her most dere and lovyng husbond."[74]

Some of Henry's actions bear the mark of a social script, an action that is expected in certain settings and that marks out the emotional terrain of the emotional community of the royal household. Whatever affection his gift may have expressed, it was also a demonstration of the bonds of fidelity and a public expression of honor that privileged personal relationships above all others. On occasions such as this one, the social script was recognized most clearly by those present who understood the explicit value placed on the material gifts, which revealed both formal and often cloaked actual motives.[75] No matter what his intentions, Henry's kind gesture helped Catherine move forward, and she began a lifetime of collecting books and supporting the intellectual careers of Desiderius Erasmus, Juan Luis Vives, Thomas More, and Alphonsus de Villa Sacra.[76]

It was not imperative that Catherine accompany Arthur to Ludlow, but it does appear to have been her choice, although it prompted most of her Spanish attendants to leave London.[77] The couple stayed at Windsor until 21 December, and then began the journey to Wales via Abingdon (then part of Berkshire), Kenilworth (Warwickshire), and Bewdley (Worcestershire). They arrived in Ludlow Castle (Shropshire) at the end of December and lived there until April 1502.[78] Ludlow and its environs were well known to Arthur, who had lived there from the age of seven, but this landscape was like nothing Catherine had ever experienced.[79] The town and castle are situated centrally in the Welsh Marches, a large administrative area covering the modern counties of Shropshire, Herefordshire, Cheshire, Gloucestershire, and two-thirds of Wales. The region is a lush, green, hilly landscape, and Ludlow Castle is located at the confluence of two rivers, the Teme and the Corve. The winter weather is chilly, damp, windy, and dark, much like British Columbia and the Netherlands. This was not the golden rolling hills of Castile or the Mediterranean climate of Granada that Catherine knew as a child. Little is known of the trip to Ludlow, but chroniclers and correspondents note that Catherine was ill during much of the winter of 1501–2. It is difficult to know precisely what caused her illnesses. She may have had the same illness as Arthur, which is often just noted as a fever. Given what we know now about medicine, the illnesses may have been due to the shock of the cold, damp climate of Ludlow on a young woman accustomed to spending the winter in Seville and Granada. They may have been due to the emotional stress of leaving home, moving, marrying, and moving again. They may also have been due to the different diet, one with few of the citrus fruits that were routinely served at court. In Spain, Catherine would have eaten more fruits, both dried and fresh, raisins, olives, and almonds. Spanish foods were heavily spiced with cinnamon, saffron, and ginger. Based on menus and household accounts, a substantial amount of the diet of English courtiers was meat. Fruits such as cherries, strawberries, apples, peaches, and pears were preserved. Oranges, lemons, grapes, and even pomegranates had been imported since at least the thirteenth century and were available at court.[80] Vegetables, some pickled, would have been familiar: onions, chives, scallions, radishes, carrots, turnips, parsnips, green beans, cabbages, cauliflower, cucumbers, and asparagus.[81] In Spain she drank wine, but she was not fond of English beer, thinking it was so bitter that it must be "the sponge of ice and vinegar given Our Lord."[82]

THE FIRST FUNERAL, 1502

During that chilly, rainy winter, Arthur, too, was very ill. By late March his illness worsened, and on 2 April 1502 he died.[83] Catherine, a wife for just four months, was transformed into a young widow who found herself in a legal and marital, and ultimately a reproductive, limbo. Reports at the time speculate that Arthur died of sweating sickness or something he caught while washing feet on Maundy Thursday. Sweating sickness is poorly understood, although recent studies on this disease that caused five devastating epidemics in England between 1485 and 1551 blame a virus, with a hantavirus deemed the most likely. There were also rumors that Catherine was the cause: "Wo worth the time that ever the lady Katharine came into this realm, for she was the cause of the death of the most noble prince."[84] Like the rumors of the consummation of their marriage, this testimony was only made public during the divorce proceedings in the 1520s and must be regarded skeptically.

Ill as she was, she grieved his death.[85] For comfort, she turned to her Spanish lady, María de Rojas, who slept with and consoled Catherine immediately after Arthur's death.[86] Rumors of a pregnancy proved false, but she remained too ill to attend the funeral ceremonies at Ludlow and Worcester Cathedral, which may explain why at the time there were no criticisms of her absence at the funeral.[87] The weather on the day of the funeral was atrocious. A contemporary report describes "the foulist caulde, wyndy and rayny day" on which the journey took place and the difficulty of bringing the coffin along the heavy roads, "in some places fayne to take oxen to drawe the chare so ill was the way." Her presence was marked by a silk-fringed bannerell emblazoned with her royal arms.[88]

Catherine's mother, Isabel, upon hearing the news of Arthur's death, had the Castilian court go into mourning for him. She ordered yards of black cloth to be made into gowns for forty-five women at her court and the women who returned after the wedding in England, including Inés Vanegas (the mother) and Beatriz Galindo, and Catherine's former chamber attendants, Nieta and Porras.[89] Catherine received strong and enduring support from the woman who smoothed this painful and difficult transition from wife to widow—her mother-in-law, Elizabeth of York, a shrewd royal mother who wisely kept her head down, not only weathering harsh political tumult but doing so quietly, with a graceful, steady force of will. She understood that she was an important counterbalance to her husband's weak claim to rule and an insecure structure of succession. For Catherine, she was a model of a queen-as-mother in very rough times who knitted together antagonistic factions. Her personal chambers were used for royal business involving other women, but high-ranking noblemen also attended these events. She carefully supervised household accounts, was influential in appointing people to high-ranking household positions, and supervised the renovations at Greenwich Palace in 1502. She took an active role in arranging marriages for her family and supported her sisters financially. This was personal work, but because it involved members of the royal family and their allies, it was not insignificant. Catherine, present at Elizabeth's court at Richmond, Greenwich, and Eltham, listened carefully, watched attentively, and took note of how to be an exemplary English queen consort. Catherine was comforted by Margaret Beaufort, the Duchess of Richmond and Derby; her Tudor sisters-in-law, Mary and Margaret; her English friend and staunch ally Margaret Pole, Countess of Salisbury; and her English attendants, Elizabeth Darcy, the manager of Arthur's nursery and childhood household, and several ladies from her household represented her at the funeral.[90] These women in her most intimate circle were the glue that held Catherine together emotionally at a time when she was exhausted from a life of travel and ill health and faced an uncertain future. In the space of a year she had gone from the familiar comfort of her mother's household to new beds, new foods, and new customs. Her grief for Arthur was no doubt real, but she was also grieving the loss of a life she had spent her entire life preparing for.

Once Catherine had recovered, she left Ludlow, probably in late April or early May, and arrived at Durham House in London, the official palace of the bishop of Durham, situated along the Strand. She lived there for seven years, until her marriage to Henry in June 1509, and probably used only parts of the house and shared the rest with the bishop and his household. Durham House was centrally located, which gave her a physical proximity to court at Westminster and Greenwich, and it had a stately appearance that faced the Strand and Thames.[91]

Most of what transpired during those years was not recorded and is lost to us. We know from the Privy Purse accounts of Queen Elizabeth of York that she eased Catherine's transition with an empathy born of an understanding of the loss of a loved one so young. She settled past due bills accrued from the wedding, paid for the yards of black velvet to cover the litter that brought Catherine back to London, ordered four yards of flannel for her, and paid for cushions for her attendants. She ordered that five bucks be sent to her household in Durham House. She invited Catherine to visit her at the palace at Westminster, paid for expenses for Catherine's barge from Durham House to Westminster for a visit, paid for the messengers that went back and forth between the two households, and had made a litter of blue velvet with cushions of blue damask that was probably given to an unnamed "lady of Spain," one of Catherine's attendants.[92]

The bureaucracy of the royal household was well established by 1501, and it stipulated that as a royal princess she was entitled to the care and support of her immediate family until she married. Catherine came to England with ample provisions, a dowry that was to be paid in installments (the payment of which was a bone of contention between Fernando and Henry VII), and hundreds of ladies and lords to accompany her to her wedding in London and make her feel at home in the new land. Once married, she and Arthur would have been supported by her husband's family until Henry VII's death, at which point she would have been granted a queen's household, with a full staff of officers and income separate from that of the king. Those seemingly well-laid plans fell apart after Arthur's death when disputes arose between Fernando and Henry concerning Catherine's dowry. Her status was unclear, and as a result, her household and finances in England were unstable and unreliable. After Arthur's death, Catherine's status as well her household and finances in England were unclear, unstable, and unreliable.

The royal household that Catherine experienced as a young widow was a precarious and sometimes lonely place where her actions and the very substance of her life depended on circumstances outside her control.[93] Except for a few letters to Fernando pleading for money, very little is known about her expenses and income.[94] As a widow she could exercise considerable power and authority as head of a household, but she had little property that she could manage on her own and so had limited social and economic autonomy and security. Kings Henry and Fernando fought over money, from the terms of the dowry to her household expenses. Her dowry was contested. Catherine was protected by her mother-in-law, Elizabeth of York, who paid some of Catherine's expenses after the death of Arthur.[95] From April 1502, she had little control over her actions except to plead with both her father and her father-in-law for financial support. Catherine, at the center of a diplomatic contest between her father, Fernando of Aragon, and her father-in-law, Henry VII, also had limited control over her destiny. Isabel continued to pay salaries for the Spanish ladies in her daughter's household at Durham House.[96] This was particularly helpful as Catherine's finances were precarious after Arthur's death, and Inés Vanegas and her daughters were vital in Catherine's transition from Spain to England. We know that Inés, the mother, died sometime around 1504 because Baeza, Isabel's treasurer, noted in his accounting that the money in 1504 was to go to her heirs, presumably her daughters.[97] Isabel sent an ambassador to England to speak with Henry VII about what to do next. Catherine's brother-in-law, Archduke Philip, was hoping that his sister, Marguerite, would marry Prince Henry; Isabel tried to get ahead of Philip and proposed that either Catherine return home with half of her dowry or stay in England and marry Prince Henry.[98]

LIFE AT DURHAM HOUSE

During those seven years, she spent hours and days in a chamber at Durham House filled with women praying, reading aloud to each other, singing, playing musical instruments, and conversing about the events at court.[99] When she needed to stretch her legs and get a bit of fresh air, Catherine and her ladies strolled through the nearby neighborhood along the Strand and took an occasional trip by barge to Richmond to visit Arthur's family. Wardrobe accounts describe orders for fur-lined velvet mufflers and cloaks made from heavy fabrics, such as buckram, that suggest they were meant as outdoor wear, and riding gowns and riding equipment (such as whips). Later wardrobe accounts note that Catherine ordered items earmarked for walking "in the mornynges," and it is likely that while at Durham she went walking for exercise and pleasure.[100] The women at her court formed alliances based on social rank and role in the household, alliances that formed the basis of personal relationships marked by gift-giving, bequests, and inheritance. They sang songs both sacred and secular, accompanied by lutes and virginals, seated on embroidered pillows and cushions and surrounded by cloths of state, which bore her royal arms and inscriptions, and tapestries on the wall that bore images of ancient Greek and Roman histories and Christian stories. Draperies enclosed spaces to create small discrete areas for more private conversations, but privacy was hard to come by. In her chamber at Durham House, even when she was desperate for money, she was enveloped by embroidered pillow-cases, cushions and chair seats covered with needlework, tables covered with needlework, and pin cases containing the materials for needlework. She and her ladies at court were surrounded by yards and yards of cloth and thread for embroidery. An outsider observing life at Durham House would have seen wealthy women seated by windows, quietly embroider-ing the cuffs and collars of the shirts worn by loved ones.

The needlework of Catherine and the ladies was not merely useful or decorative. It was a means of communication, a visual language more humble than Latin but an important way for women to express their ideas. It was a lifelong occupation. Catherine would have learned cross-stitch before she was five years old, and her first major project was probably a colored band sampler completed when she was between eight and ten years old. It was followed, a year or so later, by a whitework sampler and finally by a cabinet or casket to hold trinkets and writing materials. Needlework recorded and commemorated women's lives and their participation in a wider public world. Needlework was one of the most important creative and, for some, economic work of a woman's life in early modern England, and Catherine's skill with the needle was well known.[101]

Needlework was more than a socially acceptable way to pass the time. At a time when ornate textiles formed much of the royal wealth, all kinds of embroidered work were taken seriously as an art form. It was a creative outlet for women in Catherine's chamber that made and sustained social and political affiliations. Women's portraits were copied in embroidered textiles.[102] As the women at court embroidered, they crafted both an object and a network of relationships.[103] Catherine and her ladies operated as important political actors at court, whether in the royal household or in the wider ambit of the early modern court.[104]

Every stitch sent a message. At a time in Catherine's life when her world was turned upside down, needlework was a meditative, comfort-ing practice that linked her to her past, to her mother. It was something she had total control of, and it shaped her mental world. We sadly do not have, or do not know if we have, any remnants of Catherine's own embroi-dery, but the cupboards at the Victoria and Albert Museum in London

FIG. 9 | Unknown embroiderer, napkin, linen with inserted bands of woven linen and silk, red silk embroidery in Spanish-stitch style depicting lions and castles, bordered by narrow floral bands, ca. 1500s, possibly Spanish or Italian. Victoria and Albert Museum, London, 234-1880. Photo © Victoria and Albert Museum, London.

contain textiles from Spain from around 1500 that may have been packed in her luggage. Some of those stitches speak the visual language of Castile. When Catherine came to England, she may have brought objects like an orphrey, an ornamental stripe or border on an ecclesiastical vestment decorated with pomegranates—Catherine's most personal emblem—and an arrow, one of the royal devices also used by her mother, Isabel.[105] An orphrey may well have been packed in the baggage of a cleric who traveled with Catherine when she sailed across the Bay of Biscay in 1501. But she also brought with her a new and distinctive form of embroidery known as Spanish blackstitch, also known as double running, backstitch, stem stitch, or the Holbein stitch because it can be seen on the cuffs and collars of subjects in Hans Holbein's paintings.[106] In the sixteenth century, it was done on plain weave work so that the embroidered pattern stands out. The counted stitches are worked to make a geometric or small floral pattern that is the same on the underside. Spanish blackstitch embroidery was suitable for edging table linen. The band shown in figure 9, made from linen with inserted bands of woven linen and silk, is embellished with red silk embroidery depicting castles and lions, the heraldic devices of Catherine's heartland, Castile and León. Linen cloths such as this may have had several functions in her household: as towels to dry the hands when washed before eating, as cupboard cloths on which vessels could be placed, and as the cloths used to cover the principal table place setting

FIG. 10 | Unknown tailor and embroiderer, shirt, linen, linen thread, silk thread, hand embroidered and hand sewn, ca. 1540, made in England. Victoria and Albert Museum, London, T-112-972. Photo © Victoria and Albert Museum, London.

of salt, trencher, knife, spoon, and bread. This napkin, however, signifies more than intricate stitchery on fine linen. Spanish blackstitch embroidery, long known to be a popular sixteenth-century import into England, has been credibly dated to Catherine's arrival in 1501.[107]

Needleworkers embroidered cloth with designs that were usually derived from prints or pattern books, or copied directly from an example in hand. Catherine no doubt employed professional embroiderers and artists to draw the design on the cloth and to do much of the embroidery for more mundane objects such as sheets, pillowcases, and table linens. But she followed in her mother's footsteps by embroidering the necklines, collars, and cuffs of personal items of clothing such as shifts and shirts.[108] Anne Boleyn broke with this tradition when she refused to embroider Henry's shirts.[109] But the wildly popular designs wound up on the cuffs and collars of the fashionable men and women at the Tudor court. The hand-sewn linen shirt shown in figure 10, hand-embroidered with silk thread, was made in England after Catherine's death, around 1540. A shirt such as this was an item of underwear, but the collar and cuffs of this shirt are embroidered in a pattern of stylized columbine and leaves. The embroidery continues on the seams of the sleeves and shirt body, even though these would not be seen, as in the portrait of Henry's second wife, Jane Seymour, by Holbein.

Catherine's needlework would have been done alongside the women in her household, and together they formed an artistic and political community that structured their lives. Gathered together in a private chamber at Durham House, seated on low stools covered with embroidered cloths that may have been worked by their own hands, they appeared to conform to gender roles under which needlework would keep a woman occupied so she would be more likely to hold her tongue.[110] But through their needlework women at court found an alternative to the passivity, privacy, and silence that needlework was supposed to enforce. Women created their own patterns and shared them with each other, so that the Spanish black-stitch technique was spread first at court and then emulated by generations of royal, noble, and gentry women, as well as women of middling and lower ranks, who were both consumers and patrons of a vitally expressive art form.[111]

THREE MORE FUNERALS: 1503, 1504, 1509

Two back-to-back personal blows transformed Catherine's life in London. First, the death of Elizabeth of York on 11 February 1503 left her without an important family member, a valuable ally, and a protector. The emotional hurt was profound, but it was made worse by the tough reality of having to fend for herself in the face of her troublesome father and parsimonious father-in-law. After Elizabeth's death, Henry began to pinch pennies, and his affections cooled as he sought a second wife, tensions mounted, and Catherine's health suffered.[112] Queen Isabel, in April 1503, ordered the Flanders fleet to England to bring Catherine back to Castile. The success of Spanish troops against the French persuaded Henry VII to sign a contract on 23 June 1503 for Catherine's marriage to Prince Henry.[113] In August 1504, King Henry invited her to accompany him on a hunt at Richmond and lodge with his court for three days.[114]

Then, on 26 November 1504, her mother, whose health had been declining, died. Catherine's grief was heartbreaking to those around her at court.[115] But Isabel's death was more than a personal tragedy. It reconfigured the political landscape in Castile, as Juana was crowned queen regnant and Philip her king consort. This diminished Catherine's marriage prospects and no doubt increased her anxiety. Isabel had asked Henry VII to fulfill his agreement to the marriage of Catherine and Prince Henry and that her original dowry be used for that marriage, but it was far from certain that her wish would be fulfilled.[116] The wedding was scheduled to take place on 29 June 1506, but nothing happened, and it seemed doubtful that it ever would. Some of her Spanish ladies at court returned to Spain. María de Rojas left England around 1504 to marry Alvaro de Mendoza y Guzman and was replaced by María de Salinas, who would become one of Catherine's most devoted friends.[117] They were her comfort, her little bit of Spain in England, during the unsettled period after Arthur's death. They stayed on between 1502 and 1509 and stood by Catherine while she dealt with disarray in her household and the dismissal of two Spanish attendants. Elvira Manuel left in December 1505, when she was expelled for promoting Archduke Philip of Burgundy's interests at the expense of those of Fernando of Aragon. Francesca de Caceres was involved in gossip at court about Diego Fernández, Catherine's confessor. Catherine denounced Francesca, who briefly left court to marry the Genoese banker Francesco Grimaldi.[118] Catherine also sought friendships with English women at court. She was an affectionate older sister-in-law to Henry's sister, Mary Tudor, eleven years younger, and grew close to Margaret Pole, also newly widowed and in financial distress.[119]

After the deaths of Elizabeth and Isabel, Catherine and her father regularly corresponded, and at last we can hear traces of her voice. These letters are written in the language of someone well educated, with a wide and eloquent vocabulary and a sensitivity to both the form of the letter and the recipient. Some contain sensitive information and are written in cipher, and the tone suggests that she wrote them, or that her secretary captured her words accurately, if not verbatim. She uses the language of submission, which conveys the gender of her rhetoric: "[I] supplicate your highness to command her to be favored," "I beseech your highness for to do me a grace," and signs the letters as "the humble servant of your highness, who kisses your hands." Overall these letters are formal in tone, as if from a vassal, as when she refers to him as "most high and puissant lord." Yet they are written in the rhetoric of a daughter's love and concern for her father's realm: "All this does not weigh upon me, except that it concerns the service of your highness, doing the contrary of that which ought to be done." She was attentive to the lengthy delays of correspondence, which could take a month to arrive, and so she carefully gives him ample context for the letter to refresh his memory as she pleads her case: "because I believe your highness will think that I complain without reason, I desire to tell you all that has passed." She gradually took charge of her life. She asked her father to give dowries, to bestow favors, and sometimes simply to give her the money to pay her ladies at court. She continued to give cloth and clothing to her ladies and tried to dress impressively, even though her income was reduced. She complained that "he [Henry VII] is not obliged to give me anything. . . . I have nothing for chemises; wherefore, by your highness's life, I have now sold some bracelets to get a dress of black velvet, for I was all but naked; for since I departed thence [Castile], I have nothing except two new dresses, for till now those I brought from thence have lasted me, although now I have nothing but the dresses of brocade." As her finances grew dire, she tried to keep her frustration in check, but it spilled out, and she was not averse to shaming him: "Your highness shall know, as I have often written to you, that since I came into England, I have not had a single *maravedi*, except a certain sum which was given me for food." She was increasingly annoyed, and it showed. She complains that "each day her troubles increase," and she humbly reminds him that her debt is "not for extravagant things" but only for food and to pay her household attendants. She tried to get through to Henry VII, and she was not above using emotion and a bit of hyperbole to make her point: "I spoke to him [Henry VII], and all those of his council, and that with tears," but he did not budge and this left her "in the greatest trouble and anguish in the world." She nudges him: "My lord, I had forgotten to remind your highness how you know that it was agreed that you were to give, as a certain part of my dowry, the plate and jewels that I brought."[120]

She remained as close as one could be to her sister Juana, Juana's husband, Archduke Philip of Burgundy, and her sister-in-law, Marguerite of Austria, given the distance between London and the Low Countries.[121] In January 1506, a powerful storm blew Juana and Philip ashore while they were on their way to Spain: the "tempest of wynde" at midnight was so great that it blew down trees and tiles off houses and the weathercock from Saint Paul's.[122] Philip and Juana joined the court at Windsor, where Catherine and her sister-in-law Mary were part of the dancing, music, and revelries. Catherine wrote to her father that she and Prince Henry delighted in Juana's company and lamented that she had to leave so soon after arriving.[123] The English again noted Spanish dress as somber compared to the bright silks, cloth of gold, and purple velvet worn by the members of the English court, while Juana's Spanish entourage remained dressed in black with limited embellishment.[124] But when Philip of Burgundy died unexpectedly in September 1506, Juana was a widowed queen regnant in Castile, and Henry VII and Gaston de Foix each began to consider her as his next wife.[125] Catherine wrote to her father on 18 July 1507 expressing her concern about the negotiations for the proposed marriage of her sister to King Louis XII of France, saying that it would be more than an "inconvenience . . . it would be sending discord to the very knife into that kingdom."[126]

Her tone with her father gradually became more mature and assertive, as in 1507 when she reminded him that he "may believe I speak from experience" and familial duty ("consider that I am your daughter"). She subtly asked him to give her a good reason to remain in England. In a letter expressing her frustrations with the Spanish ambassadors, she even wondered if he did not trust her, asking that he

> command some ambassador to come here, who may be a true servant of your highness, and for no interest will cease to do that which pertains to your service. And if in this your highness trusts me not, do you command some person to come here, who may inform you of the truth, and then you will have one who will better serve you. As for me, I have had so much pain and annoyance that I have lost my health in a great measure; so that for two months I have had severe tertian fevers, and this will be the cause that I shall soon die.[127]

Fernando finally took action shortly after receiving her letter when, her illnesses notwithstanding, he appointed her as his ambassador to England. She took a more active public role at court and her health improved.[128]

She was just settling into her work as ambassador when, on 21 April 1509, Henry VII died. A few days after Masses for the king's soul were said and alms given to the poor, and after his burial in the lavish new burial chapel at Westminster Abbey on 11 May, his son Henry announced that he would marry Catherine.[129] She was about to cross yet another legal and political threshold as a royal bride and Queen Catherine.

TIME LINE: ONE WEDDING AND FOUR FUNERALS, 1501–1509

1501

2 October	Catalina and the Spanish royal party arrive at Plymouth.
October	Catalina and her Spanish party are escorted across southern England to London by English nobles and local dignitaries, stopping at Chertsey, Kingston, Lambeth, Southwark, and London Bridge.
6 November	Catalina arrives at Dogmersfeld and is met by Henry VII.
12 November	Catalina makes a festive royal entry into London with pageants.
14 November	Catalina and Arthur marry at St. Paul's Cathedral. She officially takes the name of Catherine, Princess of Wales.
15–28 November	Public celebrations of the wedding.
28 November	Fernando and Isabel pay the first installment of Catherine's dowry.
29 November	Most members of the Spanish party depart.
Late December	Catherine and Arthur travel to Ludlow Castle.

1502

December to April	Catherine and Arthur reside at Tickenhill Manor (Bewdley).
24 March	Catherine and Arthur celebrate Maundy Thursday; afterward, Arthur's health, which had been poor during the winter, worsens.
25 April	Arthur dies at Ludlow and is buried at Worcester Cathedral. Catherine is too ill to attend his funeral and burial.
May	Catherine, in mourning, returns to London and takes up residence at Durham House with members of her Spanish household.
Autumn	Queen Elizabeth of York, pregnant, and her daughters, Margaret and Mary, comfort Catherine and entertain her at Westminster.

1503

11 February	Queen Elizabeth of York dies in childbirth.
Spring	Henry VII considers marrying Catherine, a move opposed by her parents.

25 June	Catherine is officially betrothed to Prince Henry, the younger son of Henry VII and Elizabeth of York.
8 August	Margaret Tudor marries King James IV of Scotland.
26 December	Pope Julius II grants dispensation for Catherine to marry Prince Henry.

1504

Summer	Catherine is ill most of the summer.
26 November	Death of Queen Isabel of Castile.
June	Henry VII renounces the treaty of marriage between Catherine and Henry.

1505

| July | Catherine's father, Fernando of Aragon, marries Germaine de Foix. |

1506

January	Philip, Archduke of Burgundy, and Catherine's sister Queen Juana of Castile arrive at the royal court at Windsor.
Late March	Marguerite of Austria rejects the suggestion that she marry Henry VII.
25 September	Philip of Burgundy dies and his sister, Marguerite, is named regent of the Netherlands for his young grandson, Charles.

1507

| April | Catherine is named Spanish ambassador to England, the first woman in Europe to hold an ambassadorship. |

1509

| 21 April | Henry VII dies at Richmond Palace. |

CHAPTER 4

Bride Again, Queen Finally, and Mother at Last

🌿

The King my Lord adores her, and Her Highness
him.

—Diego Fernández, 1510

The suddenness of Henry's decision to marry Catherine dramatically changed her life. On 11 June, they were married privately in the queen's private inner chamber, or closet, at Greenwich. Two weeks later, on 24 June, she was anointed and crowned queen consort of England. She must have had profoundly mixed emotions at the prospect of marrying Henry after years of an on-again, off-again relationship. Their marriage was arranged originally in 1503 and a papal dispensation was received, but plans were made and broken as Henry VII and Fernando squabbled and used Catherine as a political pawn. Whatever she felt, she kept to herself, but she probably did not have much choice about whether to marry Henry. The negotiations are written in coolly transactional language that focuses on the question of the dowry from her marriage to Arthur as her dowry for this second marriage. Her father was strongly in favor of the marriage. She was his "dutiful and obedient" twenty-three-year-old daughter, and she knew full well that the seven years spent as a widow in a reproductive limbo would complicate her duty to bear children. She could not waste time.[1] As for Henry, scholars are split on whether he was a dutiful son who followed his father's deathbed wishes or an impulsive or irresponsible prince in a hurry to get on with the business of being a king.[2] For them both, political considerations may have been key to the decision, but in important ways it was not a bad match. They had known each other for seven years, had often lived at the same residence, had both grieved the death of Elizabeth of York. Catherine, five and a half years older, had known Henry since he was a ten-year-old attendant at her wedding to Arthur. Henry's sisters, Margaret and Mary, were friends of Catherine's. Margaret was closer in age, but she had left court in July 1503 to marry King James IV of Scotland. Mary was eleven years younger than Catherine, but they had grown close since Elizabeth of York's death. They were highly educated, shared intellectual interests, had mutual friends at court, and were both healthy and young. As a king of England, Henry was precisely the sort of man Catherine's parents had in mind for a husband.

There are few details of the wedding, and we are not certain who officiated. Out of respect for the mourning for Henry VII, it was a quiet celebration without public festivities, jousts, or banquets. It was, however, a momentous transformation for Catherine from princess to queen consort. At that moment, she stepped out of the shadows of Durham House and into the brighter light of the royal court, into the joys and sadness of marriage, pregnancy, and motherhood. She was present in the highly visible court, and in the first years of her marriage she was a vital adviser to Henry, but after 1514, often pregnant and then a mother, she was gradually obscured in the narrative sources by her flamboyant husband and his highly competent secretaries and chancellors. We can find traces of her in the objects she owned, wore, cherished, and gave as gifts. These reveal a fun-loving, superbly educated, culturally sophisticated, pious woman who applied the lessons she had learned at the court of Castile, and a quiet widow biding her time, waiting to take charge of her life.

Her transformation from wife to queen was marked by a joint coronation ceremony on 24 June at Westminster Abbey. It was Midsummer's Day, the feast of the nativity of Saint John the Baptist, a day that Catherine as a child in Spain would have celebrated with bonfires. She was not the focus of attention in this shared coronation, but it is significant that it took place immediately after the wedding. Henry VII, facing serious challenges to his authority, had been more cautious, waiting for two years to pass and the birth of a son before he allowed a coronation for Elizabeth of York. But Henry was supremely confident both in the legitimacy of the marriage and that he and Catherine would have children quickly and that there would be boys.

The coronation service, as outlined in the *Liber Regalis*, which dates to the reign of Edward II (1307–27), stipulated the anointing and adornment with regalia of the king and queen. The ceremony began at 6:00 AM in Westminster Hall, where both Catherine and Henry were dressed in crimson velvet and silk lined with miniver and ermine. Her hair was loose on her shoulders, a symbol of her fertility and chastity, and she wore "on her bare hede a riche cercle of golde." The chronicler Edward Hall noted that she was "beautiful and goodly to behold" in her gown of white embroidered satin, her hair cascading down her shoulders, and wearing a jewel-studded coronet. Her white satin dress had a hooped skirt, but she had to leave her *chapines* at home because the *Liber* specified that both king and queen process barefoot, walking on a rich blue cloth, to Westminster Abbey. Catherine was drenched when the canopy that covered her collapsed in a sudden deluge of rain. Margaret Beaufort did not want to miss the celebrations, so she rented a house in Cheapside so that she and her granddaughter, Mary, could get a close look at the procession.[3]

The coronation ceremony was embedded in the Catholic Mass, and for the king it had echoes of priestly ordination, which would not have been part of Catherine's coronation as queen consort. She was, however, anointed with holy oil on her forehead and her breast. After Mass, the transformation of Catherine and Henry from princess and prince to queen and king was marked by a change of clothes into purple imperial robes before being crowned by William Warham, archbishop of Canterbury. In addition to the closed imperial crown, her regalia consisted of a gold scepter and rod, each topped with a dove, and a ring. Then, at Saint Edward's shrine behind the high altar, they disrobed, laid their regalia on the altar as an offering back to God, and only Henry carried a scepter and rod out of the church. They were swathed in layers of red silk, white damask, and cloth of gold, and their entire coronation was intended to legitimize the couple as the true king and queen. None of Catherine's regalia has survived, but her royal identity is preserved in her signature on her correspondence. No longer "the Princess of Wales," she is "Katharina the Queen" when writing to her father and her nephew Emperor Charles V, and "Katharine the Quene" when writing to Henry and her English subjects.[4] Her choice of spelling her name distinguishes her from two later Tudor queens with similar names, Katheryn Howard and Katherine Parr.

A plethora of gilded pomegranates entwined with Tudor roses decorated the stages and streets. The couple processed through London and celebrated the event with banquets filled with music and dancing, tournaments, and a two-day joust, complete with chivalric backdrops of mountains, castles, a forest, and a park.[5] The poet Stephen Hawes recorded the day's events in *A Joyfull medytacyon to all Englonde of the coronacyon of our moost naturall soverayne lorde kynge Henry the eyght.*[6] Thomas More wrote a "Coronation Ode," a Latin poem for presentation to the royal couple. More devotes roughly one-fifth of the poem to an encomium to Catherine. No longer insultingly critical of the Spanish as he was in 1501, he was effusive in his praise of Catherine,[7] comparing her to heroic women from classical Greece and Rome—Alcestis, Cornelia, Penelope— and praising her patience, devotion, and love for Henry:

> This lady, prince, vowed to you for many years, through
>   a long time of waiting remained alone for love of you.
> Neither her own sister nor her native land could win her
>   from her way; neither her mother nor her father
>   could dissuade her.

The poem closes with prescient verses on children and marital devotion:

> But your queen, fruitful in male offspring, will render it on all
>   sides stable and everlasting.
> Great advantage is yours because of her, and similarly is hers
>   because of you.
> There has been no other woman, surely, worthy to have you as
>   husband, nor any other man worthy to have her as wife.[8]

In the decoration of the presentation copy of More's "Coronation Ode," Henry's arms are on the title page and Catherine's on the verso. But the most revealing image is a richly colored illustration of Catherine's emblem

FIG. 11 | Unknown artist, illumination of Thomas More, "Coronation Ode," 1509. British Library, London, Cotton MS Titus D iv, fols. 2–14, image on fol. 12v. Photo: British Library, London © British Library Board. All rights reserved / Bridgeman Images.

of pomegranates of Granada entwined with Tudor roses, the fleur-de-lis, and the Beaufort portcullis badge, all under a bejeweled imperial crown (fig. 11). The image abounds with references to sexuality, fertility, and bounty. The pomegranates are ripe, and the one nearest the rose is broken open, provocatively revealing the red seeds in a shape that the late medieval viewer would have recognized as signifying female sexuality. The red Tudor rose is shown first as a bud, then partly opened, and then in full bloom—an allusion to the progression of the dynasty from its origin in Henry VII's victory at the Battle of Bosworth Field in 1485 to its full flowering with Henry's coronation. The image is flush with the hopeful promise of a fruitful union, both a personal marital one and a political one in which the Yorkist and Lancastrian factional strife was finally put to rest. The emblem of the linked pomegranate and rose beneath an imperial crown caught on immediately and appeared in the first printed book to celebrate the royal marriage. As ubiquitous as tea towels with the royal seal and T-shirts printed with Queen Elizabeth II's corgis that appear in gift shops all across England, the hallmark of Catherine and Henry's marriage was stamped on all sorts of objects. It would have been almost impossible for the common man or woman in London or the noble at court or in the countryside to avoid. Gilt basins and silver saucers were etched with pomegranates and roses, tapestries were embroidered with the initials of their names knit together, stained-glass windows bore the heraldic devices, and a mirror with a painted wooden frame was emblazoned with the arms of England, Castile, and Aragon. Henry himself owned a dog collar embroidered with roses and pomegranates.[9]

The marriage and coronation also dramatically affected three of Catherine's personal attendants and closest friends, who personally and immediately felt the change in status. Both María de Salinas and Inés Vanegas, who had been with Catherine since at least 1501, moved from Durham House across the Thames to Greenwich, and both were present at the coronation. On 30 July at Greenwich, Inés married William Blount, Lord Mountjoy, a student of Erasmus and master of the king's moneys and keeper of the exchange in the Tower of London.[10] Margaret Pole, the Countess of Salisbury, whose family suffered under the reign of Henry VII, returned to court in 1509 and, because of Catherine's affection for her, was accorded high status at the coronation.[11]

Amid the joyous celebrations, the one deeply sad note for both Catherine and Henry was the unexpected death of his grandmother Margaret Beaufort on 29 June. Her health had been a concern for several months, but after the coronation she had become increasingly frail.[12] In her will of January 1509, she bequeathed to Catherine jewelry "such as collers and girdles," but her most important legacy was not jewelry. Her worldly toughness balanced with piety and generosity were touchstones for Catherine as she stepped into the center of the royal court and took her place as Queen of England.[13]

AN INTIMATE LIFE LIVED IN PUBLIC

The sweet sentiment that opens this chapter, that "The King my Lord adores her, and Her Highness him," reported by Diego Fernández, chancellor to Catherine's father on 25 May 1510, may actually be a fair assessment of much of the first decade of their lives together. Henry behaved publicly as the perfect courtly lover; Catherine was a beautiful, youthful wife and an audience for his chivalric posturing and his jousts.[14] Her tenure as ambassador for her father had made her a valuable political asset to the inexperienced young king, and he relied on her formidable international connections to diplomacy. Their affection appeared genuine, but the six, maybe seven pregnancies tell only a part of a successful marriage that was lived in the private chambers of their many residences but at the same time was a public event spent under the scrutiny of courtiers, ambassadors, clergy, and the populace of England. To the modern reader, mindful of the tragic events that followed later in their marriage—Henry's infidelities, Catherine's defiance of his plans for a divorce—it seems wrong to consider the early years of their marriage a success. But if we read her life backward, from the bitter end of divorce and isolation, we miss the richness of nearly twenty years of her life. If we fall into stereotypes of Catherine as the virtuous wife, the faithful foil to Henry's libidinous rake, and later the dour and bitter outcast, we see a character in a tragedy, not a woman in full. If we situate her among the other wives of Henry, we risk the fruitless game of comparing women by Henry's scale of worth. If we measure her value only as the wife who could not produce a son, if we persist in thinking of her as Henry did, as a dynastic failure, we fail to grasp the rich fullness of her life. We need to disrupt the ways scholars, and the general public, have come to understand her.

To do this, it is important to get more than just a sideways glimpse of their relationship through the narrative sources. These are sketchy and incomplete, her voice is often muffled, and even after 1509, when we sift through the words of chroniclers and ambassadors, we rarely hear her actual voice. She and Henry sent messages to one another when they were separated, sometimes through couriers, but much of what remains of their correspondence is often couched in official language and deals with work, not pleasure. It is possible, however, to get some sense of their relationship by looking at the gifts they exchanged at New Year's festivities. The highly staged rituals of gift-giving at a royal court need to be interpreted carefully, though, because they carried social obligations and reflect custom and personal taste as much as genuine affection.

Catherine displayed her Spanishness as queen, and either imported Spanish clothing or hired Spanish tailors gave Henry gifts that honored her heritage and that, at first, he seemed to like. Many of the pieces of gold and silver plate that she brought with her when she came to England were noted as gifts to Henry in the 1521 Jewel Book.[15] She introduced a new style of Spanish cape when she gave Henry a "Spanish cloak of black *frisado* with a border of goldsmith's work" in 1521. Her Spanish-style gifts to him included two mantles of purple tilsent and green velvet in the "spanysshe" fashion, two swords, a dagger, and "a payre of spanisshe buskyns enbraudrd with Roses & portcules," a Tudor emblem. The addition of the Tudor rose and portcullis makes the Spanish-style buskins an Anglo-Iberian hybrid.[16] The only recorded New Year's Day gift to her, in 1513, is lavish: a pair of gilt great pots that weighed 575 ounces (for comparison, ladies at court received little gilt pots weighing 16 ounces).[17] His gifts to her in 1516 included cloth and clothing, too, such as mantles of green velvet, and often betray a sense of largesse and extravagance.[18] The Spanish fashion spread at court and beyond as Henry gave away clothing to his courtiers and even King François of France.[19]

When they were at court, Henry and Catherine shared a palace but spent much of their time in separate chambers, a common practice for English monarchs. Her official residence in London as queen was Baynard's Castle, built by Henry VII in 1500–1501 and located on the Thames between Blackfriars and Saint Paul's Cathedral. Her court officials and household attendants formed a separate department that occupied different spaces at court and was organized similarly to the king's household. During her reign as queen, she had her own lord chamberlain and a host of men associated with cooking, dressing, tending to horses, and washing up who were permitted to work in the private female space of the household. Her Watching, or great chamber, served as a waiting room, and her presence chamber was the formal dining room, where she entertained the king and important visitors. Her privy chamber, the extensive lodgings for members of the royal family, with private and bedchambers, wardrobe, and kitchen, formed an architecture of intimacy.[20]

Catherine's private chambers were closed to almost everyone except the king, his or her attendants, and people specifically granted the right to enter. Catherine's reported reaction to the unexpected entry of Henry and twelve companions in 1510 suggests that the king rarely entered unannounced: They "came suddenly in a morning into the Queen's Chamber, all appareled in short coats, of Kentish Kendal, with hoods on their heads, and hose of the same, every one of them, his bow and arrows, and sword and buckler, like outlaws, or Robin Hood's men, whereof the Queen, the Ladies, and all other there, were abashed, as well for the strange sight, as also for their sudden coming."[21] Her bedchamber, however, was more than just a place for frisky, playful entertainment. It was a place where they expressed marital affection and sexual desire, and eventually it was a metaphor for the legal wrangling that set in motion the divorce that would propel the Protestant Reformation in England.

Catherine's private chamber was a site of entertainment that included the masque, a staged theatrical entertainment that mingled playfulness and politics and included active parts for women, with an array of other festivities accompanied by food and music. In 1514, after the Christmas revels at Greenwich, four masked lords and ladies went to Catherine's chamber to continue to dance. Afterward, she "heartily thanked the king's grace for her goodly pastime, and kissed him." She arranged "amusements of every description, the chief of which, however, and the most approved by his Majesty, was the instrumental music of the reverend Master Dionysius Memo." On Candlemas Eve in 1520, after Catherine and Henry came back from evensong, a trumpet announced the arrival of four gentlemen and a lady seated in a wagon. Catherine read a challenge in which the four gentlemen, "for the love of their ladies," participated in a tilt. Her chamber was a site of formal politically charged entertainment, as when, in 1517, Henry brought the imperial ambassador to Catherine's chamber after dinner and "made her and all the ladies pay him as much honors as if he had been a sovereign." At the conclusion of the masques to honor the French ambassadors and the signing of the Treaty of Universal Peace in 1518, the French delegation danced in Catherine's chamber with ladies who spoke French, much to the delight of the ambassadors.[22]

Catherine and Henry had friends in common who made the social events more pleasurable and meaningful. Catherine's close confidant María de Salinas was godmother in 1511 to Mary, the daughter of Henry's great friend Charles Brandon.[23] María received letters of denization (citizenship) on 29 May 1516, shortly before her 5 June marriage to William, Baron

Willoughby d'Eresby (d. 1526), master of the royal hart hounds. They were married at Greenwich, probably in the chapel of the Observant Friars (Franciscans), where Catherine and Henry had married, and were given the loan of Greenwich Palace for their honeymoon and the manor of Grimsthorpe, Lincolnshire, as a wedding present, as well as a substantial dowry.[24] Henry also named one of his new ships the *Mary Willoughby*, perhaps in honor of María de Salinas.[25] Catherine gave María a gold ring with a heart-shaped diamond and nine small rubies (it had been given to her by the bishop of Carlisle).[26] María had three children: Henry, the king's godson, Francis (both sons died young), and Catherine (1520–1580), who became the ward of Charles Brandon, Duke of Suffolk, upon Willoughby's death.[27]

Catherine and Henry circulated around the main palaces near London—Greenwich, Richmond, Windsor, Eltham, and Woodstock—as their lives followed the weekly routine of life, dictated by both the liturgical calendar and the seasonal calendar, marked by the summer season of warfare and the beginning of the harvest. They celebrated both sacred and secular festivals, most importantly Candlemas (the Purification of the Virgin Mary, 2 February, which featured a dramatic display of lighted candles), Easter, the Feast of Saint George (23 April, the investiture of the Order of the Garter), Whitsunday, All Saints and All Hallows, Christmas, and Epiphany.[28] These were opportunities for wearing crowns and donning the imperial purple attire (Christmas Day, Easter, Whitsunday, and All Saints Day), which set them apart from the nobles and the weavers, shepherds, tailors, alewives, and parish priests of the realm.[29] They held solemn courts at Easter, Pentecost, and All Saints as well, but the Christmas season and the New Year festivities were the high point of the year.

They publicly expressed the legitimacy of their marriage and the promise of heirs through the royal progress, a highly staged travel through the countryside in the summer that offered wide possibilities for political and legal work and personal communication with their subjects. Catherine's travels around Spain as a child had prepared her for a progress, which allowed them to exploit a variety of residences for the court. It was also a means of assuring political security, as the nature of hospitality offered by their subjects and overt gestures of loyalty by cities, towns, and individual hosts became tests of the quality of bond between the ruler and the ruled. The English people outside London, who were no doubt eager to see their new, exotic, foreign-born queen, gathered in large numbers to watch the processions and to present personal petitions to the king and queen.

Henry's normal notion of a royal progress was to pass time in good company, often accompanied only by a small riding household, but Catherine understood the power of charisma. A childhood spent in the company of her mother, who had a keen understanding of the importance of personal, physical contact with her subjects, had given Catherine comfort with the intimacy of public appearances. They covered about five to fifteen miles each day, which allowed ample time to rest at small villages, pray at local shrines, take part in pageants, receive gifts from dignitaries, greet the people who gathered along the roadsides, and savor the foods in season, such as the local strawberries, pears, apricots, and apples. She and Henry both loved hunting, and it was a great honor for the gentry and local elites to share in the hunt with the royal couple and indulge in venison for dinner.[30] Catherine continued to be "richly dressed in the Spanish fashion," favoring black velvet gowns with wide sleeves. But wearing black did not mean she was a dull dresser. During her first year as queen, Catherine spent a considerable sum of money to replenish her outdated and worn-out wardrobe. She probably had no Spanish tailors at court and had some of her gowns tailored to suit a more English fashion. She preferred heavy velvet and richly woven satin gowns with a stomacher, a decorated triangular panel that fills in the front opening of a woman's gown or bodice to clearly define the waistline. But English fashion was transformed by her taste for hooped skirts and black velvet. In 1519, she welcomed Henry and his entourage on progress to stay at her estate at Havering-atte-Bower in Essex, where the ladies in a masque were wearing black velvet gowns bordered with gold "with hoops from the wast dounward."[31] Her wardrobe included a dazzling array of colors and fabric, with intricate silk and gold thread embroidery, fur linings, and gemstones set in the trim.

Yet under this extravagant royal display of wealth she wore, like her mother, a modest habit of Saint Francis, and in private she wore plainer clothing as a sign of her humility.[32] On her progresses she regularly sent agents ahead of her into the towns to find people who might need her help or just want to see her in person. The human touch and sensitivity to the emotional impact she had on the English people gave her formidable power and immense popularity among them.

THE WORK OF A QUEEN CONSORT AND QUEEN REGENT

In the first five years, Catherine was a politically active queen consort and a particularly strong influence on Henry. As queen, she held lands, fees, honors, parks, and other lands in Dorset, Essex, Wiltshire, Gloucestershire, Devon, Herefordshire, and Lincolnshire and the castles of Huntingdon, Odiham, Marleburgh, Devizes, and Fotheringhay.[33] These properties, which she held throughout her marriage, created affinity relationships and generated revenue that enabled her to extend patronage. Greatly increasing her independence was her status as a *femme sole*, a legal designation which gave her the right to sue in her own name for her rents and debts. She could not, however, permanently alienate any of her properties, and upon her death these estates would return to the crown.[34] She was also five years older than Henry and highly educated, and she had experience during the seven years she had spent in England as princess dowager and as ambassador for two years for her father at Henry VII's court. After their marriage Henry routinely sought her advice. She is present in much of the official record from 1509 to 1520, and makes noteworthy appearances throughout the mid- and late 1520s. He trusted her and was confident in her loyalties. He particularly valued her active work as a key liaison with the Spanish diplomats at court and her support of amicable Anglo-Iberian relations, and she took his side in dealing with the French.[35]

In early 1513, Henry, determined to take an army to France, allied with his father-in-law, Fernando of Aragon, to fight the French, reclaim long-lost English territory in France, and subdue King Louis XII, who threatened to invade Italy. Catherine was no mere adjunct to her husband. Her support for this action was noted by Andrea Badoer, Venetian ambassador in London, who wrote in January 1513: "The King [is] bent on war[;] . . . the Council [is] averse to it; the Queen wills it."[36] Taking Catherine's advice and with her by his side, Henry mustered the troops at Dover, and on 11 June 1513 he appointed her to govern England, Wales, and Ireland as his regent while he was gone, with the elderly Earl of Surrey in charge of the military forces.[37] Henry's decision to appoint Catherine as regent was not exceptional, although the English had been wary after the contentious regency of Margaret of Anjou during the illnesses of Henry VI during the War of the Roses. In France, Louise of Savoy served as regent for her young son, François; Anne de France did likewise for her younger brother, Charles VIII; and Marguerite of Austria was regent for her nephew, Charles V.[38] The ordinariness of a female regent may account for why the only chronicler to mention the establishment of the regency, and only briefly, was Raphael Holinshed: "The .xv. day of Iune the king departed from Grenewiche, taking his iorney towardes Douer, whether he came by easye iorneys, and the Queene in his companie. After hee had rested a season in the Castell of Douer, and taken order for the rule of the realme in his absence he tooke leaue of the Queene, and entring his shippe the last day of Iune, being the day of Saint Paule: he sayled ouer to Caleys."[39]

Catherine's actions as regent are recorded in royal accounts—grants of land, expenses for provisioning the army, orders to the armorers and heralds and to the mayor and sheriffs of Gloucester. She corresponded regularly with Henry and Wolsey in France and her former sister-in-law, Marguerite of Austria, regent of the Netherlands. She was concerned for Henry's safety and the wider implications of English actions in France, and she did not miss a beat. She had substantial powers over the army and the right to elect bishops and abbots, to appoint sheriffs, to issue warrants for payment of such sums as she might require, to sign warrants with the privy seal, and to convoke Parliament.[40] She issued documents in her name as "Rectrice," using the feminine form of "regent" ("Teste Katerina Angliae Regina ac Generali Rectrice Eiusdemi.")[41] She was assisted by a highly capable, trustworthy, and seasoned small council: Thomas Howard, the Earl of Surrey; William Warham (archbishop of Canterbury and lord chancellor); Sir Thomas Lovell (treasurer of the household); and John Heron (treasurer of the king's chamber). Warham's chancellor served as general secretary, and Heron controlled the money.[42] She was actively involved in organizing the defense by ordering the mustering of troops, conveying of arms, armor, and supplies, and commanding the lords, mayors, sheriffs, and other officials to assist. She did not stay in London but moved north as far as Buckingham and Woburn Abbey in Bedfordshire.[43]

While Catherine held down the fort in England, Henry captured the town of Thérouanne and sent her an unusual gift—the Duke of Longueville, as a hostage, in person, to England. But English actions in France riled up the Scots, who were staunch allies of the French. The Scottish King James IV, married to Henry's sister Margaret, had threatened war with England if Henry went to war with France. What happened next should have come as no surprise to anyone. By midsummer, tensions along the northern border went from a simmer to a boil, and James made good on his threat. Catherine's preparation for queenship was grounded in late medieval Spanish humanist curricula and methods, but it did not explicitly include lessons on how to win a battle. Nevertheless, Catherine forged ahead and spent late July and all of August preparing for war against the Scots and her in-laws. She demonstrated skillful acumen and a genuine taste for political, governmental power and authority as she took the reins.

It was a very brief war. She did not command troops at Flodden—that would have been exceptional—but she was a key figure who kept the government running to support the military actions.[44] When the Scots began to move south in late August, Catherine marched north as far as Buckingham and reportedly made a speech that would have made her mother proud, but she did not get as far as Flodden, where the English troops won a decisive victory on 9 September. King James and most of the Scottish aristocracy (including twelve earls, the archbishop of Saint Andrews, two bishops, and two abbots) and thousands of Scottish soldiers were killed. In a terse report, the chronicler at Grey Friars Priory in London, in the only entry for 1513, said, "Thys yere the kynge went in to France, and the carreke and the Regent byrnte. And this yere was the Scottych felde, and the kynge tane and slayne, and browte to Shene."[45] Catherine wrote immediately to Henry with exuberant praise for the victory and sent Henry a bit of the bloodstained coat worn by James IV in the battle. Mindful of English sensibilities, she diplomatically held back from sending the dead king's corpse:

> My husband, for hastiness, with Rougecross I could not send your Grace the piece of the King of Scots coat which John Glynn now brings. In this your Grace shall see how I keep my promise, sending you for your banners a king's coat. I thought to send himself unto you, but our Englishmen's hearts would not suffer it. It should have been better for him to have been in peace than have this reward. All that God sends is for the best. My Lord of Surrey, my Henry, would fain know your pleasure in the burying

of the King of Scots' body, for he has written to me so. With the next messenger your Grace's pleasure may be herein known.[46]

Catherine's letter to Henry reveals a competitive nature that she had not shown before. Henry sent her a living human souvenir of his military exploits, but she joked that she was ready to send to him a dead king. It is an intimate letter, as playful as one can be when the object of the joke is a dead brother-in-law, and refers to the familiar work of the ladies—sewing the clothing and doing needlework for the standards, badges, and emblems for the army. How we understand Catherine's actions in this incident depends on whom we read. All sixteenth-century English chronicles must be read carefully because the genre had changed significantly in the century since the Wars of the Roses. These "new" chronicles displaced women from the central narrative, downplayed their public role as mediators and intercessors, and placed queens in the shadows, where their actions were minimized or neutralized as merely domestic.[47] Holinshed's *Chronicles* undercut the significance of her actions, making Catherine simply the recipient of the embalmed body of a king:

> The same day, there appeared some Scottes on an hill, but one William Blacknall that had the chiefe rule of the ordinaunce, caused suche a peale to be shot off at them, that the Scots fled, or else the L. Admiral, which was come to view the fielde, had bin in great daunger as was supposed: but now that the Scottes were fled, and withdrawen, all the ordinance was broughte in safetie to Eytil, and there remayned for a tyme. After that the Earle of Surrey had taken order in al things, and set the North parts in good quiet, he returned to the Queene with the dead body of the Scottish King cired.[48]

The *Chronicles* were not the product of a single author. Eight men of varying origins and upbringings were principally involved in the huge enterprise of writing the *Chronicles*, in collaboration with a number of printers and publishers. In their collective minds, Catherine was a passive, not active, queen regent.[49] Edward Hall's chronicle, published in 1458, includes valuable eyewitness or nearly eyewitness accounts that

"Holinshed" paraphrased and summarized, but to all of them, Catherine was on the sidelines.

Diplomatic correspondence tells another story. She corresponded often with her father and with his ambassador Eustace Chapuys about matters concerning the pope, France, Italy, and preparations for war. Even her most mundane activities were noted by diplomats at court from Madrid, Vienna, Venice, and Milan who sent their bosses lively, lengthy, and highly personal missives filled with comments on the battle. These diplomats regarded her as an active, not passive, actor. The Italians were the most enthusiastic. Lorenzo Pasquaglio, writing to the Venetian council, commented on her military work and reported enthusiastically, if not quite accurately, that the queen had taken the field. The Milanese ambassador, Paolo de Laude, wrote that "an English lady has captured three Scottish horsemen; a duke is a great gift, but she [the Queen] hopes to send him a king."[50] The Italian humanist Pietro Martire d'Anghiera, writing on 23 September 1513, placed Catherine at the center of things and gave her credit for victory: "Queen Katharine, in imitation of her mother Isabella, who had been left regent in the King's absence, made a splendid oration to the English captains, told them to be ready to defend their territory, that the Lord smiled upon those who stood in defence of their own, and they should remember that English courage excelled that of all other nations. Fired by these words, the nobles marched against the Scots . . . and defeated, humiliated and massacred them."[51] It is not surprising that Martire gushed. He was Catherine's childhood tutor after she was seven years old, and after 1501 he was her parents' chaplain. His standpoint was staunchly royalist, and he had broad knowledge of how courts operated. A prolific letter writer and court historian with a journalistic style and sometimes gossipy prose, his works recounted the deeds of Spanish kings, queens, explorers. The English people noted approvingly her role in the victory at Flodden in manuscripts (now housed in the British Library) that bear images of her emblems of pomegranates and castles. These manuscripts range from a manual on warfare to market privileges granted in 1514 to the town of Saffron Walden and are potent witnesses to Catherine's charisma.[52]

At age twenty-eight, married to a vigorous king and deeply enmeshed in the governing of the realm, Catherine was moved by the experience of war and mourned the death of James in a painfully personal way. In a gesture of familial affection, she sent a court chaplain to comfort Margaret and arrange for a truce.[53] When Margaret, pregnant and in exile from political turmoil in Scotland, returned to the English court in 1516, she and Catherine shared the experience of widowhood and remarriage. This could not have been easy, given the circumstances, but Catherine welcomed Margaret into her court and made her a part of official entertainments at court, including mixed-sex gatherings that included dancing, music, playing cards and chess, gambling, and banquets.[54] The emotional sisterly bond is evident in their exchange of gifts. Catherine gave Margaret a white palfrey for her entrance into London, and when Margaret left court in 1517 and returned to Scotland, she may have given Catherine a Flemish book of hours that was originally a gift to her from James.[55] Catherine also took her other sister-in-law, Mary, under her wing when she was betrothed to King Louis XII of France, sharing with her how to deal with the problem of communicating at a court where a different language is spoken, the importance of alliances, and the value of personal access to the king.[56] The circle of widowhood widened when Louis died in 1515 and Mary chose, controversially, to marry Charles Brandon, the Duke of Suffolk. The close friendship of Catherine, Mary, and Charles weathered the ordeals and joys of pregnancy, motherhood, and the shifting politics of Henry's reign.

After 1513, however, Catherine's role in the reign changed slowly. She was not formally shoved aside, and there was no deliberate, or at least no formally stated, exclusion of her as queen. She stepped aside partly to focus on pregnancy and childbirth, and then, after the birth of her daughter Mary, Mary's education. The ascendancy of Thomas Wolsey as royal chaplain, then almoner, and after 1515 as chancellor and finally cardinal excluded her from any direct role in the governance of the realm.[57]

THE INTIMATE POLITICS OF MATERNITY AND MOTHERHOOD

More than anything else, the first decade of Catherine's marriage was devoted to pregnancy, childbirth, and ultimately raising their young daughter, Mary. For all the attention paid to Catherine's hope for a

healthy baby boy, very little attention has been paid to Catherine's experiences during pregnancy. This is due in part to the frustrating nature of
the sources and the sketchy modern knowledge of early modern obstetrics and gynecological medicine. We know that when Catherine came
to England in 1501, she brought her own medical personnel from Spain.
Juan de Soto, her apothecary, stayed with her until her death in 1536. Her
surgeon after 1509, Balthasar Guersie, was an Italian surgeon with a medical degree from Cambridge. Beyond their names, very little is known of
their work. Midwives handled obstetrical responsibilities, but they did
not write down the experiences of childbirth. We do know that most
physicians regarded pregnancy and childbirth as natural events best not
interfered with.[58] In physicians' descriptions of pregnancy, it is not always
clear what they mean by the terms "miscarriage" and "stillbirth." "Stillbirth" very loosely meant the birth of a dead child or hemorrhaging by a
woman who thought she might have been pregnant.[59] And because the
dating of the onset of pregnancy was imprecise, it is difficult to know
whether the event occurred before or after fetal viability.

Contemporary chronicles and letters are not entirely trustworthy, and
not simply because the authors witnessed the pregnancies from a distance.
Chroniclers reported the news of pregnancy or birth or death, but they
gave few details. Itineraries tell us when the king and queen were in the
same place at the same time, from which we can infer a likely time frame
for sexual intercourse to result in conception. This uncertainty has led
physicians who know little about history to diagnose her retrospectively,
and historians who know little about medicine to speculate about diagno-
ses.[60] It makes sense, then, to follow the modern definition of a miscarriage
as the expulsion of the fetus from the womb before twenty-eight weeks of
pregnancy, or roughly the beginning of the seventh month.[61] This is not
simply a question of subtlety or semantics. What we call the event matters
because it is important to characterize as accurately as possible what was
happening. If we use modern standards and terminology, she was pregnant at least six, perhaps seven times, with only two live births—a son,
Henry, who died shortly after his birth, and a daughter, Mary, who ruled
as queen. Each pregnancy mattered to Catherine, making it important
to sift through the evidence carefully to understand each one as a significant event in her life.

Because a royal pregnancy is a public event and a social practice, careful reading of a number of nonmedical sources clarifies some of the confusion. Catherine wrote only a few letters with details of her pregnancies, so her voice is heard mostly filtered through the men around her, many of them diplomats who reported on life at court. But pregnancy and childbirth involved many people and many objects, both medical and religious. Birthing had a designated space in Catherine's chamber, women cared for her, and in some cases she subsequently bequeathed the items handled by her attendants as a way to commemorate the event and cement the personal relationships. The actual objects used by Catherine during her pregnancies and miscarriages—clothing, furniture, dishware, and jewelry—do not survive, but it is possible to glean insights from the inventories, household purchases of items for her chamber, letters, and comparison to the accounts of noblewomen. Royal wardrobe accounts report salaries paid to nurses and midwives, purchases of bed linens for a queen's confinement, and baby blankets for the child's christening or funeral. The first lady mistress of the nursery was Elizabeth Denton, but for most of her pregnancies Catherine relied on Margaret Bryan.[62]

Fine bed linen imported from the Netherlands and embellished with embroidery and lace insertions would have been ordered. After childbirth, the cradle and mother's bed were given particularly decorative sheets and pillow covers. Richly embroidered hangings for beds commonly fitted inside alcoves, with curtains to conceal the wooden structure and hide the bed during the day. A bed valance made of woven linen with pulled and drawn threadwork, with bobbin lace insertion and embroidery in silk and applied linen tassels built up from buttonhole stitch and French knots, would have hung high on the bed frame under the canopy.[63] There are no references to any special clothes having been ordered for any of Henry's wives and no portraits of the queens while pregnant, but pregnancy portraits of elite women, such as Thomas More's daughters, show that women wore gowns laced loosely to accommodate their pregnant bodies.[64] Once again, an inventory tells a richer story. Among Catherine's possessions at her death were "three smockis of fyne Hollande clothe, wherof two be wrought about the collers withe golde and the thrude wroughte aboute the collar and at the handis with silke' along with two double petticoats of holland . . . necessaries provided for the Princesse Dowager whatte tyme she laye in childe bedde."[65] These embroidered smocks and petticoats, carefully folded and tended for twenty years, convey across five centuries Catherine's deeply emotional message of what motherhood meant to her. It was not simply the duty of a queen to provide an heir; it was the powerful bond of a mother to her children, both the one who survived her and those who did not.

Catherine, like all queens consort, went to great lengths to ensure a healthy pregnancy and the safe delivery of a healthy child, preferably a boy. She turned to both medical and nonmedical practices to improve her chances of pregnancy, and, like English kings and queens since the thirteenth century, she turned to her religious beliefs and made pilgrimages to the shrine at Walsingham Priory in East Anglia.[66] The manors of Great and Little Walsingham were assigned to Catherine as part of her dower, and while on pilgrimage she would stay at one of her manors at Litcham, which had a church well known for its rood screen with depictions of female saints.[67] A very wealthy establishment that commemorated the annunciation, the priory's most important relic was reputed to be the holy milk of blessed Mary, which honored lactation. Catherine, and at least once, Henry, went there to pray to Saint Margaret, the patron saint of childbirth, and to visit the statue of the Virgin with Child. Wells at the shrine reminded the visitor of the power of the Virgin, who miraculously rescued a boy who fell into a well.[68] At the Slipper Chapel at Houghton, about a mile and a half southwest of Walsingham, pilgrims took off their shoes and walked barefoot to the shrine. The lore of shrine told of how Henry VIII walked barefoot from the town of Barsham to the Chapel of the Priory and presented the Virgin with a necklace of great value.[69]

She probably took home good-luck charms to signal a pregnancy: girdles, apotropaic gemstones such as coral (believed to have beneficial properties for fertility), or a string of semiprecious stone beads that doubled as a rosary (paternoster), such as pearls to stanch hemorrhaging, jet to quell childbirth pains, jasper to help expel the afterbirth, and amber to help with childbirth and ward off evil eye and fairy abduction and calm teething pain. Birthing girdles predate Christianity. "Our Lady's Girdle," also known as Saint Elizabeth's girdle (she was elderly and formerly unable to have children), was kept by monks in a purse at Westminster in "a long coffer of crystal . . . with three cases" and was probably used in 1502 by

FIG. 12 | Unknown artisan, Our Lady of Walsingham pilgrim badge, late fourteenth–early fifteenth century. Lead alloy, 52 × 40 mm. Museum of London Picture Library, 82.8/4. Photo © Museum of London.

Elizabeth of York for the birth of Katherine.[70] Perhaps she got an ampoule in the shape of a cockle shell marked with a capital crowned W or having a crown monogram. Such a badge could have been one of the annunciation, with the Virgin and Archangel Gabriel with a lily pot between them, or the Virgin seated with a fleur-de-lis on her right shoulder and Child on her left, or the priory and chapel with a statue of the Virgin and Child. Or Catherine may have owned a pilgrim badge that depicted the Virgin of Walsingham with the Christ Child beside her to focus her prayers for the Virgin's help during the pregnancy (fig. 12). In this example, both figures have haloes around their heads. Around the figures is a frame decorated at the sides with a zigzag and dot motif. Above their heads is a crenellated canopy. The statue of the Virgin Mary at Walsingham and at other shrines of Our Lady would have been the focus of worship for pilgrims.

On 1 November 1509, just five months after the wedding and one month before Catherine's twenty-fourth birthday, Henry wrote to his father-in-law that Catherine was pregnant.[71] He added that "the child in her womb is alive," indicating quickening, or the moment when the mother can feel fetal movements in her uterus. A first-time mother typically feels fetal movements at about eighteen to twenty weeks, suggesting that Catherine may have become pregnant soon after the wedding, as early as late June or July. After Christmas she was at Richmond to prepare for the birth. All seemed well when, on 16 and 23 December 1509, Henry gave a substantial grant of fabric for the nursery, the bedchamber furnishings, and clothing to Catherine in preparation for childbirth.[72] On 30 January 1510, she complained of a pain in her knee, and the next day she went into labor. She vowed to donate "one of her rich head-dresses" to Saint Peter the Martyr of the Franciscan Order, and sent it by one of her attendants who wished to become a nun of that order.[73] But the child, a girl, was stillborn. No records of a funeral have been found, and there is no mention of whether she was churched. The sad news was tempered a bit by the court physician, who told her that one child, presumed to be a boy, still lived in her womb. There is no record of what the court physician did that led him to this conclusion, but it is medically possible that there were fraternal twins: the stillborn child, born prematurely, and a second fetus that still lived. Catherine was skeptical, but as weeks passed and her abdomen continued to swell, it seemed that he might have been correct. Preparations were made for a second confinement, with orders on 12 March for red ceremonial cloth to cover a baptismal font, Holland linen for the bottom of the font, and yards of lightweight silk or linen to cover the font.[74] But there is no report of any hemorrhaging or expulsion of any fetal tissue, and by late spring it was clear that there was no other child. The information was not made public for over four months, and it seems that the only people at court who knew any details were Catherine, Henry, the physician, and two Spanish women at court, most likely María de Salinas and Inés Vanegas.

Catherine acutely felt the loss. On 25 May, she instructed her ambassador, Diego Fernández, to report to her father that "the last day of January in the morning her Highness brought forth prematurely a daughter, without any pain except that one knee pained her the night before. This affair was so secret that no-one knew it until now except the King my lord, two Spanish women, a physician, and I. The physician said that her Highness remained pregnant with another child and it was believed and kept secret."[75] It is unlikely that Fernández knew much beyond the bare facts, but if he did know more, he was exceptionally discreet in keeping his confidences. In a letter to her father on 27 May, she told him that she had "miscarried a dead daughter and because it was considered here an ill omen I did not write before to tell your Highness." She begged him not to reprimand her or be angry with her, saying the stillbirth had been the will of God. She put on a cheerful face and was thankful that God "has given her such a husband as the King of England."[76] Knowing that both her mother and mother-in-law had experienced a similar sadness of losing a pregnancy was probably some comfort, but it must have been gratifying to know that she could easily and quickly become pregnant. Catherine's devotion to the Franciscans highlights the influence of her mother, a patron of the Franciscans; Isabel's miscarriages and stillbirths must have been very much on her mind throughout the pregnancy. She would also have been comforted by the women at court, who helped her regain both her physical and emotional health.[77]

She got pregnant again quite quickly. Accounting for the month that a husband was advised to refrain from sexual intercourse with a postpartum wife, the earliest this could have occurred was late April or May. She could have felt quickening in late summer at the earliest, and royal officials again began to prepare for childbirth. On 29 September 1510, household accounts note payment for a bearing cloth ("beryng payne") of purple velvet to hold the baby and green wool for making curtains for Catherine's bedchamber, perhaps to separate the chamber when she gave birth.[78] Sometime before 1:30 AM on 1 January 1511, she gave birth to a son.[79] Four days later the baby was christened Henry, Duke of Cornwall, and on 8 January Catherine told her sister-in-law Marguerite of Austria about the birth and christening.[80] Henry rode to Walsingham to pray at the shrine, and in early February Catherine was churched.[81] This ritual of thanksgiving for the safe delivery of a child and a reenactment of the churching of the Virgin Mary took place at the door of the chapel, where Catherine would have been greeted and blessed by a priest.[82] She would have worn new clothes for churching, and objects needed for churching included a veil (a "care cloth"), a chrisom cloth (which wrapped the baby after he was anointed with the holy oil after being baptized), basins, and ewers. She then went to Richmond with her ladies at her side to rest and recuperate.[83] Henry rejoiced, ordering beacons to be lit in London and free wine to be distributed to all citizens of London. Churchmen processed through the streets, and celebrations for the new baby boy lasted well over a month. Henry did what came naturally. He staged a tournament at Westminster.

FIG. 13 | Henry VIII jousting before Catherine of Aragon, 1511. College of Arms MS Westminster Tournament Roll, 1511, membranes 25–26. Reproduced by permission of the Kings, Heralds, and Pursiuvants of Arms.

The Westminster Tournament, staged on 12 and 13 February 1511, was intended to promote the Tudor realm in a grand spectacle of dynastic power and military prowess. It showed the chivalric magnificence of young Henry's court, with his wife, newly delivered of a son, in an orchestrated magnificence meant to rival that of the Burgundian court. The tournament was staged as an allegorical challenge from four strange knights—*Vailliaunt desyre* (Brave Desire, Sir Thomas Knyvet), *Bone voloyr* (Good Desire, Sir William Courtenay), *Joyous panser* (Happy Thoughts, Sir Edward Neville), and *Coeure loyall* (Loyal Heart). Loyal Heart, was, of course, Henry, broadcasting his chivalric love for Catherine. The entry into the tiltyard was followed by presentation of the shields to Catherine, seated in a pavilion with her attendants. Henry, as the Tenth Worthy, wore on his helmet a gold *cointrise* (a lady's sleeve or scarf) that Catherine had given him.[84]

The manuscript evidence for this tournament, one of the first Burgundian-style tournaments held in England, is particularly rich. Two contemporary chronicles describe the festivities, and in the Revels Account, the Serjeant of the Tents, Richard Gibson, left a detailed record of the supplies necessary for the pageant that preceded the tournament and a play-by-play record of the joust. The border of the manuscript of the Westminster Tournament Challenge bears Catherine's pomegranate emblem alongside the Tudor rose (fig. 13). In a narrative scene, Catherine is seated under the pavilion, at the far left, attentively watching Henry do kingly masculine jousting. As Lady of Honor, she acts as the leader of the Court of Honor to make sure that everyone behaves with good sportsmanship and handles their horses with both competence and kindness. Serenely triumphant while Henry edges out his companions in mock battle, she watches Henry, as Couere loyall, at the left in the foreground, as he is about to "accomplish certain feates of Armes" in honour of the "byrthe of a yong prynce."[85]

But the festivities were bittersweet. A week later, on 22 February, their baby boy died. At first, Henry's concern was for Catherine, who, "like a natural woman," was devastated and "made much lamentation." He did not show his emotions outwardly, but "like a wise Prince took this dolor-ous chance wondrous wisely."[86] He did provide a suitably lavish funeral for the baby and burial at Westminster Abbey with 180 poor men dressed in black, accompanied by the Chapel Royal choristers.[87] Modern sources do not agree about the cause of death: some speculate that it was an intestinal disorder, others say a respiratory infection, and one obstetrician claims it was spirochetal pneumonitis, a common respiratory disease often confused with tuberculosis. It is likely that he was born premature, at seven months gestation, and thus would have been small and frail, with underdeveloped lungs that made nursing difficult.[88] Retrospective diagnosis, however, is not good history. All we know for certain is that in January 1511 Cather-ine gave birth to a son who lived six weeks and died of an undetermined illness.

Catherine and Henry were nothing if not determined to have another child, and despite their efforts to keep rumors at bay, on 11 Septem-ber 1511, Cardinal Wolsey speculated "that the Queen is with child," but either she was not or she experienced another miscarriage.[89] There is no evidence to suggest that she was pregnant in 1512, but by the late spring or early summer of 1513, Catherine, then twenty-eight years old, was pregnant again. That summer, Henry was in France and she was regent and deeply enmeshed in the governing of the realm and managing a war with Scotland. Catherine could have conceived no later than early June, when Henry left England for France, which would make her no more than three months pregnant in September. It is possible that in August she felt the quickening while in the north of England preparing for the Battle of Flodden. On 16 September, after the defeat of the Scots and the death of King James IV, she wrote to Henry that she hoped he would be home soon. At the end of the letter she tells him, "And with this I make an end, praying God to send you home shortly, for without this no joy here can be accomplished; and for the same I pray, and now go to Our Lady of Walsingham that I promised so long ago to see."[90] Her joy was not just for a military victory. By telling Henry that she planned to make a pilgrimage to the shrine at Walsingham, Catherine was telling Henry that she was pregnant. She took a cue from her mother, who was well known for working through all of her pregnancies, war or no war. The precise date that she went into labor is not known, but on 6 October the Venetian ambassador reported that "the Queen of England has given birth to a son," but the child was either stillborn or died shortly after birth.[91] The five-month period between Henry's departure and her delivery of a child suggests three possible ways to understand this event. If she had become pregnant in early June, it could have been a miscarriage. If she had conceived earlier, it could have been a stillbirth. Or the child could have died during or immediately after delivery, due to prematurity. It is simply not clear. Catherine's sadness was compounded by irony. Margaret Tudor was pregnant at the same time, and in April 1514 she gave birth to a son.

In June 1514, Gerard de Pleine wrote to Marguerite of Austria that "the Queen is believed to be with child, and is so, as far as the writer can judge."[92] Nicolò Di Favri of Treviso, an attaché at the Venetian embassy in London, reporting on the proxy marriage of Henry's sister Mary to Louis XII of France, casually commented that "after the King came the Queen (who is pregnant) clad in ash-coloured satin with chains and jewels and on her head a cap of cloth of gold covering her ears in the Venetian fashion."[93] Catherine's chamber was prepared for the birth as early as 4 October, as shown by an order of bedclothes.[94] But on 31 December 1514, Peter Martyr reported that "the Queen of England has given birth to a premature child,—through grief, as it is said, for the misunderstanding between her father and her husband. He had reproached her with her father's ill faith."[95] The Venetian ambassador, Andrea Badoer, reported that "the queen [Catherine] was delivered of a stillborn child of eight months—a great grief to all the court."[96] Chroniclers, too, blamed this outcome on her emotional state due to a quarrel between her father and her husband that provoked her to give birth prematurely. Based on what we know now about the adverse effects or emotional stress on the immune system, this is not at all an unreasonable speculation. The physical demands of repeated pregnancies and the emotional toll of miscarriages or stillbirths would leave even the most physically hardy woman exhausted.

There may be some truth to the anxiety felt at court over Catherine's emotional health. By September 1515, people close to the crown anxiously inquired about a pregnancy. Women and men, after repeated miscarriages and stillbirths, are often reluctant to speak too soon and will not share the news of another pregnancy until they feel it is safe to do so. But by October or November it was clear that Catherine was pregnant again. News of her father's death on 23 January 1516 was kept from her to avoid causing her to grieve and lose the child.[97] At last, at about 4 in the morning on 18 February 1516, at the Palace of Placentia, Catherine gave birth to a daughter, Mary, who would survive and rule as Queen Mary I from 1553 to 1558. Her physician, Peter Vernando, attended at Mary's birth. The labor was long, but the daughter was healthy. When Mary was christened on 21 February, the Prior of Christ Church of Canterbury and his servants were paid £4 for carrying the baptismal font to and from Greenwich for Princess Mary.[98] She was carried to her christening by Elizabeth Stafford, Countess of Surrey and wife of Thomas Howard. Her godparents were Thomas Wolsey; Catherine of York, Countess of Devon and daughter of Edward IV; Margaret Pole, Countess of Salisbury; and Agnes Howard, Duchess of Norfolk.[99] The joy at the birth of Mary was expressed visually in decorations in the *Salue radix*, a musical manuscript of motets composed by "Magister Sampson," with Catherine's pomegranate and the Tudor rose joined allegorically as a symbol of the union.[100]

Can we even imagine what she felt in that moment, after the hormonal roller-coaster of pregnancy and childbirth, following the years of heartbreak? Catherine's joy and relief at a successful pregnancy and delivery of a healthy child, and her emotions for Mary, are poignantly expressed by the fact that she kept the baby blankets. The inventory at her death in 1536 noted four small coverlets ("counterpointe of astate") that were provided for Catherine when she gave birth ("provided from the Princesse Dowager whatte tyme she lay in childebedde"). The inventory lists one quilt made of rich purple edged with ermine fur, two mattresses stuffed with wool and covered with Holland cloth for a cradle, and a linen cambric sheet fringed with gold to cover the infant. One crimson coverlet, edged with ermine, was threadbare from use, with the fur ripped in places.[101] Catherine kept these baby blankets, sheets, and mattresses for two decades. They were mementos of Mary as a baby. They reminded her of how her baby smelled, the softness of her skin, the sight of her asleep in her arms or the cradle. That cradle was rocked by the most trusted members of Princess Mary's household. When Catherine handed her new baby over to someone in the first years of her life, it would have been to Elizabeth Denton. Then Margaret Bryan took over, followed in 1521 by Margaret Pole, and Catherine Pole, later Lady Catherine Brook, nurse before the end of 1516 until 1525. All of them were compensated with clothing and livery.[102]

There is a strong suggestion that she might have been pregnant in 1517. On 13 March 1517, Charles Brandon accompanied Catherine and her sister-in-law Mary to Walsingham.[103] But this may have been wishful thinking. Either she was not pregnant or she had a miscarriage that went unreported. But we can be fairly certain that in the summer of 1518, at age thirty-two, she was pregnant again. On 1 July 1518, Henry wrote to Wolsey: "Two things there be which be so secret that they cause me at this time to write to you myself; the one is that I trust the Queen my wife to be with child."[104] On 10 November 1518 she gave birth one last time, to a son or daughter who was stillborn. The Venetian ambassador, Sebastian Giustinian, reported that "the most serene queen was this night delivered of a daughter, which to the few who are as yet acquainted with the circumstance, has proved vexatious, for never had this entire kingdom ever so anxiously desired anything as it did a prince, it appearing to every one that the State would be safe should his Majesty leave an heir male, whereas, without a prince, they are of a contrary opinion."[105] In 1519, Catherine again went on pilgrimage to Walsingham and prayed, but as far as we know she never was pregnant again.[106]

Causes for the difficulties Catherine and Henry experienced with pregnancies are vexing to determine. Looking at the maternal history of both her mother and mother-in-law for clues in their maternal histories can shed some light. Catherine's mother, Isabel, was pregnant at least seven times between 1470 and 1485. She had one known miscarriage; five children lived past birth to adulthood, and four of them survived their mother. When she was nineteen years old and not yet crowned queen, she gave birth to her first daughter, also named Isabel, born just under a year after her marriage, on 2 October 1470. Five years later Isabel was pregnant again, after a period of civil war. During this pregnancy, while on campaign her riding on horseback from town to town, she miscarried a son. In September 1477, the chroniclers note briefly that the king "stayed some days in which the Queen became pregnant," and they were right: on 30 June 1478 in Seville, Isabel gave birth to a son, Juan. A little over a year later, on 6 November 1479, her second daughter, Juana, was born. On 28 June 1482, during the war with Granada, she went into labor at the council table and gave birth to a third daughter they named María and a stillborn female twin child. On 15 December 1485, during a lull in the war, she gave birth to Catherine, her last child and probably her last pregnancy. From her mother's history, then, there is no reason to suspect that Catherine would have difficulty producing the requisite brood of boys and girls. Furthermore, her siblings easily produced healthy children. Her sister Juana had six children very quickly, and María had ten children, eight of whom lived to adulthood. Juan died shortly after his brief marriage to Marguerite of Austria, and she did not conceive. This family history does not suggest any abnormalities.

On Henry's side, Catherine's mother-in-law, Elizabeth of York, was pregnant eight times, but only three of her children outlived her: Henry VIII, Margaret, and Mary.[107] One daughter, Elizabeth, died at age three, and two sons, Edward and Edmund, died in infancy, all of unknown causes. Another daughter, Katherine, died nine days after her birth and was quickly followed by her mother.[108] The nine-day interval between the child's birth and the queen's death suggests puerperal (childbed) fever. It is clear that Elizabeth and Henry VII had no impediments to fertility, and that she could carry a pregnancy to term; three children died while young, but that was not unusual in the later Middle Ages.

Henry seems to have had healthy sperm, at least some of the time, because he had three children with other women: in 1519, a son named Henry FitzRoy with Elizabeth Blount; in 1533, a daughter, Elizabeth, with Anne Boleyn; and in 1537, another son, Edward, with Jane Seymour. But his own sexual history is not entirely clear-cut, and we may never know whether any other women with whom he had sex had miscarriages. Eric

Ives has suggested that Anne Boleyn may well have had sex with other men because she feared that Henry was impotent. Knowing that a son was essential, Ives argues, Anne may have been trying to improve her chances.[109] Jane Seymour may just have had the good fortune of a young woman, because after that no children were produced in Henry's very troubled marital history. He never had sexual relations with Anne of Cleves, Katheryn Howard's extramarital sexual life and early execution for her affair make it impossible to know if she might have ever been pregnant with a child by Henry, and Katherine Parr never had a child with Henry. She did, however, have a child after Henry's death with her third husband, when she was close to forty years old. Henry was plagued by a series of injuries and in later life was in poor health, but the most important issue here is the suggestion of syphilis. This, too, is only a speculation, because there is no evidence that Henry received any of the standard late medieval treatments for syphilis.[110] But even if he did have syphilis, we do not know the date of onset or whether this had anything to do with Catherine's stillbirths and miscarriages.

This sketchy evidence has recently been augmented by the work of bioarchaeologist Catrina Banks Whitley and anthropologist Kyra Kramer, who argue that Henry VIII suffered from McLeod's syndrome, in which the man transmits the Kell antigen to the woman. This works something like the more familiar Rh antigen. If a Kell-positive father impregnates a Kell-negative mother, each pregnancy has a 50–50 chance of being Kell positive. The first pregnancy typically carries to term and produces a healthy infant, even if the infant is Kell positive and the mother is Kell negative. But the mother's subsequent Kell-positive pregnancies are at risk because the mother's antibodies will attack the Kell-positive fetus as a foreign body. In other words, a woman can bear a child, but subsequent pregnancies may fail because of an immune incompatibility. Evidence strongly suggests the possible transmission of the Kell positive gene from Jacquetta of Luxembourg, Henry VIII's maternal great-grandmother. There was a pattern of reproductive failure among Jacquetta's male descendants, while the females were generally reproductively successful, which suggests—and I stress the word "suggests"—the genetic presence of the Kell phenotype within the family. But because with a Kell antigen incompatibility only the first pregnancy is successful, Whitley and Kramer are not convinced that Kell antigen is at the heart of the problem.[111] At present, we are left with speculation and centuries of blame heaped on Catherine for what is casually, cruelly, and wrongly termed dynastic failure. She did bear Henry an heir who succeeded him as Queen Mary I.

It is significant that Catherine as queen and partner in politics shifted from being a close adviser to Henry to being consumed with pregnancies and motherhood. She was not absent, just not part of the king's inner circle. She advised Henry and routinely received ambassadors with him, managed her estates and household, and supervised her council.[112] She continued to be an important adviser after her father's death in 1516, and Henry relied on her to negotiate with her nephew Charles, who in 1519 added the titles of Archduke of Austria and Holy Roman Emperor to his simply regal title of King of Castile and Aragon. With her sister-in-law Margaret, Catherine acted forcefully and publicly to intercede in 1517 on behalf of apprentices in London who were arrested and set to be executed for their participation in the Evil May Day riots protesting the use of foreign workers. Catherine appeared on the scene with her two sisters-in-law and successfully interceded with Henry and Wolsey to show mercy.[113]

Catherine shrewdly focused her efforts as queen on bearing healthy children. Her six pregnancies made a space for Wolsey to step into. He was valuable to Henry because he was talented, and he owed his power to Henry, not landed estates and family connections. Wolsey profited from Catherine's absence after Flodden and her subsequent decline in power from one of the king's most valuable advisers.

CATHERINE AT THE FIELD OF THE CLOTH OF GOLD

Still, Catherine remained politically significant outside the king's inner circle of advisers. The strength of their relationship was powerfully on display in a convincing show of comity, marital peace, and a talent for political theater in France at the Field of the Cloth of Gold in the summer of 1520. The French ambassador noted that "she is held in greater esteem by the King and his council than ever she was."[114] This famous meeting of the English and French monarchs, seventeen days filled with lavish ceremonies and tournaments, was designed by Cardinal Wolsey to craft an

alliance between the two realms.[115] It posed distinct diplomatic problems
for Catherine, though, with roots in the relations between the Habsburg
emperor Maximilian and Henry. They disagreed on the best way to handle
relations with France: Henry usually preferred peaceful means to balance
power, while Maximilian wavered between threats of war and overtures of
peace. The death of Maximilian in 1519 and the succession of his grandson and Catherine's nephew, Charles, persuaded Catherine to view the
French as a threat to the best interests of both her husband and her
nephew.[116] Rather than directly challenge Henry and Wolsey, she met
with her council and voiced her objections to an alliance with the French,
which prompted the French ambassadors to report to Henry that she "had
made such representations, and shown such reasons against the voyage,
as one would not have supposed she would have dared do, or even imagine."[117] A queen's audacious act such as this could have gone badly, but
Catherine's instincts were sound. Henry interpreted it not as a threat to
him but as an expression of a sentiment shared by many of the English
nobles. Catherine gained influence at court, and Henry gained lever-
age in the meetings with the French. She worked with the regent of the
Netherlands, her sister-in-law Marguerite of Austria, to get their nephew,
Emperor Charles V, to meet with Henry before the Field of the Cloth of
Gold. Catherine made an emotional pitch to Henry, saying that she hoped
that "she might see Charles, which was her greatest desire in the world."[118]
This may read to our ears like a persuasive ploy couched in the language of
emotional hyperbole, but it has the ring of truth.[119] It had been fourteen
years since Catherine had seen any of her family. Her parents and three of
her siblings had died, her mentally fragile sister, Queen Juana of Castile,
was largely absent from court, and the two sisters rarely, if ever, communi-
cated. Charles was one of the few family members still alive, but she had
never met him. He replied to her, thanking her for organizing the meeting and saying that it would give him "the greatest satisfaction" to meet
with her and Henry.[120] The meeting took place at Canterbury in May 1520,
where Catherine's clothing signaled her loyalties. A gown of cloth of gold
embroidered with the Tudor roses and a necklace made of five strings of
pearls with a pendant with Saint George wrought in diamonds showed
off her Englishness, while a luxurious Flemish headdress was a nod to her
family ties to Marguerite and Charles.[121] When they met, she "embraced

her nephew tenderly, not without tears."[122] Catherine corresponded regularly with Charles, and he remained her strongest advocate in the coming decades. She made the point that Henry and François could negotiate a flawed peace treaty, but she would stay true to her nephew and the growing global power of the Spanish Empire.[123]

Catherine and Henry then left England for the meeting with François I at the Field of the Cloth of Gold in France, an extravagant public display of power and political theater in a series of tournaments, banquets, and masques. Catherine very skillfully used livery and her own clothing and appearance to communicate visually her sentiments and her own complex personal and dynastic identity without challenging Henry. She was accompanied by an entourage of the highest-ranking noblewomen in England and her closest friend, María de Salinas. She would dress in Tudor colors of green and white, but her entourage bore her distinctive badge with pomegranates and gold sheaves of arrows.[124] Catherine and her French counterparts, Queen Claude and her mother-in-law, Louise of Savoy, competed for attention in the spectacle of costly and lavish fashion. Catherine, aware that all eyes would be on her and her court, closely supervised the livery of fifty-five guardsmen and twelve yeomen and grooms, ordering yards and yards of green and russet velvet for coats and doublets and black velvet bonnets. On 12 June, the Venetian ambassador reported that "the headdress of the English Queen was in the Spanish fashion, with a tress of hair over her shoulders and gown, which last was all of cloth of gold; and round her neck were most beautiful jewels and pearls." But she was also true to the English crown, as when she wore a petticoat of silver tissue, a gown of cloth of gold lined with purple velvet with roses of England embroidered in gold thread.[125] She made a very positive English statement later when she wore round her neck "five large strings of pearls, with a pendant St. George on horseback slaying the dragon, all in diamonds."[126] The livery of her servants featured the Tudor rose embroidered along with cloth-of-gold sheaves of arrows, the heraldic emblem of her mother. In her chambers, Catherine displayed nine tapestries of gold and silk embroidered with flowers and foliage.[127] The women of her chamber "were well arrayed," "ornamented in the English fashion," and wearing sumptuous jewels.[128] But Catherine favored the styles of her homeland. She wore sumptuous dresses "in the Spanish fashion," which meant sleeves slashed to reveal white undersleeves and bands covered in jewels and gold embroidery, with her braided hair covered by a gold and jewel-encrusted Spanish coif that hung down her back. Her litter was covered completely in cloth of gold and embroidered with crimson satin and gold foliage.[129] The gift exchange had the desired effect of impressing the guests with the wealth of both sides. Equestrian gifts were popular. Catherine gave Louise of Savoy a saddle and harness, and she gave Queen Claude several palfreys and hobbies (later known as hackneys), very large Irish or English horses with a long, smooth, ambling gait suitable for women to ride comfortably.[130]

The Field of the Cloth of Gold marks a turning point in Catherine's life. One of Queen Claude's attendants, Anne Boleyn, was probably in attendance, although her name is not listed. After Anne's father, Sir Thomas Boleyn, brought her back to England in 1521, she was placed in Catherine's household and made her first recorded appearance at court at a masque on 1 March 1522, where, presumably, she caught the eye of the king.[131]

TIME LINE: BRIDE AGAIN, QUEEN FINALLY, AND MOTHER AT LAST, 1509–1519

1509

21 April	Prince Henry succeeds to the throne.
11 June	In a private ceremony, Catherine and Henry marry at Greenwich.
24 June	Catherine and Henry are crowned in a joint ceremony at Westminster Abbey, followed by days of public festivities to celebrate the marriage and coronation.
29 June	Margaret Beaufort dies.
1 November	Catherine announces her first pregnancy.

1510

30 January	Catherine gives birth to a stillborn child, probably a premature delivery. There is a suggestion that a twin survived, but by March it is clear that this was not true.
March	England and France sign treaty of peace.
Late spring	Catherine becomes pregnant, probably in May.
Summer	Henry and Catherine make a grand royal summer progress, staying with Lord William Sandys at the Vyne in Hampshire, Dorset, Corfe Castle, Southampton, Salisbury, and Woking.

1511

1 January	Catherine gives birth to a son, named Henry.
5 January	Prince Henry is christened.
Late January	Henry makes a pilgrimage of gratitude to the shrine of Our Lady at Walsingham Priory in Norfolk.
Early February	Catherine is churched, marking her formal reentry into the court after giving birth.
22 February	Prince Henry dies.
Summer	Henry and Catherine make a summer royal progress to Northampton, Leicester Abbey, Coventry, Warwick, and Nottingham.

November	Fernando of Aragon and Henry sign the Treaty of Westminster, a move designed to offset the growing power of France and Navarre.

1513

Late spring	Catherine is visibly pregnant.
15 June	Henry appoints Catherine regent to secure territory in the north while he leaves England with the army to fight in France.
9 September	Catherine, as regent, supervises the English army's preparations to fight the Scots at the Battle of Flodden. The Scottish army is defeated and King James IV of Scotland dies, leaving Margaret Tudor a widowed young mother.
6 October	Catherine gives birth to a child, perhaps premature and presumed to be a son, who dies shortly after delivery.

1514

March	Henry signs a truce with King Fernando of Aragon, King Louis XII of France, and Emperor Maximilian.
June	Catherine is rumored to be pregnant again.
9 October	Princess Mary marries King Louis XII of France.
Late November or early December	Catherine gives birth to a child who may or may not have been christened on or shortly after the third day after birth.

1515

1 January	Louis XII of France dies.
3 March	Widowed Princess Mary marries Henry's close friend Charles Brandon, Duke of Suffolk.
Summer	The court stays at the residence of Cardinal Thomas Wolsey, newly appointed chancellor. His authority at court begins to displace that of Catherine.

1516

23 January	Catherine's father, Fernando of Aragon, dies, and his grandson Charles succeeds him as King of Spain, the united realms of Castile and Aragon.
18 February	Catherine gives birth to a healthy, and perhaps full-term, daughter, Mary.
20 February	Mary is christened at the Observant Friars church at Greenwich.
Summer	The court spends most of the summer in London or at Wolsey's residence.

1517

May	Catherine, with her sisters-in-law Margaret, dowager queen of Scotland, and Mary, duchess of Suffolk, intervenes in the Evil May Day riots on behalf of the rioting apprentices.
Summer	A bout of the deadly "sweating sickness" breaks out at court, and Henry, and probably Catherine, spend most of this time outside of London at Wolsey's residence.

1518

Easter	The court stays at Woodstock, at the Abbey of Abingdon, to avoid the plague in London.
1 July	Catherine, at Woodstock, announces her pregnancy.
5 October	The Treaty of London formalizes the betrothal of Princess Mary to the French dauphin, François, Duke of Brittany, and Mary is taken on an official royal progress to mark the event.
10 November	Catherine gives birth to a child who is stillborn, or who dies soon after birth. This is her last known pregnancy.

1519

5 January	Henry commissions a joint tomb at Windsor for his burial with Catherine.
Summer	Henry and Catherine go on a royal progress to Sussex, Kent, staying with Edward Stafford, the Duke of Buckingham, at Penshurst, and Catherine's manor at Havering-atte-Bower in Essex.
15 June	Elizabeth Blount, a member of Catherine's personal household and Henry's mistress, gives birth to an illegitimate son, Henry FitzRoy.

CHAPTER 5

A "Humble and Loyal" Queen

I have been to you a true and humble wife.

—Catherine of Aragon, 1529

A PORTRAIT OF QUEENLY POWER, CA. 1520–25

Around the time that Catherine and Henry met with François I at the
Field of the Cloth of Gold, perhaps a little after, but definitely sometime
between 1520 and 1525, an anonymous artist painted a pair of portraits of
Catherine and Henry (fig. 14). Although curators once thought that the
female portrait was of Henry's sixth wife, Katherine Parr, the style of her
dress dates to the 1520s or 1530s and the facial features match far more
closely with portraits of Catherine of Aragon.[1] Double portraits such as
this were not uncommon at the time and would have been produced in
multiple versions, some of them based on copies. In the early 1520s, they
might have been commissioned as a pair, and they are now hung side by
side at the National Portrait Gallery in London. It is not known who
commissioned these portraits and for what purpose, but they may have
been painted to commemorate an event as a visual representation of the
power and sophisticated cosmopolitan culture of the Tudor monarchy.
They are noteworthy as among the earliest examples of an artist painting

FIG. 14 | Unknown artist, *Catherine of Aragon*, ca. 1520. Oil on oak panel, 520 × 420 mm. National Portrait Gallery, London, on loan from Church Commissions for England, ID no. L246. Photo © Stefano Baldini / Bridgeman Images.

directly from a sitter, not a copy and not based on an idealized imagining of a queen or king, although the artist used a drawing to trace out the composition, which is conventional. Portraits as a genre were increasingly popular in the sixteenth century and often symbolized loyalty to the king, which was particularly important during the turbulence of the divorce and religious reform in the late 1520s and 1530s. The painter, likely a male artist either from the Netherlands or influenced by fellow artists from that region, painted the two portraits at roughly the same time using oil on an oak panel of about the same size for each (roughly 20 × 16 inches).

The paintings are stylistically a matched set. Both Catherine and Henry are depicted wearing lavishly embroidered velvet clothing and ostentatious jewelry, seated before a similar green damask background; both are shown with serious facial expressions; and both look off to one side. The portrait of Henry has survived better, with minimal restoration, so that his is a more sensitive rendering. Catherine's portrait has suffered from awkward restoration and overpainting, and as a result it feels less vibrant and rich. Nevertheless, it is a remarkable portrait of Catherine at a crucial moment in her marriage.

The artist depicts Catherine as confident, assured, and serene, precisely what one would expect if one visited a thirty-five- or forty-year-old queen consort of England, the mother of the heir to the throne, and aunt of Emperor Charles V. As befits a royal portrait, the artist paid close attention to fashion and jewelry as a way to convey the charisma and majesty of a queen. She wears a Spanish hood, the sign of her foreign fashion sensibility, that is adorned with goldsmiths' work and red-orange jewels, perhaps corals, perhaps rubies. Restoration has revealed a bluish-black veil with soft folds and pale highlights that glimmer subtly against the deep green damask-patterned background. The gabled headdress has gold and red bands, with white linen lappets that cover her ears and hair, held in place by a pin. She wears no crown, meaning that she may have sat for the portrait on an ordinary day of the week. The artist wants the viewer to know that this clothing and those gems are the ordinary attire of a queen consort of a wealthy, powerful man. The red velvet dress has a gold band at the embroidered square bodice with buttons or studs at the left and right corners. It is not flashy or outrageously ostentatious, but it is most certainly luxurious. Slit sleeves of black velvet peek out from an ample oversleeve of gold brocade, with a hint of embroidery on the cuffs of her linen shift. Her jewelry is an impressive display of three strands of large white pearls with a large round pendant set with four pearls, one large central gem (perhaps a ruby) surrounded by four cabochon gems. The pendant recalls the work of Toledan goldsmiths. In a few years, Holbein would use this design in depicting pendants and bracelets referred to as Moorish or Damascene ("Moryse and Damasin"). Catherine wears no earrings, or at least none are visible, though she brought with them with her from Spain and started the fashion in England. The very simple, elegant, stirrup-style ring is set with a red ruby or garnet, and it rests midknuckle on the third finger of her right hand (Henry's rings are similar in simplicity).[2] The jewels are important because so many jewels from this period were dispersed after her death or destroyed during the Reformation, and if they are indeed what she wore for the sitting, she had rather simple taste in rings. All in all, her clothing and jewelry are unexceptional for a queen.

Her facial expression is striking, however. She is tight-lipped, her jaw appears to be clenched, and she has a steely-eyed gaze. Unlike Henry's face, which is delicately soft, with warmth of color and modeling, hers appears stern, not alluring or charismatic, not the sort of woman who attracted throngs of English men and women when she came to town on a royal progress. Is the tenseness in her lips and eyes due to Catherine's mood or age? Did the artist intend to portray her as wooden, stiff, and cold? Or did the artist catch her at a moment when the youthful promise embodied in the young woman Juan de Flandes painted in 1497 has been tested by her difficult pregnancies (see fig. 7)? Or does she look harsh because conservation treatments restored some of the original subtlety of color but sharpened the lines of her face? Retouching of the face and chest darkened the colors, reinforced her eyebrows, added dark shadows to narrow and define the nose, added bright highlights to the eyes, and adjusted the mouth with a line of brown overpaint separating the lips.

If in fact this portrait was painted from life, then it is likely to be an actual portrait of Catherine created during a period of relative stability in her marriage. Under ordinary circumstances, she and Henry would have settled into a period of maturity and faced together the challenges posed by religious reform and global expansion. But we know, from our vantage point, that no matter how confident and self-assured she may have seemed to the artist, by the early 1520s there were cracks in her serenity. She knew that she would have no more children, yet her marriage was cordial. She was no longer the first person Henry turned to for advice—Wolsey was. Still, the success of the Field of the Cloth of Gold and her meeting with Charles V showed that she was an important part of Anglo-European diplomacy. She kept busy with supervising the management of her estates and was an increasingly important patron of art and literature. She was part of the official diplomacy at court, meeting with the King and Queen of Denmark; she accompanied Henry to interview with the King of Scotland, and was asked to intercede for arrested Spaniards.[3] Yet in more significant matters her influence had begun to wane. In May 1521, she begged Henry in vain to spare the life of her old friend and staunch supporter Edward Stafford, the Duke of Buckingham, who ran afoul of Wolsey and behaved treasonously when he boasted foolishly that if Henry were to die without a son, the men in the Stafford family would be the next kings of England.[4] His trial and execution revealed the precarious position of the Princess Mary in a family that feared rule by a woman. Again, with our hindsight, we know that Catherine's serenity and poise would be tested by unexpected challenges coming not from enemies on the continent or heretics, but from within her marriage.

CRACKS IN THE MARRIAGE BEGIN TO SHOW

If there is one fact about Henry VIII that just about everyone today in the Western world knows, it is that he had several public sexual affairs. Young unmarried women, and sometimes the married ones, too, caught his amorous gaze. Catherine knew well that kings could be unfaithful to their wives and suffer few consequences. Kings expected their wives to tolerate their affairs and not make a public fuss about the rivalries, children, or political consequences. Her father, Fernando, had a number of sexual liaisons and fathered at least four illegitimate children, two of them before he married Isabel. Isabel could not, or simply did not, stop her husband's liaisons, but as a queen regnant she had resources not available to Catherine. And Isabel used them to good effect. She understood the implications of feminine and masculine characteristics and combined aspects of maternal femininity and masculine sovereignty to prevent his affairs and his children with other women from seriously threatening the marriage.[5] It was not that she did not feel the hurt of his wayward affections, but Isabel had a realm of her own to rule. And as a queen regnant, even in a political culture that did not explicitly prohibit women from ruling in their own right, she had powerful enemies who wanted to see her fail. Whatever her personal feelings, she did not make a public fuss about other women or children in Fernando's affections, but she was neither passive nor docile. She used political gestures and personal rhetoric to express her sentiments. Rather than challenge Fernando's public assertion of his masculine sexuality, she counterbalanced it with the customary wife's duty to sew his shirts and a queen regnant's duty to govern her realm. She used feminine norms to her advantage, and earned the respect of her subjects. She listened to her confessor, Hernando de Talavera, who advised her to be "much more constant in the love and respect due to such an excellent and worthy companion, much more constant and certain and true in every agreement and promise."[6] By our standards this would seem hypocritical, an admission of the weakness of femininity. But by her standards it was using the tools she had to govern a society that limited her options for action.

Catherine, growing up at her mother's side, witnessed this and, judging by her later actions during the divorce, took it to heart. The deeper message, one that informed her own actions when she had to deal with Henry's sexual affairs, was Talavera's advice to avoid doing anything that would make the king anxious about his masculinity. Without the powerful tools of a realm of her own, Catherine took Talavera's advice to heart when she pondered her motto, "Humble and Loyal." The message for Catherine as she embarked on a life as a queen consort was that her role was not to rule, but to bear children, while the king's role was to use his virile masculinity to exert his power as king. She, too, would sew her husband's shirts and keep her tongue in check. Catherine's reactions to Henry's liaisons were neither all passive nor all saintly. Both she and her mother were deeply pious. They took to heart late medieval church teachings about men and women. But they also were realists who knew that more was at stake than simply their husband's delicate masculinity or their own emotional pain. They had realms to run and children to raise. Humble and loyal. Those words, sadly ironic in retrospect, resonate across the 1520s as Catherine publicly tried to remain calm and dignified as Henry plucked a succession of young women from her court, directly in front of her, to satisfy his desires.

The women in Catherine's court in the 1520s came from a relatively small group of interrelated aristocratic families with close ties to the reigning dynasty. They formed an inner circle of courtiers and ladies who curried favor with the king, the queen, and the royal family to secure patronage for themselves, their kin, and their own households. Their proximity to the king made their families wealthy and politically powerful, and the families were not above using their daughters and wives in the sexual economy of the royal court. Catherine's privy chamber had a staff of about sixteen women. Some were there because their husbands were at court. Mary Boleyn Carey's husband was a member of the king's privy chamber. Many of them had worked for Elizabeth of York and stayed on. Agnes Tylney, the Duchess of Norfolk, served Catherine for sixteen years. Some were Henry's kin, such as Gertrude Courteney, Marchioness of Exeter; Lady Elizabeth Stafford; and her sister Lady Ann Stafford. Margaret Pole, Countess of Salisbury, a member of Catherine's household from the wedding, was sent away when her family fell out of the king's favor, came back, and was Princess Mary's governess from around 1520 to 1533.[7] Two women who came with Catherine from Spain profited well from the experience. Inés de Vanegas, daughter of Catherine's nurse when she was a child, married William Blount, Lord Mountjoy. María de Salinas, one of Catherine's closest Spanish friends, became fully acculturated in England as a baroness when she married William Willoughby, Baron of Eresby (one of her more prominent descendants was Diana Spencer [d. 1997], first wife of Prince Charles). Webs of affiliation, reciprocity, obligation, duty, and friendship cemented the personal bonds of the court. The women at court had an allegiance to their immediate families, who sought to protect the personal reputations of their daughters for a marriage match that benefited the family's interests. Their families' wealth and power also made them vulnerable to the dangerously shifting factions at court, and to the king's attention. The royal court was a perilous place for unmarried, pretty, decorous young women who were skilled at singing, dancing, playing musical instruments, and speaking French. Their proximity to the king brought them to his attention, their families benefited from the liaisons, and Henry was able to present himself publicly as a virile, desirable, lusty man. His liaisons with women at court began as early as 1510, but became more seriously dangerous for all parties as more and more of Catherine's pregnancies ended without a male heir.

Henry's choice of women for his liaisons reveal his preference for selecting his next lover, and sometimes his next wife, from the women serving his current wife at court. It is very disturbing for us today to think about this, and it was for some of them, too. But women at court were a commodity in a courtship ritual that was prelude to a well-matched marriage exchange. Proximity to the king complicated the plans of even the most careful parents, however. Ambitious and powerful parents considered a daughter who caught the king's eye the price they had to pay for a seat at the table next to the king. The most vulnerable were the maids of honor, who came to court around age sixteen. Gossip in the household about Henry's liaisons began around 1510, when there was talk of a scandal at court when Edward Stafford, the Duke of Buckingham, discovered that Henry had cast his eyes on his sister Anne, Countess of Huntingdon. It is not clear whether he had a sexual affair with her, but both Anne and her sister Elizabeth, Countess of Sussex, were caught in the web of innuendo and scandal.[8] Later, two women in Catherine's household were sexually involved clearly and openly with Henry—Elizabeth Blount and Mary Boleyn Carey, sister of Henry's second wife, Anne.[9] Blount, a lady-in-waiting to Catherine, first came to court around 1512, when she was twelve years old. She was a cousin of William Blount, husband of Catherine's personal attendant Inés Vanegas. At Christmas 1514, Elizabeth took part in a masque where she was one of four ladies who "came into the Quenes chamber with great light of torches and daunced a greate season" with Henry. She accompanied Catherine to Shooter's Hill on May Day 1515 and took part in the betrothal ceremonies for Princess Mary and the dauphin of France in October 1518. In June 1519, she bore Henry's illegitimate son, Henry FitzRoy, when Henry's daughter Mary was just over a year old.[10] Mary Boleyn's husband, William Carey, was a member of the king's Privy Chamber, and her liaison with Henry was no secret. Her son Henry, born in 1525, was named after the king, who was also his godfather but did not admit paternity to the boy. Mary's sister Anne Boleyn was "a fresh young damsel" who could sing, dance "passing excellence," and speak French. She was brought to court by her mother, Elizabeth Boleyn, and Anne was one of Catherine's maids at court before she became the king's favorite mistress, and later his second wife.[11] Nevertheless, they preserved the fiction of marital harmony.

RESONANT OBJECTS: A ROSARY AND A MUSIC MANUSCRIPT

Catherine took respite from Henry's affairs and their growing estrangement in a familiar way: she turned to her friends. Outside of her immediate family in London, one of the most significant people for Catherine at this point in her life was Marguerite of Austria, daughter of Emperor Maximilian of Austria and Mary of Burgundy, and regent of the Netherlands from 1507 to 1515, and again from 1517 to her death in 1530.[12] Marguerite was five years older than Catherine, and they first met in the autumn of 1496, when Marguerite came to the Spanish court to marry Catherine's brother, Juan. After Juan's death five months after the wedding, Marguerite stayed in Castile until 1499, and spent some of her time at court teaching Catherine how to speak French. They had very similar personal histories. Both were educated to be the wife of a duke or king. Both learned how to practice diplomacy from skilled women, Catherine from her mother and Marguerite from Anne de France (Beaujeau), regent from 1483 to 1489 for King Charles VIII (Mary of Burgundy had died when Marguerite was two years old) and author of a handbook of advice for elite women, *Lessons for My Daughter* (1517–21).[13] This face-to-face education was a strong preparation for both of them to govern a court and a realm. They also were educated formally by prominent humanist tutors, and they had a serious taste for visual art, music, and learning. Their lives crisscrossed because their siblings married each other in a double royal wedding: Juan and Marguerite, Juana and Philip. They both married while quite young, were widowed within months of their weddings, and had difficult pregnancies. Both experienced the early death of a brother—Juan in 1497 and Philip in 1506. Both were politically active throughout their lives, and during their second marriages both governed as regent for a husband or nephew. There are some differences—Marguerite was widowed twice and never had a child survive to adulthood, Catherine had to endure the infidelities of her husband—but until Marguerite's death in 1530, they stayed in touch across distances on a range of subjects both personal, as when Catherine needed a recommendation for a physician for Henry while he was in France, and political, when they helped people seeking places at court.[14] And they exchanged gifts.

As women in positions of power, they were obliged to offer gifts to cement the diplomatic and familial ties. This high-level gift-giving was part of the "household of magnificence" and was fixed in its substance and meaning. Neither of them needed to be present to provide their gifts; messengers could be dispatched with money, plate, or other gifts, and could return with the approved offering from the monarch.[15] What makes the gifts from Marguerite to Catherine and Henry more significant than most is that they were more than a political act. They reveal powerful personal and familial ties. Two gifts in particular, believed to have been sent by Marguerite to both Catherine and Henry but particularly significant to Catherine, speak eloquently of the closeness of the personal bond and convey subtle but important messages of meaning and emotion.

The first gift sent was an exquisitely carved boxwood decade rosary created in a workshop in Flanders (figs. 15 and 16). To be used daily, a decade rosary was a devotional object, intended to stir the imagination by stimulating both sight and touch in order to inspire silent and oral prayer. It was both a key element of her piety as well as a memento of her family. This one is an extraordinary work of art. As a material object, it is both image and signifier, object and iconography; it represents craft, use, and experience. By 1500, the most advanced princely patrons competed openly with each other to acquire art, to have possessions produced by a "big name" artist. Precious metals, gems, rare textiles, and exquisite artisanal craft created the illusion of sky instead of blue paint, flesh instead of boxwood. It is a finely crafted, costly, useful, and enchanting objet d'art.[16] Intimate in size and delicately carved, not quite 23 inches long, it consists of ten small faceted "ave" prayer beads (1.5 inches in diameter) and a larger "paternoster" bead (2.1 inches in diameter), with a carved crucifix on the end of the string of beads, attached to a carved ring that could slip over a finger or a belt. It is tactile, heavy and compact, soft and smooth, polished from frequent touching, and tiny enough to loop around a belt.

The paternoster bead, known popularly as the "prayer apple" and carved in the shape of a nut, could be carried in the palm of one's hand.[17]

A rosary such as this, part of a late medieval fascination for incredibly small masterpieces, highlights the complex and profound intertwining of Catherine's life, art, and piety. Boxwood, prized for its consistent grain, was hard enough to hold its shape and was believed to have been one of the woods used to make Christ's cross. Using tiny two-inch-long tools, artisans carved with exquisite detail religious scenes within the beads. Each bead is carved in the shape of a walnut, which symbolizes three aspects of Christ: the outer sheath represents Christ's flesh, the shell is his cross, and the core symbolizes Christ's death.[18]

Catherine's physical devotional act would begin with securing the beads to her belt or her finger.[19] The finger ring signified the identity of the owners, with the royal arms of England and two inscriptions. One is the motto "Honi soit qvi mal y pense" of the Knights of Garter (Evil be to him who thinks evil) and the other is the opening verse of Psalm 70, "posvi dei adivtorivm mevm" (O God, come to my assistance), from the vespers sung in honor of the Virgin Mary. Then she would touch the crucifix, with its image of the crucified Christ and the four evangelists on one side and the four Latin church fathers on the other. She would secure the beads in the palm of her hand and recite the ave beads, one by one. Each bead was carved with Latin inscriptions of scriptural texts on large scrolls held by apostles and prophets. The ave beads told a biblical story of the prophets, apostles, miracles, and martyrs, some with dozens of characters in full regalia and action. Then her fingers would reach the large paternoster bead with images depicting the incarnation, life, and passion of Christ and the redemption of mankind. Finally, the paternoster bead would be opened and the intricate sculpture inside would be contemplated. What makes this rosary even more meaningful to both Catherine and Henry, and to viewers five centuries later, is that when the paternoster bead is opened there is a very small carved image of Catherine and Henry. They are dressed in contemporary Flemish fashion and seated together in a gallery above an altar, hearing Mass. This minute detail, almost invisible to the naked eye, is one of the few surviving portraits of the two of them together in the same visual frame.

FIG. 15 | Decade rosary of Henry VIII and Catherine of Aragon, ca. 1509–26. Boxwood, 472 mm long × 57 mm in diameter, ave bead 38 mm in diameter. Photo © The Devonshire Collections, Chatsworth. Reproduced by permission of the Chatsworth Settlement Trustees / Bridgeman Images.

FIG. 16 | Detail of Chatsworth decade rosary, the paternoster bead (opened). Photo © The Devonshire Collections, Chatsworth. Reproduced by permission of the Chatsworth Settlement Trustees / Bridgeman Images.

It is highly likely that the rosary was from Catherine's sister-in-law Marguerite of Austria, but the maker, the date of creation, and the circumstances of the presentation of the gift are not known. It was made in the workshop of a Netherlandish carver, Adam Dirckzs (and perhaps by his hands). Because it was a royal gift to both Catherine and Henry, it most likely was created between the wedding and their estrangement, between 1509 and 1526. If it was sent in 1509, as a wedding gift, Catherine would have used this rosary both as joyful prayer for her marriage and hope for successful pregnancies and to comfort her as she recovered from a miscarriage or stillbirth. If it was sent in 1516, as a gift to celebrate Mary's birth, the rosary would have been part of her rejoicing in the birth of a healthy child. And if it was sent in 1522, when Charles V came to England, it would have been meant as a symbol of her family allegiances on the continent. Charles was welcomed with an elaborately staged and very costly welcome entry into London.[20] No matter when the rosary was sent and for what event, it would have been an important part of Catherine's prayers as Henry's affections cooled and the divorce loomed.

The Tudor heraldic emblem signifies that the rosary was owned by both Catherine and Henry, but we are not entirely sure who would have used it personally. For several reasons it makes sense that Marguerite or Charles had Catherine, not Henry, in mind when they commissioned the rosary, making it more hers than his. A rosary is closely associated with late medieval Marian devotion among women, especially after 1500, and it was predominantly, but not exclusively, a form of piety that spoke powerfully to women.[21] Two images in the halves of the paternoster bead—the Mass of Saint Gregory, which affirmed the sacrament of transubstantiation, and a Virgin of the Apocalypse—illuminate both the prayers to the Virgin Mary and the more controversial theme of the immaculate conception.[22] This tight linkage of images and the act of prayer would have created for Catherine, a wife and mother, an empathic devotional act to the Virgin Mary. It is not clear when rosaries became widely used in England, but by the late fifteenth century there were rosary confraternities in Castile associated with the Dominican Order and references to the liturgy for a rosary at Eton College.[23] Given her deep allegiance to the Church of Rome, Catherine probably kept the rosary until her death. After that it changed hands several times. Henry restricted the use of rosaries in 1538 and banned them outright in 1547, and this one was owned by a Catholic bishop and a Jesuit priest in France until its purchase by the Duke and Duchess of Devonshire. The purchase by the Dukes of Devonshire may also link the rosary back to Catherine and her daughter. The provenance is a tangled thread, however, that goes back to Gertrude Blount Courtenay, Marchioness of Exeter and Countess of Devon (d. 1558). She was a close member of Catherine's circle at court, a relationship commemorated by a lavish gift to her from Catherine of a crucifix studded with diamonds and a pearl.[24] Gertrude was also a relative of Elizabeth Blount, the mother of Henry FitzRoy, one of the godparents of Mary, and a fierce opponent of Anne Boleyn. But no matter how it came to be in the collection of the Duke of Devonshire, the boxwood rosary signifies the survival of Catholicism after the Reformation, Catherine's death, and the destruction of shrines such as Walsingham. It is just one of many devotional objects in motion that moved back and forth across the English Channel as religious politics shifted hands in the mid- to late sixteenth century.[25]

But an exquisite rosary was not the only meaningful and beautiful gift from Marguerite. She also used gift-giving to send a deeply personal private message of comfort to Catherine sometime after her last miscarriage in 1518 but before the divorce of 1529, a time when her marriage was faltering and she needed emotional support. Marguerite well understood the physical ordeal of a miscarriage and not only the emotional distress of the loss of a child, but also the sense of failure that Catherine felt when it was clear she would not have another child. Marguerite also understood the political sensitivities of the moment, and rather than send an official gift of state, she commissioned a sumptuous presentation manuscript of music, "Book of 28 motets, 6 Latin secular pieces, and 1 canon," created by Petrus Alamire, a music scribe in her service. At first glance, based on the illuminations, the manuscript appears to have been addressed to both Catherine and Henry, depicting the banners of England and Castile flying from twin towers, embellished with the Tudor rose and pomegranate (fol. 2v), their emblems combined together in the initial (fol. 3) and the letters H and K written in flowers on these folios (fig. 17). It is inscribed "Katherina" and "Henricus rex" in the text of the motet "Adiutorium nostrum" (fols. 4v–6r).[26] The gift was addressed to them both, but as with the boxwood rosary, Marguerite had Catherine in mind when she commissioned it.

FIG. 17 | Sheet music for motets, decorated written music with decorated initials and voice parts for a choir. Motets for unaccompanied mixed voices. Photo © British Library Board / Robana / Art Resource, New York (AR9119933).

Musicologist Jennifer Thomas argues, however, that the more import-ant message from Marguerite to Catherine is textual, not visual, and is embedded in the complex text, which contains allusions to Dido and Aeneas, rumors, doubts about the legitimacy of a marriage, a lost or unre-sponsive lover, and the loss of a child. Thomas argues that this manuscript was not intended for Henry's eyes but was instead an exceptionally sensi-tive and intimate gift to a friend and sister-in-law. Thomas points out that many manuscripts collect motets on liturgically appropriate texts for practical use, but this one commemorates many significant biographical events in the lives of Marguerite and Catherine. Further, the themes that are so dominant in the lives of the two women also echo those of a third royal woman, Anne of Brittany, who also suffered several miscarriages despite many pregnancies and who was once thought to be the intended recipient.[27]

For example, the text of motets 27–31 (fols. 50v–56r), the "Dulces exuviae," "Relics once dear," derives from Dido's lament at the end of book 4 of the *Aeneid*:

> Relics once dear, while fate and heaven allowed,
> Take this my spirit and loose me from these woes.
> My life is lived; I have fulfilled the course by fortune given, and
>   now my shade
> Passes majestic to the world below.[28]

Thomas notes that this five-part repetition of a motet was unusual, and it is the only text repeated in this manuscript. She argues convincingly that the tragedy of this moment in the poem, when Dido is abandoned by Aeneas, resonated personally and deeply with the twice-widowed Marguerite, who intended these motets to convey sympathy covertly to her sister-in-law.

The last line of motet 32, the "Absalon fili mi," "Daughters of Jerusalem, tell my beloved that I languish with love," takes on a startling and pointed meaning as a narrative of Catherine's life after 1518. It may reflect her estrangement from Henry, her inability to speak to him directly, and the hurt she felt at Henry's affairs with Elizabeth Blount and Mary Boleyn.[29] The manuscript also contains strong associations with the Virgin Mary, such as in the motet "Ave sanctissima Maria," and this links back to the boxwood rosary, which contains a carving of the illumination of the Virgin. These feminine themes and texts link Catherine to the Virgin Mary as sympathetic mothers who both suffered the loss of a son. Thomas also notes that the references to Catherine's pomegranate emblem in the "Descendi in ortum meum" are sly allusions to fertility and pregnancy:

> I went down into my garden to see the fruit of the valleys,
> to see if the vine was in bloom and the pomegranate in bud.
> Return, return, return, that we may look upon you.[30]

Taken together, this manuscript and the boxwood rosary are far more than just a devotional object and a sumptuous musical text. They are personal communications from one close friend to another who shared a family history. Their messages of emotional expression echo across the centuries, telling us of the costs of physical and political failure borne by women who failed in the duty to provide a male heir. This must have been deeply frustrating for Catherine, whose own mother was witness to the fact that a woman could indeed inherit and rule successfully. For her, a daughter was not dynastic failure, it was a joy. In the early 1520s, Catherine devoted herself to her daughter, Mary, the center of her emotional world and, she believed, the anchor of her marriage and status as queen consort. That anchor, however, was in danger of slipping away as Henry's quest for a son to succeed him led him to question the legitimacy of their marriage, of their daughter, and of Catherine as queen.

EDUCATING MARY

As Mary grew from a toddler to a precocious and lively little girl, Catherine focused much of her attention on providing an education in an intellectual milieu where literacy was expected and cultural patronage the norm. She knew that Mary, whether she would succeed and rule in her own right or govern alongside a husband, would need an education at least as good as the one she had received. She took her cue from her mother, Isabel, and was much more involved in promoting learning than Henry. She made sure that Mary's education stressed the ideas of the proper social role of a princess while providing her a rigorous education to prepare her for whatever challenges she might face.[31] Her careful attention to Mary's education is a natural extension of her life surrounded by learning and literature. In a stained-glass window in the chapel at the Vyne (Hampshire), Catherine is shown kneeling before her patron saint, Catherine, and reading a book, in meditative contemplation.[32] Since childhood, and for as long as she lived in England, books were a refuge for Catherine from her troubles. We need only think back to her visit to Henry VII's library at Richmond in 1501, which he hoped would ease her homesickness: "to a lybrary of is, wherein he shewed unto her many goodly pleasaunt bokes of werkes full dilitfull, sage, mery, and also right cunning, both in Laten and in Englisse."[33]

Books were, of course, more than a respite from a crumbling marriage. They were fundamental to her identity and her work as queen. She was a patron of culture in the broadest sense of the word, both publicly at court and more privately in the royal household and beyond, encompassing Spain, England, the Netherlands, and Austria. With her sister-in-law Marguerite of Austria she shared an aesthetic taste and probably art dealers and book publishers. Inventories of her possessions and household accounts reveal a bibliophile, a lover of fashion, and an avid patron of art and humanist writers. Her piety and alliances with the Catholic Church were sources of her power as she navigated a political culture transformed by confessional disputes. She was said to have been a member of the third order of the Franciscans, and she was a generous benefactor to the Observant Friars at Grantham and Greenwich, where the friars' church was probably the site of the wedding of Henry and Catherine and royal baptisms.[34] She actively supported scholars at Oxford and Cambridge and promoted learning at court by surrounding herself with noble men and women who valued lively intellectual conversation.[35] She used her wealth as a patron of the College of Stoke-by-Clare, a small, wealthy institution in Suffolk. This college, customarily under the control of the queens of England, associated with the royal households, and closely linked to academics from Queen's College and Saint John's College at Cambridge, was part of Catherine's patronage of learning.[36]

Catherine was a bookish queen, and the British Library manuscript collection includes some of the books she owned with Henry, including a devotional text commissioned by Piers de Champagne from Richard Faques (printed 1509) that bears a woodcut of their combined arms.[37] But she owned and ordered illuminated manuscripts and books on a range of subjects, and, like many of her possessions, they are scattered and have never been studied as a coherent whole. Some of the manuscripts and printed books are noted in the inventories of the royal library, and some are currently in other collections. Some of the books listed in Henry's collection were most likely commissioned by Catherine, given as gifts from Spanish courtiers or ambassadors, or brought by her to England in 1501. Other works commemorate her frequent visits to and patronage of favorite religious sites, such as a devotional text at Syon Abbey commissioned by a nun at Syon, the daughter of Catherine's vice-chancellor.[38] And some are no longer in England, such as a book of hours illuminated by William Vrelant (ca. 1460) known as the Hours of Catherine of

Aragon, currently in the royal library at The Hague.[39] For example, the 1542 inventory of the books in the royal collection notes copies of works by Sallust, Dante, and Petrarch translated into Castilian, a language that Henry did not read. It is also likely that she owned a Spanish translation of Erasmus's *Enchiridion militis Christiani* (as *El enquiridion o manual del caballero Cristiano*, published in Alcalá de Henares in 1527). Erasmus thought more highly of Catherine as an intellectual person than of Henry, and this volume first belonged to Catherine before it passed into Henry's library at an unknown date. We can be more certain that she owned two anti-Protestant reform treatises by Alfonso de Villa Sancta, his *De libero arbitrio aduersus Melanchthonem* (1523) and his *Problema indulgentiarum: aduersus Lutherum* (1523), written at Catherine's request and dedicated to her. A copy of this manuscript in the Vatican contains an illumination with Catherine's personal emblem, the pomegranate (Vat. Lat. 3731, 2 r). Villa Sancta, a Franciscan, her confessor and a close friend of Thomas More, gave Catherine the title *Fidei Defensor*.[40] It is likely that "Salustius with songis in Spanysh" (original lost), a popular Spanish translation by Francisco Vida de Noya first printed in 1493, belonged to Catherine.[41]

Catherine's influence extended beyond court. Her encouragement of learning dramatically altered the possibilities and responsibilities for educated women in England.[42] As patron of humanist luminaries, Catherine encouraged intellectual interests for women in general. She asked Thomas More to translate Juan Luis Vives's *De institutione feminae Christianae* into English, and he hired Richard Hyrde to do the translation as *A very fruteful and pleasant boke called the instruction of a Christen woman*.[43] She asked Sir Thomas Wyatt in 1527 to prepare an English translation of Petrarch's *De remediis utriusque fortunae* (Remedies for fortunes), but he did not complete it; instead, he presented her on New Year's Day 1528 with Plutarch's less politically volatile *De tranquilitate et securitate animi*, translated as *The Quyete of Mynde*. She owned a copy of Vives's *De concordia et discordia in humano genere* (On concord and discord in humankind). Now housed in the Chapter Library of the College of Saint George at Windsor Castle, it bears the arms of Henry VIII, Catherine's personal emblem, the pomegranate, and the arms of Castile.[44] And she was the recipient of at least seven book dedications that would have been inscribed in a presentation copy, such Juan Luis Vives's *De institutione feminae Christianae* in

English and Spanish. Together they owned at least a dozen illuminated books of hours, some they commissioned and some they inherited.[45] In addition to books that have been named and cataloged in museums and research libraries, twenty-one unnamed volumes were counted among her own possessions at Baynard's Castle at her death: "one prymmar written in vellom, covered withe clothe of golde, havinge two claspis of silver and gilte," "three bookes covered withe red leather, garnysshid withe golde foyle, and tyed with grene reabande," and seventeen "smalle and greate." It is likely that these books were given to her by her mother in 1501 when she left Spain to marry Arthur, and Castilian treasurer's accounts note payments for gold and silver decorations and bindings for books for Catalina as "princessa de Gales."[46]

It was as natural as breathing for Catherine to hire powerful intellectuals such as humanists Juan Luis Vives, Thomas Linacre, and Giles Du West as tutors for Mary.[47] When Mary was seven, Catherine invited Vives to England to guide the curriculum. He sought to balance conventional ideas on women's place in a household with more open-minded ideas on educating women for life beyond domesticity. Vives wavered on what that should be, however, as he advised her to be wary of the company of men, to rely on others for advice, and to avoid public life in any form. In 1524, he outlined a curriculum in *De ratione studii puerilis*, advocating cultivation of eloquence and recommending that Mary read more pragmatic texts such as Plato's governmental writings, Thomas More's *Utopia*, and Erasmus's *Education of a Christian Prince*.[48] But he continued to believe that chastity and silence were best for females, whose study should lead them to moral lives centered on the household, not the court. In his preface to *De institutione feminae Christianae*, he complimented Catherine as an example of erudition, noting that Mary "shall read these instructions of mine, and follow in living. Which she must needs do if she is to order herself after the example that hath at home with her."[49] Also in 1524, Catherine commissioned Desiderius Erasmus to write a book on marriage, the *Institution of Christian Marriage*, for Mary when she was eight. Vives's *Satellitium sive Symbola*, a collection of advice and moral maxims, has a lengthy preface dedication to Mary as Princess of Wales, an echo of Catherine's title when she married Arthur that reinforced Mary's status as heir to the throne.[50] It was assumed, however, that even if she were her father's sole heir, she would cede the official work of governance to her husband, so Richard Fetherstone, her tutor as late as 1525, did not emphasize governmental instruction. By contrast, Henry FitzRoy, her illegitimate half-brother (born to Elizabeth Blount), was two years younger than Mary but was being educated in the expectation that he would govern something, even if just his landed estates.[51]

In 1518, as Princess of Wales, Mary was a very desirable diplomatic asset as potential bride for the infant French dauphin, François. When the treaty to seal peace with France unraveled, her cousin Charles, fifteen years older and King of Castile and Aragon, began to look attractive as a marriage candidate.[52] Catherine strongly supported the match, and in 1520 Mary was introduced to Charles, then Holy Roman Emperor, on his state visit to England just before the meeting of the royal families of England and France at the Field of the Cloth of Gold. In 1521, the Treaty of Bruges set out the terms for a future marriage, and a six-week visit in 1522 gave Charles a chance to get to know his six-year-old prospective bride.[53]

To mark that meeting, Princess Mary chose Charles as her valentine and wore a jewel with his name, which may have been the badge she wears in the miniature painted by Lucas Horenbout (fig. 18). Pearls abound in this miniature—the badge is surrounded by them, her French hood headdress is studded with them, her necklace is a double loop of pearls, and three large pearls dangle from a diamond cross-shaped pendant. She wears a white shift embroidered with Spanish blackstitch under the black gown, and she has the childish face of a pretty little girl whose hint of a smile contrasts with the solemn expression of her more serious mother in the portrait by Juan de Flandes (see fig. 7).

This portrait of Princess Mary is the earliest known example of the English miniature. Painted between 1522 and 1525, it may have been commissioned by Catherine to celebrate the Treaty of Windsor on 16 June 1522 and Mary's betrothal to Charles or have been part of a set of miniature portraits exchanged between Henry, Catherine, and Mary.[54] Mary's aesthetic tastes were cultivated by her mother, a noted patron of Flemish painters, and Catherine was influential in bringing Netherlandish artists to the English court, such as the siblings Susanna and Lucas Horenbout. Susanna came to London in 1522, hired by the king but officially part of Catherine's chamber. Catherine imported Flemish religious

FIG. 18 | Lucas Horenbout (attributed), *Princess Mary*, ca. 1525. Watercolor on vellum, 35 mm in diameter. National Portrait Gallery, London, 1999 (6453). Photo © National Portrait Gallery, London / Art Resource, New York.

art and owned a copy of Rogier van der Weyden's *Three Kings Altar*, the original of which was painted in 1455 and donated to the church of Saint Columba in Cologne.[55] The taste for Netherlandish art transferred across generations, from Isabel to Catherine to her daughter Mary. After Catherine's death, Susanna Horenbout stayed on at court and worked for Anne Boleyn and Anne of Cleves. The Horenbouts painted from live sittings without intermediary drawings, and most of their works exist in several versions. Using a technique refined in their work in manuscript illumination, the Horenbouts painted on vellum. Most of the images are circular (there are two rectangular ones), about 1–2 inches in diameter, with a medium blue background, an inner circle of gold (powder, not gold leaf), and mounted onto a card.[56] The Horenbouts were central to the rise in popularity of the miniature, which quickly became one of the most popular forms of art for the royal family and wealthy patrons in the sixteenth century. These small works of art were deliberately framed and adorned to rest on the body as though it were a wall in the most private chamber.[57] Recipients of painted miniatures literally kept them close to the chest and talked to them as though they were alive, animating them and keeping alive an emotional bond across hundreds of miles and decades of separation. [58] They were shared as keepsakes and bestowed a dash of royal charisma on the owner. Catherine was also credited with the first known instance of a miniature worn as a jewel—a jeweled tablet that formed a double-miniature portrait of Henry and Catherine given to Maud Green, who passed them to her daughter, Katherine Parr, Henry's sixth wife.[59]

The portrait survives, but Mary's betrothal to Charles did not last. It was called off when the imperial army defeated the French at the Battle of Pavia and dramatically upset diplomatic relations. Charles chose to marry Isabel of Portugal, and this affected Mary's position at the head of the line of succession, which led to a crisis in Catherine and Henry's marriage. Angry at both Charles and Catherine, Henry retaliated with an ominous move when he knighted Henry FitzRoy and granted him the title of Duke of Richmond and Somerset. Catherine objected loudly to this move, which put FitzRoy too close in the line of succession for her comfort. Henry retaliated by sending Mary, then nine years old, to Ludlow Castle in the Welsh Marches to learn how to supervise a household of roughly 340 people and how to govern the Council of Wales.[60] This was her longest separation from Catherine, who wrote to Mary regularly with bits of news and a recognition of the awkwardness of not being able to speak directly, in person. In her first letter, Catherine writes:

> I pray you think not that any forgetfulness hath caused me to keep Charles [the messenger] so long here, and answered not your good letter, by the which I perceive you would know how I do. I am in that case that the long absence of the King and you troubleth me. My health is meetly good, and I trust in God, he that hath sent me the last dooth to the best, and will shortly turn it to the first to come to good effect. And in the mean time I am very glad to hear from you, especially when they show me that ye be well amended. I pray God to continue it to his pleasure.
>
> As for your writing in Latin, I am glad that ye shall change from me to Master Federston, for that shall do you much good to learn by him to write aright. But yet some times I would be glad when ye do write to Master Federston of your own editing when he hath read it that I may see it. For it shall be a great

comfort to me to see you keep your Latin and fair writing and all. And so I pray you to recommend me to my Lady of Salisbury. At Woburn, this Friday night. Your loving mother, Katharine the Queen.[61]

Without knowing what was happening at court, Mary would have read this as an ordinary letter from a mother who is sad to see her daughter grow up a bit, leave home, and strike out on her own. Catherine says she feels bad that it took her so long to write back, that she is a little bit lonely in a nest empty of her husband ("the King") and daughter, and she prods Mary gently about her studies. The English syntax is interesting, particularly her use of "ye," the nominative form of "you." Originally plural, it had become the formal alternative to the informal "thou" (accusative "thee"). By the beginning of the sixteenth century, "thou" began to be seen as insulting and demeaning, except when used between people who were familiar with each other. It was still commonly used in addressing children, and it is interesting that Catherine does not do that with her daughter. Her use of "ye" is a sign that her relationship with Mary was both familiar and formal.[62]

Her close, watchful eye on Mary's Latin, and her pride in her daughter's intellect, are clear when she says that she is "glad that ye shall change from me to Master Federston." This is part of a social script of a mother to a child newly parted. She is glad that Mary has a new tutor so she will not lose her Latin skills but may well have been less "glad" that she was not able to keep her eye on Mary's progress with Latin. She encourages Mary to take her Latin a step further when she speaks of Mary's "own enditing," that is, "inditing," composing or writing literature.

This tells us that Mary could do more than just read Latin. She could compose in Latin. She was only nine, so it may not have been profound or eloquent, but this is a veiled hint that she should use that Latin to write home, a sentiment shared by many parents who want to stay close to their child. It is, however, more than a maternal desire to get letters from her daughter. It pushed Mary to be skilled enough to translate Latin into English, as she did with Erasmus's *Paraphrase on St. John's Gospel*, published in 1547.[63] Catherine is encouraging her to go even further, to be as fluent in Latin as the men who would surround her at court so that she could listen closely to every conversation and read every word of every letter. This would allow her to govern as an intellectual equal to kings and popes.

She is content knowing that Mary is in good hands with both Fetherstone and her close friend Margaret Pole, the Countess of Salisbury, and closes as "your loving mother." Given the amply documented loving relationship of Catherine and her daughter, her words are more than formulaic flourishes. What Catherine left out in her letter to Mary in 1525 is significant, however. Her physical health may have been "meetly good," but she was very troubled emotionally by the state of her personal relations with Henry. His actions regarding Henry FitzRoy were ominous enough, but his eye had begun to wander toward one of Catherine's ladies at court, Anne Boleyn.

When Catherine wrote letters to Mary, she would have had a writing box like the one described in an inventory of Baynard's Castle, "covered withe blacke velvette, and garnysshid withe gilte nayles." It had two coffers, one of ivory "garnysshid withe imagerye, having a handille, locke, and jemewis of silver" and another covered with crimson velvet, "garnysshid with gilte nayles, having foure tilles therein, the fore fronte of every of them gilte."[64] These coffers strongly resemble a writing box like the one shown in figure 19. The inside cover depicts Henry's coat of arms and figures of Mars, Venus, Cupid. The side lids show the head of Christ and Saint George and the dragon, and the inside is lined with leather and covered with the heraldic badges of both Henry and Catherine. Curators catalog it as a possession of Henry VIII, but there is evidence to suggest that it belonged to Catherine. Yes, Henry VIII inherited his parents' love of books and the vast library started by his equally bookish grandparents, King Edward IV and Elizabeth Woodville. But Henry admitted that he found the business of letter writing "somewhat tedious and painful."[65] And by the mid-1520s he was a big, burly man, more inclined to rough-and-tumble physical activity than writing. This writing box is quite small, about 5 cm high, 43 cm wide, and 25 cm deep, and I am inclined to think that Catherine used it as much if not more than he did.

The writing box was almost certainly made in the royal court workshops in England by Lucas Horenbout, no earlier than 1525, when he first came to court, and no later than 1527, when Henry began divorce proceedings against Catherine. It was constructed of oak and walnut, decorated

FIG. 19 | Writing box, ca. 1525, possibly made in London. Walnut and oak, lined with painted and gilded leather and silk velvet, later shagreen (possibly sharkskin) outer coating. Decoration painted by Lucas Horenbout. Victoria and Albert Museum, London, 29:1 to 9-1932. Photo © Victoria and Albert Museum, London / Bridgeman Images.

with painted and gilded leather. It has a sloping top and a double lid, the outer enclosing a shallow tray contained in the inner lid, which opens to disclose three divisions, two with lids. The fall-down front encloses three drawers, the center one divided into partitions and those on the side fitted with sliding lids. There is a small drawer with compartments fitted at the right side.

The decoration includes painted heads in the style of miniature painting, which became popular after 1520, and includes both late Gothic features and early Renaissance ornament. The interior is covered with leather painted and gilt. The inside of the outer lid is decorated with interlaced strapwork, enclosing the badges of Henry and Catherine with the letters H&K joined by a lover's knot, the pomegranate, and a sheaf of arrows.[66] The inner lid bears the arms of Henry encircled by the Garter, and with putti blowing trumpets as supporters. On either side are figures of Mars in armor, and Venus, the goddess of love and fertility, with her son Cupid, each under Renaissance canopies. The compartment lids are painted with the head of Christ and figures of Saint George and the Dragon. The front has a male and a female head in profile. The falling flap is decorated with a ground of arabesques and profile heads of the legendary Greek figures Paris, prince of Troy, and Helen, the Spartan queen whom he abducted.

The leather-lined interior is painted with the heraldic badges of Henry and Catherine, and the royal coat of arms. The exterior is covered with shagreen (possibly sharkskin) and fitted with metal-gilt angle mounts, loop handles, and ball feet, all added during the eighteenth century. The interior surfaces of the compartments are lined with red silk velvet (probably added during the nineteenth century). The writing surface and the large compartment have been relined very crudely with crimson silk velvet, the appearance of which is considerably older than that of the red velvet. The front, above the three small drawers, is decorated with a male and a female profile head and scrollwork designs; and the rim below the outer lid is covered in parchment and bears an inscription in classical lettering (much rubbed) to Henry.

This is a rare survival of luxury furniture made by the royal workshops. Such small writing boxes were used on tables, to hold the paraphernalia associated with writing, such as ink and quills and other small items. It has the characteristic sloping lid of a desk, but it was not until the seventeenth century that the desk developed as a specialized form of table with drawers. The inventory taken at Henry's death in 1547 lists similar boxes or desks with their contents. For example, in a closet next to the King's Privy Chamber at Greenwich Palace were three desks covered with leather, one of which was "furnysshed with boxes without Counters with a penne knyfe and a payer of sisorres."[67] This costly object was an innovation from continental styles crafted in workshops in Ghent and Bruges. It could have been a royal gift and might have passed out of royal ownership soon after it was made. The physicality of this small desk, which shows evidence of having been used (but we do not know how often or for how many years), gives day-to-day meaning to a delicately painted work of art. It was a piece of furniture made not only to delight the user but also to be used. It was meant to be touched by Catherine's hands, to hold the ink and pens and bits of paper on which she wrote letters to her father and her daughter.

THE PLEA OF A "STRANGER BORN OUT OF YOUR DOMINION"

What Catherine left out in her letter to Mary in 1525 is significant, however. Unable to imagine a Tudor dynasty without men, Henry fretted over Mary's status as legitimate heir. He had already made an ominous move that threatened Mary's standing in the line of succession when he named his son with Elizabeth Blount, Henry FitzRoy, to the title of Duke of Richmond and Somerset. By around 1526, her father's romance with Anne Boleyn was warming up and diplomatic tensions were high, complicated by tense relations with Charles V and François. Catherine allied with Charles and was frustrated that she was unable to influence events.[68] In May 1527, Wolsey had begun a formal inquiry into the validity of the royal marriage.[69] She refused to relent to Henry's wishes that they separate and she enter a convent.[70] Henry declared war against Charles in January 1528, which inflamed Catherine even more. But their disagreements over foreign relations were simply sideshows to Henry's anxiety over a male successor. To keep Mary near him, he recalled her from Wales. When Mary returned to court, she naturally favored her mother as the marriage deteriorated and taking sides became personally dangerous.

Personal, dynastic, and diplomatic matters complicated the next years for Mary. Henry's anxiety over the fate of his dynasty if a legitimate daughter were to take precedence over an illegitimate son led him to pursue lengthy and politically divisive legal proceedings, which, in turn, intensified the anxiety for both mother and daughter. The events that led to the divorce of Catherine and Henry are well known, described in terms of theology and both canon and secular law. The proceedings were lengthy, prolonged by procedural questions of who had the authority to decide the outcome—a secular royal court in England or a religious papal court in Rome—and centered on whether the marriage was truly licit, whether or not she had had sex with Arthur, and whether biblical texts regarding a man marrying his brother's widow had legal force.[71] If we trust that she told the truth in 1503 about never having had sexual intercourse with Arthur, and that she was in fact a virgin when she married Henry and that he knew it, what remains is simply the fact that Henry would not tolerate a queen regnant of England. It will not spoil the ending of this chapter to reveal that in the end Henry got his divorce and then, perhaps to his eternal chagrin, he was succeeded by not one, but two Tudor queens regnant. But Henry's conscience, legal wrangling, and theological hand-wringing are not my main concerns here. Catherine is.

Above the noisy chorus of men, her voice emerges forcefully. To hear her, we rely on George Cavendish, an intimate member of Cardinal Wolsey's household, whose biographical essay *Thomas Wolsey, Late Cardinall, his Lyffe and Deathe* (ca. 1554–58) draws on his observations and experiences at court.[72] The "King's Great Matter" was brought to trial at a court organized under the auspices of the papal legate, Lorenzo Campeggio, at Blackfriars in London in June 1529. On 18 June, Catherine appeared in person at the legatine court at Blackfriars with a formal protest in which she denied the impartiality of the legates and her appeal to Rome. On 21 June, she and Henry both appeared. The sources differ considerably in their accounts of what happened, but it is clear that Henry, Wolsey, and Catherine all spoke, Henry setting out his case, Wolsey defending his own impartiality, and Catherine appealing to her honor and that of her daughter and of the king to justify her appeal to Rome. Cavendish sets the scene: The two cardinals, Wolsey and Campeggio, with the archbishop of Canterbury, William Warham, were seated at tables, benches,

and bars to make the room look like a consistory court. To dignify the
participants, a cloth of estate was placed under Henry's chair, and Catherine sat "a distance beneath the king." Cavendish was an eyewitness,
although he did not write his account until decades later. He combines
historical fact and fiction with a strong moral purpose, and he gives a
sympathetic portrait of her.

When Catherine was called to respond to the crier, she did not reply
to him but rose up out of her chair and, because "she could not come
directly to the king for the distance which severed them, she took pain to
go about unto the king, kneeling down at his feet in the sight of all the
court and assembly, to whom she said in effect, in broken English":

> Sir, I beseech you for all the loves that hath been between us, and
> for the love of God, let me have justice and right, take of me some
> pity and compassion, for I am a poor woman and a stranger born
> out of your dominion, I have here no assured friend, and much
> less indifferent counsel: I flee to you as to the head of justice within
> this realm. Alas! Sir, wherein have I offended you, or what occa-
> sion of displeasure have I designed against your will and pleasure?
> Intending (as I perceive) to put me from you, I take God and all
> the world to witness, that I have been to you a true and humble
> wife, ever conformable to your will and pleasure, that never said
> or did anything to the contrary thereof, being always well pleased
> and contented with all things wherein ye had any delight or dalli-
> ance, whether it were in little or much, I never grudged in word
> or countenance, or showed a visage or spark of discontentation. I
> loved all those whom ye loved only for your sake, whether I had
> cause or no; and whether they were my friends or my enemies.
> This twenty years I have been your true wife or more, and by me
> ye have had divers children, although it hath pleased God to call
> them out of this world, which hath been no default in me.
>
>   And when ye had me at the first, I take God to be my judge,
> I was a true maid without touch of man; and whether it be true
> or no, I put it to your conscience. If there be any just cause by the
> law that ye can allege against me, either of dishonesty or any other
> impediment to banish and put me from you, I am well content

to depart, to my great shame and dishonor; and if there be none, then here I most lowly beseech you let me remain in my former estate, and received justice at your princely hand. The king your father was in the time of his reign of such estimation through the world for his excellent wisdom, that he was accounted and called of all men the second Solomon; and my father Ferdinand, King of Spain, who was esteemed to be one of the wittiest princes that reigned in Spain many years before, were both wise and excellent kings in wisdom and princely behavior. It is not therefore to be doubted, but that they were elected and gathered as wise counsellors about them as to their high discretions was thought meet. Also, as me seemeth there was in those days as wise, as well-learned men, and men of good judgement as be present in both realms, who thought then the marriage between you and me good and lawful. Therefore is it a wonder to me what new inventions are now invented against me, that never intended but honesty. And cause me to stand to the order and judgment of this new court, wherein ye may do me much wrong, if ye intend any cruelty; for ye may condemn me for lack of sufficient answer, having no indifferent counsel, but such as be assigned me, with whose wisdom and learning I am not acquainted. Ye must consider that they cannot be indifferent counsellors for my part which be your subjects, and taken out of your own council before, wherein they be made privy, and dare not, for your displeasure, disobey your will and intent, being once made privy thereto. Therefore, I most humbly require you, in the way of charity, and for the love of God, who is the just judge, to spare the extremity of this new court, until I may be advertised what way and order my friends in Spain will advise me to take. And if ye will not extend to me so much indifferent favour, your pleasure then be fulfilled, and to God I commit my case!

She knelt as she had at Westminster Hall in 1517 when she begged for the lives of the London apprentices after the Evil May Day riots, and as she had when she begged for mercy for Edward Stafford in 1521. Here, however, she was kneeling out of deference to the office of king, not as

a supplicant seeking his intercession. She then stood up, curtsied to the
king, turned around, and left. The crier called her back "by the name of
Catherine, Queen of England." But she did not turn back, and replied,
"On, on, it maketh no matter, for it is no indifferent court for me, therefore I will not tarry: go on your ways."[73]

This is a famous speech, one often depicted in plays and films with an
emphasis on the femininity of Catherine as a "poor woman and a stranger"
and "a true and humble wife" in contrast to the brash masculinity of
Henry. It is not possible to know how much of this is an accurate rendi-
tion of what she said, but it has enough details of the room, the people
who were in attendance, and their mood to instill confidence in the
veracity of the story. In Cavendish's telling, as an eyewitness to the event
and recorder of Wolsey, it rings true to her character from other sources.
Taking a cue from her mother, who so skillfully balanced masculinity and
femininity, Catherine reminds Henry of the pleasure they took in each
other's company, how she never said or did anything to criticize "all things
wherein ye had any delight or dalliance," a clear jab at his sexual liaisons.
Her plea that her marriage was based on principles of truth, honesty, and
wisdom resonates loudly with her intellect and education. She relies on
both the legal weight of her memory of events in the royal bedchamber
with Arthur and her spotless reputation as Henry's wife. She uses a range
of rhetorical tones to make her case, most strikingly the hendiadys, as
she expresses a single idea by two words connected with "and": justice
and truth, pity and compassion, will and pleasure, delight and dalliance,
shame and dishonor, wise and excellent, order and judgment, wisdom and
learning, will and intent. Catherine's use of these verbal pairs slow down
the rhythm of thought and perception, breaks complex ideas down into
more elementary units, and leaves her listeners just slightly out of joint.
It creates a kind of double take that forces the listener to pay close attention to her every word to take heed of the only two things that matter:
Catherine and Henry. She uses "ye" here much as she did in her letter
to Mary, as a sign that she had both a familiar and a formal relationship.
When she addresses Henry directly and reminds him that "when ye had
me at the first," she is making both a personal and a political statement.
He "had" her both sexually, in a physical joining of two human bodies as
wife and husband, and metaphysically, in a joining of two political bodies

and queen and king. When she tells him that at the moment of sexual union she was "a true maid without touch of man," she is claiming her status as both wife and queen.

She calmly states that the Christian scriptures are the only authority that matters. She clearly asserts that she would only allow a papal trial to determine the fate of her "true" marriage when she was a "true maid." She values tradition instead of the "new inventions" of a "new court." She denounces the bias that denied her "indifferent counsellors." But, in a clear jab at the toadies and yes men in Henry's court, she unleashes her emotions in a sharply worded denunciation of the fearful men who, unlike her, are afraid to challenge Henry. Her "loves" of many sorts—personal, sexual, religious, maternal—shared with Henry were the foundation of her legitimate marriage. If Cavendish got the tone right without any exaggeration, it is no wonder people still pause for breath before they applaud at the performance of a queen superbly balancing femininity and masculinity, righteous anger and legal argument, all while begging for pity and compassion.

Like modern readers and audiences, Henry paused. After a long moment of tense silence, he tried to control the damage and agreed that yes, she was a good woman and yes, he was sad to lose her. The next day, when both Wolsey and Campeggio came to see her privately in her presence chamber, she met them "with a skein of white thread about her neck." She had been doing her needlework, "thinking full little of any such matter" as the divorce. Speaking to them in English, she reiterated her emotional and financial poverty, her lack of true friends and legal counsel to guide her. They went into her privy chamber, where what they said could not be heard by anyone but them. On 16 July, Pope Clement VII agreed to try the case in Rome. A week later Campeggio, with Wolsey's agreement, adjourned the court for the summer vacation.

"REGINA KATHERINA EIUS UXOR"

After her appearance at Blackfriars, Catherine acted publicly as though little had changed. She was queen and so she stayed at court, dined with Henry, took part in official ceremonies, and spent as much time as possible with her daughter, but Henry's actions left many people feeling very uneasy about whether and how to support her without enraging him. Charles Brandon and Thomas More tried to shift the responsibility from Henry to Wolsey, a handy device to deflect blame to counsellors they despised.[74] People in the regions where Catherine held property (East Anglia, the Thames Valley) denounced the divorce and remained loyal to Mary.[75] But Erasmus betrayed his own uncertainty about the divorce when he wrote to Juan Luis Vives in September 1528, telling him that bigamy would be better than divorce, using a metaphor of how it was no problem that two Junos (Catherine and Anne) can share one Jove. Erasmus also suggested to William Blount, Lord Mountjoy, that Catherine should read his treatise *Vidua Christiana* (On Christian widowhood), published in 1529, which falls back on stereotypes of femininity.[76] Catherine did not need advice on how to cope with the death of a husband. She could have used some advice on how to cope with his infidelity.

At times of political strain, the flickers and shadows cast off by art can reveal sentiments that the narrative facts obscure. Three miniature portraits of Catherine created in the mid- to late 1520s subtly reveal the anxieties stirred up by the divorce and suggest some ways that people closest to her conveyed personal, often political messages of her transformation from queen consort to ex-wife. In one miniature from around 1525, Catherine appears at first glance quite conventional (fig. 20). Her attire marks her as a woman of high rank, wearing the familiar headdress with her hair pulled off her face, but there is neither text nor emblem to remind the viewer that she is a queen. She wears a crimson gown, probably velvet, with a square neckline edged with gems and pearls and an embroidered edge on the smock undergarment. Her jewelry is not flashy or ostentatious, simply softly gleaming pearls in two strands of a necklace and along the edge of the headdress. She wears two pearl and gem-encrusted necklaces, one with a large cross. The embroidery, the by-then-famous Spanish blackstitch, edges the undergarment and shows off the middle bow, which delicately protects her modesty. The emblem IHS is embroidered or pinned to her bodice, and we are certain that it is Catherine before the divorce began because Horenbout included an inscription, *Regina Katherina eius uxor* (Queen Catherine, his wife). This miniature was probably painted when she was a forty-year-old mother of a nine-year-old daughter. She is modest

FIG. 20 | Lucas Horenbout (attributed), *Catherine of Aragon*, ca. 1525. Watercolor on vellum stuck onto plain card, 38 mm in diameter. National Portrait Gallery, London, 1969 (4682). Photo © National Portrait Gallery, London / Art Resource, New York.

but fashionable, with her slit sleeves and ornate edging on the neckline of her red velvet dress. She looks out with a direct gaze, but is neither a seductress nor a schemer. As Horenbout makes abundantly clear, she is indubitably a queen.

Horenbout reveals her as an individual, not an idealized synthesis of what people expected a queen to look like. Her features are softly rendered, enlivened by a small dot of bright red at the corner of her eye. This is a portrait of a queen at home, someone easy to imagine as a mother who read to her daughter, as a wife who dutifully embroidered her husband's shirts, and as a patron of artists, authors, and universities. She seems almost alive. This is a woman who would indeed save, until the day she died, the blankets and bedsheets from her lying-in with her daughter.

The owner of the miniature who wore it on the bodice of a dress or the collar of a jacket clearly understood the significance of the Spanish-style hood and the Catholic message of the design of the necklaces. The wearer of this miniature would be identified as someone who considered Catherine a legitimate queen. He or she had an incentive for wearing a portrait that repeated a younger, beautiful likeness of Catherine while conveying, perhaps, an intelligible iconographic message to her adherents. As time passed and the divorce heated up, the wearer might cleverly conceal this miniature under a lace ruffle, but it was a marker of identity, much like the pomegranate or sheaf of arrows embroidered on a napkin or emblazoned on a livery badge.

Two other miniatures, painted a little later, send more subtle, slightly different politically charged messages. In one, in the collection of the Duke of Buccleuch, Catherine appears at her most English, with her hair hidden beneath a dark velvet gabled headdress. The dress is luxuriously full, with a boxy bodice and a white girdle, with enormous oversleeves of ermine and ruffled cuffs that peek out from under pearl-studded pierced velvet undersleeves. She wears gem-studded rings instead of necklaces, and at her bodice she wears a modest sheer linen shift with Spanish blackstitch embroidery. There is nothing extraordinary about what she is wearing. What is unusual is what she holds in the crook of her left arm—a marmoset, which she is feeding a peanut. Marmosets and other monkeys were believed to be a remedy for loneliness and melancholy, easing the burden of worries.[77] Catherine's marmoset is part of an early modern fascination among the elites with ownership of exotic animals from the Americas and Asia. It marks this portrait as part of the imperial voyages of exploration and conquest that were key to the vast wealth of Catherine's nephew Charles V and that the English were just beginning to exploit. It was one more way for her to be depicted as foreign. But comparing this with the miniature from the National Portrait Gallery shows that the exaggerated, angular features of the earlier image have given way to a softer face with a more pleasant, gentle expression (see fig. 14).

This is not, however, the only image of Catherine holding a marmoset. One other, in a private collection, shows the monkey being offered a coin, which it ignores, reaching out instead for the jeweled crucifix that Catherine wears at her breast (fig. 21). This portrait derives directly from the Buccleuch miniature, but the subtle alterations to the iconography make it a painting with a message. Bendor Grosvenor suggests that encoded within this miniature is a more specific allusion to Catherine's precarious position at court during the divorce proceedings. Grosvenor argues that this portrait was commissioned, probably not by Catherine, but in support of her belief in the sanctity of her marriage to Henry. It bears an inscription that is a near anagram of the name "Thomas More," which would have been meaningful for an audience schooled in allegory. Grosvenor notes that "the coin being rejected by the monkey is clearly an English coin, in this case a groat [a commonly used silver coin that weighed about 3.1 grams]. And on the other side of a groat . . . is a portrait of Henry VIII. The portrait of Katherine may therefore be seen not only as her rejection of riches in favour of faith, but of Henry himself." [78] It is not clear for whom this was painted, when, or why, but Catherine's creature expresses his obedience to the church by recognizing that the cross is more precious than money. It is arguably one of the most daring images of the Tudor period.[79]

For an ally of Catherine, it would have been delightful to detect a deeper, parallel reading that critiqued the divorce by saying that piety and eternal salvation are more important than earthly reward. The portrait miniatures of Catherine with her marmoset and a silver coin were more than just flattering likenesses of a queen who was spurned in place of a younger rival. They can also be read as a calculated piece of propaganda and a move in a very high-stakes personal, religious, legal, and political game.

In a more daring and more publicly open demonstration of support for Catherine, an anonymous playwright wrote a decidedly risky work that captured the mood of people on edge. The *Interlude of Godly Queen Hester* was first published in 1561 but was probably written in the fall of 1529. It was not uncommon for authors of controversial works to seek cover under anonymity, and we do not know, and may never know, the author's identity. It was clearly someone aware of who was in and who was out at court, and who may well have known Catherine: the play was produced when Catherine presided over the Christmas revels that year, and clues in the text strongly suggest that it may have been performed under the auspices of Catherine's own chapel to console her in a time of peril.[80]

The *Interlude* is a retelling of the events narrated in the Old Testament book of Esther, from King Ahasuerus's decision to seek a wife, to his choice of Esther, the execution of his evil adviser Haman, and the pardon of the

FIG. 21 | Portrait of Queen
Catherine of Aragon,
early 1530s. Oil on oak
panel. Private collection.
Photo © Philip Mould
Ltd, London / Bridgeman
Images.

Jews and restoration of their fortunes. The *Interlude* is not, however, a simple retelling of the story. It is an allegorical reflection on contemporary events, with Catherine as the model for the Jewish queen. In the *Interlude*, Hester (Esther) is not the beautiful, young, sensual figure from the book of Esther, but a more mature woman who is the king's first wife, chosen for her wisdom and her high status, not her beauty. The playwright praises Hester's triumphs over enemies, a likely reference to Catherine's regency and the defeat of the Scots at the Battle of Flodden. Hester is praised for her intercession, as Catherine interceded on behalf of the apprentices of London in 1517. Hester worked behind the scenes to protect the Jews, just as Catherine was working with her allies to defend her faith.

The play is more than just a Christmastime entertainment. It is a study of queenship. The prologue addresses women directly, and, if it was produced at court, at least one female member of the audience would have immediately grasped the point: a good marriage of king and queen is one where the two work in harmony. She would have been saddened to hear the character of Assuerus (Ahasuerus) say,

Then, doute I not, but the wysdome of vs two,
Knytte both to gether in parfytte charyte,
All thynges in thys realme shall cumpas so.[81]

The play then turns to the dangers of speaking openly before a king, as
Catherine would know well after her performance that summer at Blackfriars. Hester speaks openly, but she is not foolhardy or reckless; she speaks
when invited, as Catherine did at Blackfriars, and says, "To speake before a
king, it is no childes playe, / Therefor, I aske pardon of that I shall saye."[82]
The playwright then has Hester recite her thoughts on what virtues a queen
should possess—wisdom, justice, fidelity, truth, and concern for the safety
of the realm. Hester continues with a short discourse on queenship:

No queen there is, but by marriage of a prince,
And under covert, according to the lawe.
So that the jurisdiction of the whole province,
To the king pertaineth, this is the trewe sawe;
Albeit, sometyme more for love than for awe,
The king is content to bee counselled by the queene,
To many sundrye cuases, as ofte hath been seene.[83]

The emphasis is on marriage as the maker of legal queens and queens
as good advisers, unlike the evil Haman. Catherine would have understood precisely who the playwright had in mind as he stressed that Hester
comes to the king "a virgin pure, / A pearl undefiled, and of conscience
clear."[84] Audiences who attended performances of the *Interlude* during the
Christmas season anywhere in London or Westminster or at court would
have recognized Catherine as the "pearl undefiled," the white of the pearl
symbolic of purity. The audience would have perceived that Catherine's
marriage was legitimate and that Mary was the legal heir to the throne.
They would have been reminded of the unprecedented events of the prior
summer, which left Catherine's marriage in legal limbo, and would have
been mindful of the dangers they faced as the divorce proceeded.

1520

Summer — The court, probably with only Henry most of the time, spends the summer at Wolsey's residence.

June — Catherine and Henry, with a large official retinue, stage an official, high-level meeting with King François I at an event known as the Field of the Cloth of Gold (Guisnes, France).

15 June — Pope Leo X excommunicates Martin Luther as a heretic for the publication of the Ninety-Five Theses.

1521

Summer — Royal progress is confined to towns and houses close to London to avoid the plague—Windsor, Woking, Guildford, Wolsey's residence, and Elsings, home of Sir Thomas Lovell in Middlesex.

11 October — Pope Leo X names Henry the Defender of the Faith for his defense of orthodoxy against the reforms of Martin Luther.

1522

1 March — Anne Boleyn first appears at court as part of a masque.

5 June–July — In a highly staged elaborate joint progress, Henry and Emperor Charles V go to Greenwich, Windsor, Hampton Court, Winchester, and Wolsey's residence. They agree to the betrothal of Charles to Princess Mary, then six years old, and court painter Lucas Horenbout begins work on a portrait miniature of Mary.

November — The royal court stays at Hertford Castle to avoid plague at Greenwich, Richmond, and London.

1523

Summer (?) — Catherine invites Juan Luis Vives to court as tutor for Princess Mary, and he begins two works on education, *De ratione studii puerilis epistolae duae* (On the Program of Studies) and *The Education of a Christian Woman* (*De institutione feminae Christianae*), which he dedicates to Catherine.

1524

March   Henry is seriously injured and near death from an accident at a
                       jousting competition.

May   William Tyndale, a leading figure in the English Reformation, is
                       expelled from the Catholic Church.

Summer   Henry spends the summer at Wolsey's residence.

1525

24 February   Defeat of François I of France by imperial troops at the Battle of
                       Pavia; he is taken prisoner, an action that disrupts diplomatic
                       relations between England and Emperor Charles V.

5 June   Henry FitzRoy is made Knight of the Garter, Duke of Richmond
                       and Somerset, and Earl of Nottingham.

August   Catherine's public rage at the elevation of Henry FitzRoy prompts
                       Henry to order the reorganization of the household of Princess
                       Mary; she is sent to Ludlow, Wales, to preside over the Council of
                       Wales and the Marches.

Summer   Henry holds court at Wolsey's residence.

1526

Summer   A "grand sweep progress" of seven counties—Surrey, Sussex,
                       Hampshire, Wiltshire, Berkshire, Buckinghamshire, Bedfordshire—
                       takes place, with Henry staying often at Wolsey's residence.

1527

6 May   The Sack of Rome and capture of Pope Clement VII by imperial
                       troops led by Charles V disrupt diplomatic relations across Europe.

17 May   A tribunal meets at Cardinal Wolsey's York Place residence at
                       Westminster to discuss the legality of Catherine's marriage to Henry;
                       Catherine is not informed.

22 June   Henry meets with Catherine in private, in an emotional meeting,
                       and announces his intention to have Wolsey begin an examination
                       into their marriage.

August   Princess Mary returns to court after nineteen months in Wales.

1528

Summer   A bout of sweating sickness at court prompts Henry to spend the
                       summer at Wolsey's residence.

8 June   Cardinal Lorenzo Campeggio is named papal legate in England to
                       begin the examination into the validity of marriage of Catherine and
                       Henry.

8 October   Cardinal Campeggio arrives in London.

8 November   Henry meets with nobles and legal authorities at Bridewell (London)
                       to discuss the legal implications of a divorce from Catherine.

December   Catherine and Henry celebrate Christmas at court, with Anne
                       Boleyn in attendance.

1529

31 May	Papal tribunal into Catherine and Henry's marriage begins at Blackfriars.
21 June	Catherine appears before the papal legatine court at Blackfriars to defend the legality of her marriage.
25 June	Catherine is accused of contumacy for failing to appear a second time before the tribunal at Blackfriars.
23 July	Cardinal Campeggio adjourns the papal legatine court, leaving the decision on the marriage to be adjudicated by the pope.
9 August	Thomas Wolsey is stripped of his government office as chancellor; his property, including Hampton Court, is seized, but he is permitted to remain archbishop of York; on his way to Yorkshire, he is accused of treason.
Autumn	Imperial ambassador Eustace Chapuys arrives at court.
9 October	Wolsey is officially charged with praemunire, a law prohibiting an assertion of papal supremacy in England.
October	Thomas More is appointed lord chancellor to replace Thomas Wolsey.
Christmas	Catherine and Henry hold court together at Greenwich for the last time.

CHAPTER 6

Resistance, Mortality, and the Power of Memory

God and Nature had done great injury to the said
queen in not making her a man, for she might have
surpassed in glory and fame almost all the princes
whose heroic deeds are recorded in history.

—Thomas Cromwell, 1533

RESISTANCE

When scholars who study Catherine of Aragon assess her life in the years
after Christmas 1529, during the agonizing legal standstill of several years
spent waiting for a ruling from the pope, she is typically depicted as sad,
pathetic, tragic, passive, and powerless. But when we do that, we risk seeing
her life from its ending, which was indeed tragic. But her actions in this
period are more complex than that, and the ending was not foreordained.
And her actions were hardly passive. She was a fighter. Thomas Cromwell
correctly sized her up as a formidable figure, even though he had trouble
with the fact that "God and Nature" did not make her a man. Cromwell
could not see beyond her sex and beyond thinking of power in masculine
terms. But we must. If not, we, like him, will underestimate her power.

It is power, not passivity, that forms the dominant thread of all her
actions after Blackfriars. It is not the sort of power that commands armies

or enacts laws. Her power is her resistance, a countervailing form of power, not to be taken lightly and dismissed as a lesser form of power.[1] Every act, no matter how seemingly mundane, sent the message to Henry that she was not only still alive, but still his wife, still allied with powerful friends, and still very much a powerful force. She marshaled her defenses to defend her marriage, her status as queen, and her daughter Mary's legitimacy and right to rule. She actively used her intellect, experience, personal charisma, and network of loyal allies in a powerful, steadfast refusal to relinquish her status as legitimate queen. She tenaciously held on to things that mattered, to "relics once dear," from loved ones who served as shields and weapons as she struggled to remain queen and protect her daughter from Henry's retaliation. She continued to supervise her lands and exercise authority through patronage, but lost them once the king stripped her of her titles.[2] Timothy Elston points out the irony of Henry's actions: that because he acted more like a domineering husband, his efforts to control her body, wealth, and influence actually supported her claim that he was still her husband.[3] She retained enough charisma as wife and mother to muster a dignified show of dynastic, marital, and maternal power. She resisted Henry's actions, which were based on a not unrealistic fear that Catherine's supporters would rise up and defend her. Some of her supporters were gentry, like Sir John Wallop, who stated that the "Queen was beloved as if she had been one of the blood royal of England; and the Princess in like manner. Also that should the divorce take place, the King will be at war with the Emperor and with Scotland."[4] But many supporters came from middling and lower ranks, both men and women, for a variety of reasons. Some simply disliked Anne Boleyn, calling her "a goggyll yed hoore."[5] Some feared the power of the king to divorce his wife, calling Henry "a wretch, a caitiff, and not Christian man, having two wives and a concubine."[6]

In the end, no matter how strong her charisma and popular support, she was overmatched by him. But her failure was not a sign of powerlessness. Her resistance to Henry stemmed from experience, beginning with her mother's example of how to weather the storms of marital conflict and separations from loved ones. After Arthur's death, Catherine endured widowhood and neglect but persisted, learned to cope, and sought guidance from powerful political and personal friendships in England and across the continent. These relationships are key to her survival, as the court became an increasingly dangerous place. And so, after 1530, with impressive tenacity, she embodied and enacted Henry's fears, and his fear is a clear sign of the power of her resistance.

It is truly tragic that despite all her efforts, nothing—not even calculated pieces of propaganda, beautiful objects from dear friends, and a life lived as a highly respected, honorable, and faithful Queen of England—could undo the injury done to Catherine by Henry. As the divorce proceeded, the personal, religious, legal, and political maneuvers intensified, but her anger and pain rarely surfaced. Her outward demeanor matched the tight-lipped image of her painted around the time of the Field of the Cloth of Gold (see fig. 14). Until her banishment from court in the summer of 1531 and the dismissal of most of the members of her household, she soothed the hurt much as she had as a young widow at Durham House, surrounded by her closest friends in her household, working on her needlework, reading and being read to, and corresponding with allies and friends outside of court. In the summer of 1530, religious reform and expressions of power over the pope marked a sharp turn in the marriage of Catherine and Henry, who were still officially living together. Writs of praemunire, an offense under English law of appealing to or obeying a foreign court or authority that challenged the supremacy of the Crown, were issued against fifteen clergy who dared to assert the primacy of the pope in religious matters in England. In September, Anne Boleyn demanded that Catherine's courtiers be forbidden to visit her, and on 29 November Cardinal Thomas Wolsey died. These "troubled affairs" and "tribulations" prompted Catherine to write directly to Pope Clement VII on 17 December, saying that Henry was being led around by bad advisers.[7] This very common argument made by someone who does not want to provoke the wrath of the king would be repeated in many of her letters. Catherine knew that to protect her marriage was her best way to protect her daughter's legitimacy, and so she did not leave her husband's side until ordered to do so, and even continued to sew his shirts after divorce proceedings had begun.[8]

The year 1531 marked a turning point from truly bad to even worse. In March, Mary spent several weeks with Catherine at court, and in July they went hunting at Windsor. But later that year Henry forbade Mary from visiting her mother. She was kept from court, and her status as princess was uncertain. Catherine stayed at Windsor Castle until July, where she had what would prove to be a tense final meeting with Henry on 14 July. A few weeks later, Catherine was banished from court and sent to live at the More in Hertfordshire, a house once used as a hunting lodge by Cardinal Wolsey. Princess Mary had visited her mother for the last time in May, but the struggles of her parents seriously affected her emotionally. This, in turn, affected her physical health and prevented her from making the journey to whatever castle far from London Catherine was inhabiting. Catherine did not yield, and the legal wrangling dragged on without clear resolution. But Parliament bent to Henry's will and strengthened his powers relative to the church. In 1432, the situation became dire. In March, the Parliament passed the Supplication Against the Ordinaries and the Act of Conditional Restraint of Appeals. In a letter to Charles V dated 22 April, Catherine expressed her hope that he would be able to persuade Pope Clement VII to decide in her favor.[9] The language of the letter is a very carefully crafted expression of hope (*esperança*), a sign to anyone who might intercept the letter before it reached Charles that she was fully aware of the writs of praemunire. This carefulness is a hallmark of all her actions, both public and private, as she pushes back against Henry, fully aware of the very dangerous legal implications of every word.

In May 1532, the Submission of the Clergy meant that the Catholic Church in England lost the power to enact any church laws without the assent of the king. In protest, Thomas More resigned as chancellor in May, and the king's Privy Council ordered Princess Mary to stop using that title and call herself "Lady Mary." Her ally and staunch opponent of the divorce William Warham, the archbishop of Canterbury, died on 22 August and was succeeded on 1 October by Thomas Cranmer, a supporter of the divorce and a proponent of religious reform. That same day, Henry sent the Duke of Norfolk to get Catherine's jewels for Anne to wear for her meeting with the King of France. She vigorously objected: "it was against her conscience to give her jewels to adorn a person who is the scandal of Christendom, and a disgrace to the king who takes her to such an assembly."[10] After that, it was impossible for Catherine to appeal any decision on her marriage to Rome. But, true to her upbringing as an *infanta* of Castile and heeding the lessons in queenship of her mother, she did not passively submit to Henry's actions, which stirred up opposition both in England and abroad.

She turned to her powerful family and friends outside England. Henry had deliberately deprived her of most of her possessions and refused to allow her to entertain visitors, so she turned to writing letters that are eloquent expressions of resistance and love, sadness and anger. Her strongest ally in terms of political clout was her nephew Emperor Charles V, whose dominion over vast realms in Europe and the Americas gave him fearsome economic and military power. Charles's ambassador to England, Eustace Chapuys, served as a conduit for their communication, and his letters to Charles during this period shed light on the living conditions and emotional state of both mother and daughter. Chapuys is clearly an ally of Catherine, but it is hard to doubt the truth of his reports of anguish Henry caused. Chapuys adamantly insisted that Catherine lodge a formal protest after Henry married Anne on 14 November, an action that began a formal break with the Roman Church and demoted Catherine to princess dowager. Writing to Charles on 15 December, just a day before her forty-sixth birthday, she expressed fears that "no good can come of the cause" and that Christendom was in peril if she should fail in her suit to the pope, who should put aside his fears and apprehensions and rule in her favor. She closed the letter with "from the More, separated from my husband without ever having offended him, Katharina, the unhappy Queen."[11] She may have been unhappy, but she still saw herself as queen.

Though the loyalties of her Spanish and English friends at court were tested during the divorce, they remained steadfast. They had been with her since her marriage to Arthur, had shared in the joy of her marriage to Henry and coronation, had been with her during her pregnancies, miscarriages, and stillbirths and the birth of Mary, and they showed no signs of deserting her. The personal loyalty of María de Salinas and Margaret Pole put them in a precarious position that risked Henry's very dangerous wrath. María's service at court and personal loyalty prompted Catherine to say of her that "in all my suffering, she is the only one who gives me consolation."[12] María had been ordered to leave Queen Catherine's service in 1532, but she continued to correspond with the cast-off queen and sent her news of Mary. Margaret Pole, a staunch Catholic, had weathered Henry's anger and retaliation before, and her faith provided ample grounds for her defense of Catherine.

The women of her court and household who stood by Catherine after the divorce risked family fractures. Elizabeth Howard, Duchess of Norfolk, was driven from court when she opposed the divorce, while her husband, the Duke of Norfolk, was actively advocating for Henry's marriage to Anne Boleyn. Anne, Lady Hussey, unlike her more cautious husband, opposed the divorce and the break with Rome. She continued to call Catherine's daughter Princess Mary after it was illegal to do so and was imprisoned in the Tower of London. Like many of Catherine's close friends, she refused to take the Oath of Supremacy in 1534, which required any person taking public or church office in England to swear allegiance to the monarch as Supreme Governor of the Church of England.[13]

The divorce strained family ties, too, in ways a fractured marriage always will, by testing loyalties. Henry's sister Mary and her husband, Charles Brandon, Duke of Suffolk, openly supported Catherine. Brandon was a good friend of Henry and had been close to the couple from the beginning of their marriage, and he had to walk a very fine line to maintain relationships with them both.[14] Other friends tried valiantly to take a moderate path. Catherine's chancellor, William Blount, Baron Mountjoy, whose second wife, Inés Vanegas (d. ca. 1515), was one of Catherine's closest friends from Spain, was one of the lords who signed the open letter to Pope Clement VII urging the divorce in 1530. But he remained Catherine's chamberlain and was ordered to stay with Catherine to prevent her escaping from England. In July 1533, as head of the delegation to Catherine at Ampthill, he failed to persuade her to submit to the king's new marriage and acknowledge herself dowager princess. He requested to be replaced as chamberlain, saying in a letter that "what business I have had in this matter since it first began, as well in the Cardinal's days . . . , I have good cause to have it in remembrance, for the high displeasure that I have had for the same. And I do perceive well, the further I do wade herein the more shall be my business, and yet it shall not lie in me to accomplish the King's pleasure herein."[15] His daughter Gertrude, Marchioness of Exeter, was close to Princess Mary, and when Mary came to the throne as queen regnant in 1553, she was rehabilitated and made a lady-in-waiting. Catherine's legal and political allies—Chancellor Thomas More, Cardinal John Fisher (formerly the bishop of Rochester), Cuthbert Tunstall (bishop of Durham), Nicholas West (bishop of Ely), John Clerk (bishop of Bath),

Henry Standish (bishop of Saint Asaph), William Peto (head of the Franciscan observants of Greenwich), Nicholas Wilson (archdeacon of Oxford), Stephen Gardiner (bishop of Winchester), and theologian Reginald Pole, son of Margaret, Countess of Salisbury—did their best in the face of a king bulldozing his way to a divorce, but, of course, they failed.[16]

It truly was all over in January 1533 when Henry privately married Anne Boleyn, then pregnant. In April, Henry ordered Charles Brandon to Buckden Palace (Cambridgeshire) to tell Catherine that in the eyes of the king she was no longer queen, and a month later Archbishop Cranmer declared officially that the marriage of Henry and Catherine was null and void. With her marriage to Henry now official, Anne was crowned on 1 June, and their daughter, Elizabeth, was born on 7 September.

Charles Brandon was sent to Catherine by Henry on numerous missions to impress upon her the reality of her new marital state. It was an unenviable task. In July 1533, when Catherine was declared princess dowager, Henry sent Brandon to deliver the news. Clearly not happy about it, he said that Catherine protested "that she was your Queen, and would rather be hewn in pieces than depart from this assertion." In December of that same year, Brandon was ordered to disband some of Catherine's servants and move her to Somersham in Cambridgeshire. The royal order tested Brandon's loyalties. He personally supported Catherine but, as the king's subject, he had to bend to Henry's will or risk arrest. Catherine defiantly locked herself in her room, and Brandon worried that he would have to tie her with ropes to get her to move.[17] María de Salinas told Chapuys that Catherine relented only when Brandon admitted that he wished something dreadful had happened on the road that would have made it impossible for him to carry out his duty to Henry.[18] The divorce was deeply unpopular among the English, and some officials did risk Henry's wrath. Chapuys reported that Henry had to order his officials to prevent the poor from coming to Catherine because he feared that she would use alms to buy their love. Her charisma and reputation had power, so much so that when she moved from house to house, the local inhabitants, in spontaneous emotional displays of support, crowded the streets to see her pass, prompting Henry to tighten the controls on her seclusion.[19]

During 1533 and early 1534, Catholic resistance to Henry's actions against Rome and dislike of Anne Boleyn took the form of scattered risings in Lancashire, unrest in London, and the dangerous prophecies and visions of Elizabeth Barton ("the maid of Kent"), which led to her hanging on 20 April 1534. This all mingled with support for Catherine to create a volatile atmosphere. Through it all, she refused to raise a rebellion against her husband, despite rumors. Imperial ambassador Chapuys wrote to Charles V in 1533 that "I have always found her so over scrupulous in her affection and respect for the King that she would consider herself irretrievably doomed to everlasting perdition were she to follow any other path that might provoke a war between Your Majesty and this king. However, some days before my writing to Your Majesty the Queen sent me word that she would willingly look out for another remedy to the evil, and that she placed herself entirely in my hands as to what that remedy was to be."[20]

A SHORT LESSON IN QUEENSHIP FOR PRINCESS MARY

All the legal wrangling and personal hostility put Princess Mary in a truly untenable spot. Her mother was no longer queen, her household was reduced significantly, she was demoted to illegitimacy, and she had a newborn half-sister who held the title of Princess of the Crown that she once held.[21] One day after Parliament passed the First Act of Succession, which invalidated Henry and Catherine's marriage, Pope Clement judged in favor of Catherine on 24 March 1534, with no right to appeal the decision.[22] Henry named himself Supreme Head of the Church of England and made Elizabeth his heir but did not explicitly exclude Mary from the succession. In a final blow, Catherine lost both control of and revenue from her reginal estates when they were transferred to Anne Boleyn. These months of head-spinning, contradictory legal decisions left Catherine weary from all the wrangling, yet she resisted pleas to give up and enter a nunnery or to fight back and call on her subjects to defend her.

But why? Why not call on her ardent supporters throughout England and in her nephew's continental realms? Why not rouse the rabble and, at the very least, use that support as a bargaining chip to regain her dignity, if not her title and privileges? Was her status and that of her daughter not worth the risk? To ask these questions presumes her inaction was a sign of feminine passivity, when in fact, it is a sign of a decisive deference. She was true to her motto, "Humble and Loyal," which at first glance seems conventionally feminine, until we ask an important question: To whom was she humble and loyal? Henry, of course, but she was also humble before the realities of her own family history. She was a daughter of Spanish monarchs whose immediate family history schooled her in the perils of royal coups. The scandals, bloodshed, and attempted coups of fifteenth-century Castile were finally resolved in the marriage of her parents. She knew the value of patience when her marriage to Arthur was delayed as her parents waited for Henry VII to eliminate the challenges of pretenders to his rule.[23] She stayed true to her conscience and remained loyal to the Crown. Patience was a strategic use of the one tool remaining to her—a dignified and steadfast resistance to Henry's overwhelming power. And her loyalty to her husband was more complex than just marital fidelity. As a queen, she was loyal to the realm. What may appear to be passivity was actually a combination of humility, obedience, and loyalty to the institution of monarchy. This loyalty was linked inextricably to the fate of her daughter, and ultimately Catherine's patient action protected her daughter's life and inheritance from Henry's wrath.[24]

The brutal reality of Catherine's political strategy of patience is evident in a personal letter that she wrote in early 1534 to Mary, who had just celebrated her eighteenth birthday. The letter may be a reply to a letter from Mary, now lost. It is not dated, but judging from context and substance, it is likely that she wrote it before 1 May, the deadline for all the king's subjects, regardless of rank or condition, to formally accept the Act of Submission.[25] In mid-May, Catherine's court was moved from Buckden to Kimbolton. Henry had seized most of her possessions, but he had not stripped her of basic writing materials. She did not have a secretary in her household, so the original may have been written entirely in her own hand.

Catherine does not waste time. She comes straight to the point without any pleasantries about her health, and there is no clear mention in the letter of Henry's love or affection for Mary. She begins with a report of news that she heard, perhaps from the ambassadors at court or a trusted friend, of "such tidings today that I do perceive, if it be true, the time is come that Almighty God will prove you; and I am very glad of it, for I trust He doth handle you with a good love." Catherine trusts God's goodness to continue to protect her daughter. This "He" clearly refers not to Henry but to God, who will handle her with "a good love." She does not explicitly tell us what this news is, but she likely means the news of Pope Clement's decision and the First Act of Succession, which would indeed test Mary's strength and will. What comes next in the letter is less clear, however, and this touches on the heart of the dilemma that Mary faced: To whom does she owe her obedience? God? Or Henry?

This dilemma centers on ambiguity in the pronouns. Who precisely is "He"? In the second sentence, for example, Catherine says, "I beseech you agree to His pleasure with a merry heart; and be you sure that, without fail, he will not suffer you to perish if you beware to offend Him." "His pleasure" seems to refer to God's will, which is the subject of the prior sentence. But given the "tidings," "His" could also refer to the First Act of Succession, which Henry wanted Mary to accept and, if she is safe from his anger and "will not suffer you to perish if you beware to offend Him." She then advises Mary to offer herself to "Him." Is this Henry? If so, that would go against Mary's loyalty to Rome. If it's God, that places her in peril with her father. Catherine advises Mary that "if any pangs come to you, shrive yourself; first make you clean" and then "take heed of His commandments, and keep them as near as He will give you grace to do, for then you are sure armed." Read as a statement of theology, "pangs" can mean mental anguish or thoughts of sin, which here would be to defy Rome, which should be resolved with confession and absolution ("shrive yourself"), and then "He will give you grace to do" and "take heed of His commandments" to arm herself. Read as advice to follow the dicta of the pope rather than her father, this bordered on treason, as Catherine knew. By then, the executions of Thomas More and John Fisher had made it clear that Henry would not tolerate resistance of any sort. If, however, the capitalization of the pronouns signifies the royal honorific, then the masculine "He" and "His" would be Henry. Read this way, she is advising Mary that the best course of action is to obey Henry, even though it goes against her conscience, and then perform confession, safe in the knowledge that God loves her and will protect her.

No matter how you read it, this is very subtle phrasing from an erudite woman with rhetorical skill who knows the risks of the familial and political terrain. Catherine knew that there were spies in her court and her letters were intercepted. She notes, "And if this lady [Anne Shelton] do come to you, as it is spoken, if she do bring you a letter from the King, I am sure in the self-same letter you shall be commanded what you shall do." Catherine had heard talk at court that Shelton was the trusty courier who bore the order from Henry to comply with his command. But Catherine trusted that Mary could read between the lines, that she could read her careful use of ambiguity in her choice of pronouns. This sort of subtlety might drive a lawyer to drink but ultimately could save Mary's life, and perhaps her legitimacy and her right to inherit.[26]

The next few sentences are clearer. Catherine refers to Henry as "the King" when she advises Mary to keep a calm demeanor and "answer you with few words, obeying the King your father in everything, save only that you will not offend God and lose your own soul; and go no further with learning and disputation in the matter. And wheresoever and in whatsoever company you shall come, [obey] the King's commandments. Speak you few words, and meddle nothing." This is prudent advice. She knew that Henry would not take kindly to Mary arguing with him about matters of theology and politics, and that such a challenge from a young woman to his authority would rouse his anger. Yet she also tells Mary that she should take care not to offend a much higher authority than Henry, to "not offend God and lose your own soul." Resistance was a risky tactic, one Catherine used skillfully and successfully when in 1529 she refused to give way at the legatine court at Blackfriars. She knew well how the rules of gender were stacked against her daughter, that outright defiance was risky as Henry had increasingly got his way. This strategy was a clear test of just how far the king would go to compel obedience from his daughter.

This passage is a canny piece of political rhetoric designed to guide Mary as she faced what they both knew would be Henry's wrath. It contains a veiled suggestion that Mary should follow her conscience, even it meant resisting her father. This is as close as Catherine would ever come to using the support of her nephew and supporters in England as way to regain her dignity, title, and privileges. Yet she seems to suggest that her status, and that of her daughter, were worth the risk. Is she giving Mary

permission to risk political martyrdom for the sake of her soul? By not
spelling it out, Catherine trusts Mary to decide.

She wants to guide Mary in her absence and promises to send her
two books in Latin, the *Vita Christi* with a declaration of the Gospels,
and the *Epistles of Saint Jerome*. The *Vita Christi* had personal meaning
for Catherine because her aunt, Sor Isabel de Villena, had written a Catalan retelling of the life of Christ intended for women. She hopes that
"in them I trust you shall see good things." What are those "good things"
that Catherine wants Mary to see? With the *Vita Christi* in mind, the
good things would have been guidance on how to accept the limitations
of her sex while subverting them to achieve both secular and spiritual
good.[27] The letters of Jerome would guide her as she sought to balance
the earthly concerns of marriage with spiritual demands. Catherine's
notions of queenship drew from familiar Spanish intellectual and spiritual touchstones such as Juan Luis Vives, Pere Torellas, and Juan de Flores.
She should turn to music and play her virginals and lute for consolation.
She has Mary's future in mind, knowing that her marriage prospects
hinged on giving in to her father, who dangled the possibility of a Scottish or French match. She says that "one thing specially I desire you, for
the love that you do owe unto God and unto me, to keep your heart with
a chaste mind, and your body from all ill and wanton company, [not]
thinking or desiring any husband, for Christ's Passion; neither determine
yourself to any manner of living until this troublesome time be past; for
I dare make you sure that you shall see a very good end, and better than
you can desire."

The letter then turns deeply emotional when Catherine tells Mary
that "I would God, good daughter, that you did know with how good
a heart I do write this letter unto you. I never did one with a better, for
I perceive very well that God loveth you. I beseech Him of His goodness to continue it; and if it fortune that you shall have nobody to be
with you of your acquaintance, I think it best you keep your keys yourself, for howsoever it is, so shall be done as shall please them." The next
line is heartbreaking in its sad reckoning with the inevitability of what
she is certain will happen: "And now you shall begin, and by likelihood I
shall follow. I set not a rush by it; for when they have done the uttermost
they can, then I am sure of the amendment." She sadly admits that the

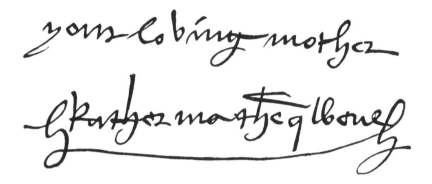

FIG. 22 | Signature of Catherine, "Your loving mother Katherina the Qween." Private collection. Photo © Look and Learn / Bridgeman Images.

divorce that has fractured the court has made friends take sides, and she asks Mary to send her best greeting to Margaret Pole, Countess of Salisbury, who was part of Mary's household, and "pray her to have a good heart, for we never come to the kingdom of Heaven but by troubles." This is a personal, almost intimate expression of a woman who keenly longs to see her daughter but maintains a steely dignity in both her intellect and her demeanor in the face of neglect and disrespect. She is fully aware of the contradictions and responsibilities of queenship that Mary will face. But Catherine assures her that even though she had fought a long battle and lost, they are of the same mind on the matter of the divorce and the Act of Succession.

The closing of the letter is not the least bit ambiguous. Catherine signs herself "Your loving mother, Katharine the Queen." That simple declaration of herself as queen, rather than the title Henry demanded she use—princess dowager—is a clear rebuke to Henry that makes an important political statement. With her signature (and her handwriting remains one of the few tangible marks she left) she conveyed the political message that Mary was still princess and heir to the throne (fig. 22). The language of the rest of the letter skillfully straddles the line between subtle and overt in articulating her resistance to Henry's actions, but she knew that it could be read by enemies. She knew that her signature as "Katharine the Queen" could provoke a swift and severe response, but she used it anyway. It would have been very cold comfort to her to know that her worst fears were not realized. Mary continued to defy her father for nearly two more years, refusing to agree to the Act of Succession until after her mother's death in January 1536.

This letter is more than just any mother's advice to her much-loved daughter at a moment of grave peril. Catherine's advice comes from her experience as counselor, having served as her father's official ambassador to King Henry VII and her husband's unofficial adviser for the first fifteen or so years of their marriage. It is advice from a queen consort who was regent of England in 1513 during the Battle of Flodden, when the English troops defeated the Scottish army and killed King James IV, and a valuable asset to diplomacy in 1520 at the Field of the Cloth of Gold.[28] It is part of a tradition of queens giving counsel, imparting reason and prudence to a queen-in-training, and teaching her to temper truth with an awareness of decorum. It is part of a growing body of literature on female sovereignty that advised queens to combine forceful action with accepting counsel from advisers, being willing to listen, and emulating regal ancestors like Margaret Beaufort, Matilda of Scotland, and Margaret of Scotland.[29]

In some ways, this letter resembles the "mirror of princesses" literature, most strikingly Anne de France's *Lessons for My Daughter*, written around 1504.[30] Like Anne, a French princess and regent for her brother King Charles VIII, Catherine makes a strong case for virtue, not only the specific feminine virtue of chastity but also the more general virtues of filial love and obedience, all of this tempered by a strong sense of ethical responsibility and reliance on trustworthy friends. Catherine's expressions of maternal love are wrapped skillfully around carefully worded advice on how to handle the news. Her advice to Mary on how best to navigate dangerous political dynamics is also a brief summary of Tudor queenship written at a key moment in English history. As a political statement, in this brief lesson on Tudor queenship, she shares with Mary the contradictions and responsibilities of queenship.

Much like the rhetoric of her statement at Blackfriars, which emphasized the "two bodies" of monarchy, the physical and political, here she also shows the two sides of queenship, regnal and maternal. She loved her daughter. Mary was more to Catherine than just an heir and symbol of dynastic legitimacy and security—she was the center of her emotional world. Mary was her only child, the much-loved daughter she cared for and educated. She felt acutely the absence of Mary, and when Mary fell ill in February 1535, she begged Henry to let her "care for her with my own hands." Fearing that his enemies were plotting to take Mary away to the court of Charles V, he refused to allow Catherine to give the "comfort and mirth" of a mother to a daughter.[31]

Her signature also conveys love of the realm and care for the institution of queenship. She was protecting Mary as the princess who would be queen. She knew that a queen was expected to be a noble, beautiful, virtuous, and chaste protector of her family. These sentiments are familiar: duty and humility. These ideas on queenship in this letter are intertwined with those of kingship. Recall, for example, the illuminated page from the "Coronation Ode" composed by Thomas More in 1509 (see fig. 11). In this image, Henry's Tudor Rose and Catherine's pomegranate entwine, symbolizing not only the dynastic marriage but also the joining of a king and queen into a monarchical pair. These forms of queenship and kingship have roots in both Castile and England. Her father, father-in-law, and husband were conventionally late medieval kings—masculine, tough-minded, and fully in charge of realms whose monarchies were based on a preference for rule by a king. Catherine also was a realist with an unwavering conviction, based on the example of her mother, that Mary could rule legitimately in her own right. Matilda's reign in the twelfth century was bitterly contested during a civil war, but the English accepted queens as regents as stand-ins for a king or prince. Their mottoes vividly express the role of a Tudor queen: Elizabeth of York was "Humble and Reverent" and Catherine was "Humble and Loyal." Catherine knew a different political reality from her mother's motto—"Tanto monta, monta tanto, Isabel como Fernando," or "as much Isabel as Fernando." She knew that that there could be another way, or least that kings and queens could work together. This knowledge gave Catherine a perspective that tested the "humble" and that informed her counsel for Mary. From her own experience as queen, she knew the power of men's hostility to women and their belief that women by nature were unruly, unable to control themselves, and unfit to govern others.

MORTALITY AND MOURNING: "MY LIFE IS LIVED; I HAVE FULFILLED THE COURSE BY FORTUNE GIVEN, AND NOW MY SHADE PASSES MAJESTIC TO THE WORLD BELOW"[32]

It is deeply ironic that Catherine ended her life as she began it, on the move, traveling from castle to castle, from Richmond, Windsor, the More, Bishop's Hatfield, Ampthill, Buckden, and, last, Kimbolton, her final home after living in so many places in Spain and England. She was attended by only a few servants: Henry VIII's physician, Dr. Butts, and her own doctor, Miguel de la Sá; her apothecaries, Juan de Soto and Philip Grenacre; her chaplain, Jorge de Ateca, bishop of Llandaff and master of Saint Catherine's hospital; and her chamberlain, Francisco Phelippes (*maître de salle*). María de Salinas, a widow since 1526, tried to spend time with her dear friend, but was often thwarted. In winter 1535, they both fell ill, but Catherine suspected that her daughter was far worse than she was told. She asked Chapuys to ask Henry for permission to for Mary to come to Kimbolton, "as that will be a great joy for them both, mother and daughter." She insisted that "no extra servants will be required, as she herself will attend to her wants, make her share her own bed, nurse her, and sit up with her when needed."[33] This request was a break with tradition, which called for nurses, not the queen, to care for the royal children, and it serves as a poignant reminder of the strength of the emotional maternal bond. And, like so many other requests from Catherine to Henry, it was denied.

Catherine's health deteriorated quickly in the fall of 1535. Just after her fiftieth birthday, on 30 December, María wrote to Henry's chancellor, Thomas Cromwell, and begged him to allow her to visit her friend. She held nothing back: "When I sent my servant to you he brought me word that you were in such importunate business that you could not despatch me or any other body. But now I must put you to pain, for I heard that my mistress is very sore sick again. I pray you remember me, for you promised to labor with the King to get me licence to go to her before God send for her, as there is no other likelihood."[34] Her angry, sarcastic tone challenged the cruelty in Cromwell's refusal to abide by a promise to try to persuade Henry to allow María to see Catherine. She berated him for his excuse that he was just too busy to be bothered to extend compassion for the friend of a dying woman.

She defied his orders. On 1 January 1536, María left her London home of Barbican and arrived at Kimbolton around 6:00 PM. She did not have formal permission to enter, but Sir Edmund Bedingfield, the custodian, allowed her to visit Catherine, after María lied to him. She told him that she had fallen from her horse, could go no further, and needed to come inside to tend to her injuries. She was joined by Eustace Chapuys, who arrived on 2 January and stayed until 5 January. As she lay dying, Catherine had a copy of Erasmus's *De praeparatione ad mortem* (Concerning the preparations for death).[35] María remained with Catherine and Jorge de Ateca, and they were there at Catherine's death on 7 January, around 2:00 PM. María and three other ladies did the women's work of mourning. They watched over Catherine's body until it was embalmed and taken to the chapel, where she remained for a week, from 16 to 22 January, in a coffin covered in a cloth of estate and adorned by fifty-six wax candles.[36] Plans for an effigy remained only that, as there is no evidence that it was ever constructed.

Early in his reign, Henry had considered a joint burial with Catherine at Westminster Abbey, but given the dramatically changed circumstances, he ordered instead a modest tomb for her, made of black marble with gilded letters and decorations. He ordered that she be buried at the Benedictine Abbey at Peterborough. Henry did allow her a measure of dignity. Her hearse was covered with a black sarsenet cloth, covered with images of the four evangelists and gold crowns, but he would not allow her the privilege of queen: the cloth was made not by the royal wardrobe but by the Painter-Stainers. On 22 January, mourners placed her coffin in a hearse to honor her as Princess of Wales, but not as Queen of England. Henry ordered Lady Bedingfield to take charge of organizing the funeral garments for the mourners. Eight principal mourners were present at the five days of Masses: María de Salinas; her daughter, Katherine, Duchess of Suffolk as second wife of Charles Brandon; Elizabeth Somerset, the Countess of Worcester; Elizabeth de Vere, Countess of Oxford; Frances Howard, Countess of Surrey; and three other baronesses. When the mourning robes for the mourners arrived on 26 January, the funeral procession began with a nine-mile journey to the Cistercian abbey at Sawtry, then to her burial place. One thousand wax candles lit the chapel for her funeral Mass, said by Bishop Ateca. The chief mourner was Lady Eleanor, the younger daughter of Charles Brandon and his first wife, Mary Tudor. Eleanor, with the eight original mourners, offered, by the hands of the heralds, three ells in three pieces of cloth of gold to be laid on her coffin and to make "accoutrements" for the men of the chapel, who were to hold a service annually on 29 January. Each of the mourners placed palls on the coffin: the chief mourner placed four, the duchess three, the countesses two each, and the baronesses one each. She was then buried in the north aisle to the left of the high altar, with a simple black cloth over the site, leaving the hearse where it stood.[37] No major male dignitaries, no members of the town council, and no foreign ambassadors were allowed to attend her funeral. Only Sir Richard Guildford, the comptroller of her household, attended. Chapuys refused to attend on principle, because she was not buried "as Queen."[38]

ERASURE

Attempts to remove traces of Catherine from public and private view started early. At Greenwich and other royal residences and places Catherine and Henry visited, Catherine's arms and badges on the stained glass were replaced with Anne Boleyn's. Some of the glass remains, such as the image of Catherine in the stained glass at the Vyne in Sherborne St. John, the estate of Sir William Sandys, a prominent figure in Henry's court.[39] In 1539, Henry had Peterborough Abbey dissolved, then reconsecrated in 1541 as an Anglican cathedral. Oliver Cromwell's soldiers seized the gilding in 1643, and in the 1700s a dean of the cathedral used the marble for his summer house. In the late nineteenth century, Katherine Clayton, a wife of one of the cathedral's canons, and supporters of Catherine started a public appeal to all the Catherines in England to donate to replace the marble slab. This slab and a gilt grille identifying this as Catherine's tomb are all that remain of her burial, unburial, and reburial.

In the strict sense of English law, as a woman covert (her legal status after the divorce), she could not bequeath manors or lands. Henry's associate Richard Rich had already informed the king that although Catherine died a *femme sole* (a woman whose marriage has been annulled or is otherwise independent of her spouse, as by owning her own property), he could devise legal means to seize her property.[40] But in a final assertion of her rights, just before she died, she dictated a list of her final requests to Eustace Chapuys.[41] She asked to be buried in a Franciscan convent, unaware that Henry had dissolved the order in 1534. She asked that Henry send someone on pilgrimage to Walsingham, but he had suppressed that shrine in 1538. She asked that five hundred Masses be said in her memory, but that, too, was refused her. She bequeathed to her daughter Mary a collar of gold that she had brought with her from Spain, and asked that her gowns be sewn into liturgical articles for the convent where she hoped to be buried. In Mary's will, she asked that her executors remove her mother's corpse from Peterborough and rebury it near her own tomb and that there be suitable monuments for them both. Like her mother's final requests, this, too, was ignored.

What was not ignored, however, was Catherine's advice in her last letter to Mary. Mary continued to defy her father, repelled every one of his rejections, and rebuked his humiliations as he stripped her of resources and bullied her to force submission to him. Her most devoted attendants were sent away, replaced by people loyal to Anne Boleyn. Her tutor was sent to the Tower. She lived in an atmosphere of petty malice and secret danger, surrounded by spies, fearful of poison, and threatened with physical violence. Yet she resisted and deflected his attempts to prevent her from having her meals prepared separately and served to her in her own chamber. The lesson she learned from her mother—to be steadfast in her resistance to a superior secular power and instead trust the higher power of God and the pope—shaped the political sensibility of Mary as she survived her father's next five wives, who suffered beheading, death from childbed fever, and rejection, before the last one managed to outlive him. She attempted to reconcile with her father by submitting to his authority as far as "God and my conscience" permitted, but she was eventually bullied into signing a document agreeing to all of Henry's demands. After that, she kept her counsel and kept her head down.

We know now what Catherine did not know then, that after the deaths of Henry in 1547 and his son Edward (1537–1553), Mary would rule as a queen regnant. As queen from 1553 to 1558, Mary would take some of the lessons from her mother. In the 1550s, humanist writer Henry Parker, Lord Morley, gave her some advice based on the exemplary life

of her great-grandmother, Lady Margaret Beaufort, as well as earlier
queens Matilda and Margaret of Scotland, as models for queenship, but
those queens consort lived in distant time and had little to offer a queen
regnant.[42] She could take more from the experience of her Castilian grandmother, Isabel, who did not share the Crown of Castile with Fernando.
They ruled their own realms more or less separately, with carefully delin-
eated areas of overlap in matters of war and relations with the pope.[43] Like
Isabel, Mary ruled in her own right, while her husband, Philip II of Spain
(1527–98), was king consort, second to her authority in her realms. Like
both Isabel and Catherine, Mary was a staunch ally of the pope, intolerant of anyone who violated Catholic orthodoxy. But Catherine's lessons
on queenship were predicated on a late medieval religious and political
reality far different from the one Mary faced in 1553. For those uncertain
and deeply troubled times, she unfortunately did not have a helpful advice
manual.

A SENSE OF MEMORY

Like many of Catherine's other possessions, some of the books from the
inventory at Baynard's Castle probably ended up at Westminster amid
Henry's books. Others were destroyed at the time of King Edward VI's
injunction of 25 February 1551 to purge the royal library of all Catholic
books. This may well have been the fate of a vellum primer, or book of
hours, "Primer written, coverid with cloth of golde"—and the three books
in red leather, which may well have been devotional books, remarkable
primarily for the designs on their bindings, were probably destroyed as
well. The seventeen books in the chest listed in the 1542 inventory, on
the other hand, lead us to other entities in the 1542 inventory, books that
confirm and deepen the conventional view of Catherine's abilities and
interests, that is, a woman musically sophisticated and pious, "of great
sense and saintliness," as Erasmus said in a letter to Petrus Mosellanus in
1519.[44] Catherine was a learned woman and a good wife and mother, and
her mind turned seriously to book patronage in the early 1520s, when she
was in her late thirties, unlikely to conceive again, and concerned with two
related issues: heresy and the possibility of a female succession in England.

FIG. 23 | The
Howard Grace Cup.
Ivory-mounted, silver-gilt.
English, hallmark for 1525–
26. Victoria and Albert
Museum, London, inv.
no. M.2680-1931. Photo ©
V&A Images, London /
Art Resource, New York.

Some of her gifts to loyal courtiers and friends have survived. One
object in particular is linked to Catherine and her Catholic allies at court
(fig. 23). The Howard Grace Cup is an exquisite ceremonial cup made of
turned elephant ivory (which may date to the twelfth century and Saint
Thomas Becket, but this has not been definitely determined), studded with
silver-gilt mounts set with gemstones and pearls. It is embellished with
images of the Knights of the Garter, Saint George in armor, and Catherine's pomegranate emblem engraved in a circle around the lid of the cup.
The cup is not large, but it is substantial, standing 26 cm tall and weighing
1135 grams. It contains Latin mottoes, or graces, that refer to the pleasures
of drinking and the importance of sobriety. It was hallmarked in 1525 and
most likely was a New Year's gift to William Fitzalan, Earl of Arundel,
serving at the royal court. The cup was carefully preserved, most likely by

Catholics who kept it underground during the reigns of Edward VI and
Elizabeth I. It surfaced in 1614 when it was in the collection of the Catholic Howard family. For a wealthy family such as the Howards, the value of
the cup was measured not just in terms of pounds and shillings but also in
the direct link to the royal court and to Catherine as an emblem of Catholic recusants.[45]

Some of the objects that have survived bear witness to those who
wanted to remove all traces of her, including a lavish book of hours that
belonged to one of Catherine's ladies at court. This book on vellum, richly
illuminated with miniatures and borders, is addressed to a lady and signed
by Henry VII as "your lovynge maistre," with later autograph inscriptions of Henry VII, Elizabeth of York, Henry VIII, Catherine of Aragon,
Margaret Tudor, and Princess Mary. It contains a translation from Latin
to English, done by Princess Mary when she was eleven years old, of "The
Prayor of Saynt Thomas of Aquune." Folio 192v contains an inscription:
"The prayor of Saynt Thomas of Aquyne, translatyd oute of Latyn unto
Englyshe by the moste exselent [Prynses, words defaced, partly expunged]
Mary, doughter to the moste hygh and myghty Prynce and Prynces kyng
Henry the viij. and [Quene Kateryne hys wife, words defaced, partly
expunged], in the yere of our Lorde God m.'ccccc.xxvij. and the xj yere
of here age." A later owner, either an ardent Protestant or at least an ally
of Henry, used a sharp object to deface the names "Prynses" and "Quene
Kateryne hys wyfe" from the rubric.[46] In a similar act of posthumous
destruction, the cover of the copy of Alfonso de Villa Sancta's *Problema
indulgentiarum aduersus Lutherum* (1523), presented to both Catherine
and Henry, had Catherine's pomegranate badge cut out from the cover
of the book and replaced with the cock, one of Henry's badges.[47]

The survival of the books in their defaced condition shows that Catherine was not an easy woman to forget. To deface a valued possession
violates it but does not destroy it. It leaves marks that transform it into
something else. It is no longer only a book of hours; it takes on a political and personal significance that transcends the meaning. In the case of
books meant to erase Catherine and Mary, it radiates its political energy,
creating a ripple across time and space that still reverberates.[48]

The violent erasure bears the animus, or perhaps just the religious
zeal, that promoted an anonymous reader to scrape her name from the

text of a book. Her powerful family on the continent prompted fear of rebellion, coup, and civil war that led her enemies to try to obliterate all traces of her. In the last few years of her life, she was unable to reclaim her status as queen and barely saved her daughter's legitimacy, yet Henry and his allies tried their best to destroy and erase the power and allure of her memory. Their rancor is still visible in a collection of motets for Anne Boleyn that is illustrated with her emblem, the falcon, picking furiously at pomegranates.[49]

Still, how do we explain scholarly neglect? As noted above, tempers cooled, England grew more secular, and during Elizabeth I's disputes with Philip II of Spain in the 1580s, Catherine was dangerously Spanish. The memory of her faded—but only a bit.

COMMEMORATION: THE NEVER-ENDING TASK OF NOT FORGETTING CATHERINE

Despite all of Henry's efforts to deny her deathbed requests, one appears to have been fulfilled. She had asked "that Mr. Whiller be paid of expense about the making of my gown, and besides that of xx £ sterling. . . . Item, may it please the King my good Lord, that the house ornaments of the church be made of my gowns, which he holdeth, for the serve the convent thereat I shall be buried."[50] A chasuble, now in the Shropshire Museum at Ludlow, made from a bit of cloth from what once was Catherine's gown, bears an embroidery of her pomegranate emblem. The history of the chasuble is a bit of a mystery. At present, there is not a clear record of ownership of any of the gowns Catherine gave as gifts to her ladies-in-waiting. The silence surrounding the gifts is not surprising at all. Catholics who allied with Catherine were careful to hold their tongues before and after Mary's reign to avoid charges of treason. Curators do not know for certain where the gown came from or how it was used to make the chasuble, nor are they sure how the chasuble itself passed from one owner to the next. Here's what they have pieced together so far.

Curators speculate that after Catherine's death, her ladies-in-waiting, perhaps at Mary's request, gave the gown to either Elizabeth Throckmorton, abbess of Denny, specifically, or to the Throckmorton family of

FIG. 24 | Mawley Hall
(Catherine of Aragon)
chasuble, sixteenth
century. Shropshire
Museums, Ludlow, RCDS
2012.00001. Property of
the Catholic community
at St Elizabeth, Cleobury
Mortimer and St Peter,
Ludlow, on loan to the
Shropshire Museums.

Coughton Court (Warwickshire). It is not clear whether the gown was worn or simply stored away, or when it was cut up to make the chasuble, but curators are reasonably confident that it remained in the Throckmorton family. The chasuble then went to the Blount family of Mawley Hall and finally was given to the Catholic Church at Cleobury Mortimer (Shropshire) in 1959. At some point, Mary, wishing to respect her mother's final religious requests, appears to have had several of her mother's gowns made into liturgical garments, such as the chasuble at Ludlow and a cope at Coughton Court.[51] We will not know if they are in fact from the same gown until textile conservators perform a thorough analysis of the dyes, threads, fabrics, and stitching of both garments. But we do know that there are bits of old and new fabric used in the final crafting of both garments, with the embroidery of the gown stitched to a base of velvet fabric not part of the original gown. It is safe to say that the Mawley Hall chasuble and Coughton cope are made from fragments of a gown owned and presumably worn by Catherine, stitched together from other pieces of fabric to make a new garment meant to commemorate her.

Catherine's bequest was part of a tradition for women of all ranks, but especially queens, to bequeath their clothing to their attendants, who would give them to churches to make into liturgical garments.[52] For queens, the practice dates to at least as early as the eleventh century. Queens Emma of Normandy (wife of Æthelred the Unready and Cnut the Great), Edith of Wessex (wife of Edward the Confessor), and Matilda of Flanders (wife of William I) were generous donors of liturgical garments to monasteries and convents. These gifts of vestments were visible to the faithful, not stored in a cupboard, and served to link the queen to the church. Liturgical garments have deep religious significance and are strongly gendered. Vestments were worn by the male clergy as a means of distinguishing them from the laity and to emphasize their role as intermediaries between humanity and the divine. Women were not supposed to touch the altar, a consequence of longstanding male concerns about women being weaker and more sinful than men. But vestments acted as a material manifestation of the ecclesiastical hierarchy, with the chasuble for the priest when he officiated at Mass and the cope a processional garment worn by the clergy and cantors. Vestments were restricted solely to men, a distinction that became blurred when female images were depicted on the orphreys, or when women's garments were stitched into the chasuble or cope.[53]

The Mawley Hall chasuble and the Coughton cope have religious features similar to other pre-Reformation vestments in Catholic churches. They show the same floral patterns, winged figures on wheels (from the book of Ezekiel), seraphim, fleurs-de-lys (symbols of the Trinity), and scroll shapes.[54] However, these two vestments differ in that they have pomegranate motifs applied to the velvet background, the same in color, shape, and size, and both use the same stitching and the same green-and-yellow braid around the edges. Large pomegranates in red pile on cloth of gold appear on the orphreys on both sides of the Mawley Hall chasuble. The embroidered emblems appear to have been taken from elsewhere and applied to the velvet background. This applies especially to the cloth-of-gold orphreys on the chasuble, which have been made by cutting a single larger cloth into four separate pieces so as to form a cross on the back and a single strip on the front. Such drastic cutting of a valuable cloth of gold would have been justified by the pomegranate pattern on the cloth, linking the vestment with Catherine. The cloth of gold itself may have been from one of Catherine's gowns, brought with her from Spain. On closely examining the velvet and embroidered patterns, the restorers had already commented that the chasuble "must have been put together from something else," and in its prerestoration condition it showed signs of having been made hurriedly. Finally, the choice of the color of the velvet material of the chasuble is also significant if it was intended to be used to offer Mass for the dead. If indeed bits of Catherine's gown were incorporated from a single gown intended to form a pair of liturgical garments, they do not match perfectly. The Coughton cope is purple and the Mawley Hall chasuble is dark blue, an alternative to black.

Catherine's request that her dresses be remade into a liturgical garment should not have ruffled any feathers, but it did. Thomas Cromwell tried to prevent this gift of her gowns, deeming it "an unnecessary and vain bequest, one which could not really be carried out, inasmuch as there was a superabundant quantity of ecclesiastic robes and ornaments in the churches of England. Instead of that, some endowment might be made to the abbey in which the Queens body would be interred, which would be, a more suitable donation and one far more worthy of notice than that of her own robes and vestments."[55] Cromwell was known to pinch pennies, but it is likely that his objections were intended to cut her more deeply. A chasuble had significant theological significance as part of the concern for the bodily purity of the priest, the prayers for vesting the priest, the rituals of cleansing in the Mass, and ultimately the core Catholic belief in transubstantiation, the act of transforming wine and bread into the blood and flesh of Christ. For queens to insert themselves into the creation and donning of priestly garb was, until the Lutheran reforms, a completely ordinary thing to do.[56] Cromwell, a follower of Protestant reformers, knew well the debates over transubstantiation. Later that year he ordered the dissolution of the monasteries and the removal of all Catholic imagery from churches in England. Catherine's donation of garments to be made into chasubles posed a grave threat to the new religion and to the Act of Supremacy, which made Henry supreme head of the Church of England.[57]

We are fortunate that Cromwell failed to prevent the bequest, for these fragments of personal fashion put to posthumous service in the Catholic liturgy are evidence of both affection for Catherine and a Catholic religious piety that risked the wrath of a newly Protestant king. Women outside the court and nobility also played their part in the dispersal of the liturgical textiles. After the dissolution, the monastic land was beyond the means of most people, but a much broader group would have been able to afford these textiles.[58] It is a sly, quiet gesture by recusants who kept faith with both their Catholicism and the memory of Catherine.

Not all the commemorations of Catherine's life were quite so subtle or so quiet. Rumor had it "that on the day that Anne [Boleyn] was beheaded the tapers round Catherine's grave [at Peterborough] had spontaneously kindled themselves, and that 'this light contynuyng from day to daye' was a token of the restoration of the old order."[59] Chapuys told Charles V that "the Queen's arms had been removed from her barge, and rather ignominiously torn off and cut to pieces. He had severely reprimanded that lady's chamberlain, not only for having caused the said arms to be removed, but for having appropriated the said barge, lately belonging to the Queen, when there were in the river many others equally fit for the Lady's service."[60] Poets and playwrights working later in the sixteenth century wrote of Catherine's patience, using the character of Griselda as a model for the long-suffering wife. William Forrest dedicated the *History of Grisild the Second* (1558) to Mary I, and William Shakespeare and John Fletcher's *Henry VIII* praises her as a dutiful, almost saintly wife and memorializes her in the Blackfriars scene.[61] Not all the books that bore traces of Catherine were defaced. As noted above, manuscripts created throughout her life, now housed in the British Library, bear Catherine's emblems of pomegranates and castles and testify to the affection of her English subjects.[62]

Beyond England, on the continent, Catherine's relatives at the imperial court kept a small part of her memory alive with a small (53 mm diameter) boxwood gamespiece for a backgammon set that bears her portrait. She is shown in profile to the left with her head covered by a hood, wearing a dress cut with a low square décolletage edged with a narrow frill. Around her neck are a gold chain and pendant. On the back an inscription reads, "Catherine Wife of Henry VIII." The profile bears a close resemblance to contemporary portraits of Catherine, is similar to one in a set owned by

Marguerite of Austria, and the lettering appears to be sixteenth century and similar to that of Holbein.[63] Catherine was a devotee of chess and backgammon, with four game sets and chess pieces among her possessions at Baynard's Castle for playing "foxe, chestys, and other games."[64]

After her death, the Reformation in England transformed the religious character of England and, along with it, how Catherine was remembered by people who had not known her personally.[65] She was a useful figure to rally both Catholics and Protestants in the increasingly hostile atmosphere of religious reforms. To Catholics she was accorded a secular saintly status for her pious defense of Catholic orthodoxy and papal authority. Her adamant stance against Henry's actions gave her a heroic status, as a Tudor-era Wonder Woman for Catholics who, after her death, found themselves increasingly at risk. Her dresses that became chasubles for Catholic priests were visual reminders that sent subtle but powerfully evocative messages of her resistance to Henry's actions.[66] To Protestants, she was a threat to religious reform whose death paved the way for a more enlightened piety based not on allegiance to Rome but on faith and adherence to Scriptures. The five queens who succeeded her all followed Protestant teachings, and Henry's sixth wife, Katherine Parr, published four works, *Psalms or Prayers*, *Prayers or Meditations*, *The Lamentation of a Sinner*, and her *Personal Prayerbook*.[67] During Mary's reign, resurgent Catholics made a martyr out Catherine. During Elizabeth I's reign, she was considered an intolerant toady to the pope whose tarnished image was linked to the derisive portrayal of her daughter as "Bloody Mary." This negative portrayal of Catherine the Catholic queen was part of the redemption of Anne Boleyn, meant to glorify Elizabeth.

Perhaps the one thing both Catholics and Protestants could agree on was her promotion of the education of women.[68] Dramatists in the later sixteenth century relished the dramatic and romantic aspects of her life, and with them much of the mythology of Catherine took shape. These portrayals of her as a wronged victim of a serial philanderer, a pious saint, or a dowdy, unattractive, and intolerant old woman have influenced the many cinematic versions of her and the other wives of Henry, and now the girl-power musical *Six*.[69]

Catherine's family kept her memory alive. Her sister Queen Juana of Castile kept a portrait of Catherine (and their mother, Isabel). It was in the inventory of her goods after her death: "dos tablas de la ymagen de la prinçesa de gales e dos papeles de pinturas de la dicha ymagen." But the inventory does not describe the image nor associate it with any artist, so we cannot be sure what this portrait looked like.[70] Remnants of her life fill the inventory at Baynard's Castle. Her sewing and embroidery consumed her day, with pin cases ("two covered with clothe of golde") that contained needlework. A rich cloth of fine linen with a picture of Christ "wroughte in gold withe nedilwork." Cushions covered with needlework, little stools covered with black velvet embroidered with gold thread, some fringed and embellished with silk and gold thread. Bedsheets of fine Holland cloth "wroughte withe Spanysshe worke" of black silk with gold buttons. Tables covered with "nedillworke" depicting the image of Christ, the Virgin Mary, Joseph, Saint Anne, and Saint Francis. Working stools covered in velvet and embellished with silver and gilt threads.[71]

Beyond the family, even the lacemakers in the Midlands commemorated Catherine, honoring her decision to support them during a slump in the lacemaking industry's fortunes by burning all her lace and ordering new lace made. Recalling that Saint Catherine was the patron saint of spinners, lacemakers in Northamptonshire devised a "Queen Katharine" lace pattern and a "Kat Stitch."[72] The faithful who congregated in the Cathedral of Worcester, where Arthur was buried in the cold, windy, rainy April of 1502, in the chantry to the right of the high altar, would have seen Catherine's pomegranates entwined with Arthur's arrows, carved in the stonework surrounding his tomb.[73]

TIME LINE: RESISTANCE, MORTALITY, AND THE POWER OF
MEMORY, 1530–1536

1530

Summer	Writs of praemunire are issued against fifteen clergy.
September	Anne Boleyn forbids Catherine's courtiers to see her.
29 November	Cardinal Thomas Wolsey dies.

1531

May	Princess Mary visits Catherine, but a prolonged bout of illness keeps her from further visits to her mother.
31 May	A delegation led by the Dukes of Norfolk and Suffolk is sent to Catherine at Greenwich to persuade her to agree to the divorce; they are unsuccessful.
July	Catherine is in residence at Windsor Castle accompanied by a court of about two hundred people, including thirty maids of honor.
14 July	The final meeting of Catherine and Henry takes place.
Late summer	Catherine is sent to live at the More (Hertfordshire), once Wolsey's hunting lodge.

1532

March	Parliament passes two acts to strengthen the king's authority over that of the pope: the Supplication against the Ordinaries and the Act of Conditional Restraint of Appeals.
May	The Submission of the Clergy orders that the Catholic Church in England give up the power to enact church laws without the king's assent.
16 May	Thomas More resigns as lord chancellor.
July	Catherine, despite vigorous protests, relinquishes her jewels to Henry, who gives them to Anne Boleyn.
Summer	Princess Mary suffers from a serious illness; Henry's privy council orders Mary to stop using the title of princess and to call herself "Lady Mary."

22 August	William Warham, archbishop of Canterbury, one of Catherine's staunch supporters, dies.
1 October	Thomas Cranmer, an advocate of the divorce, is appointed archbishop of Canterbury to replace Warham.
14 November	Henry and Anne Boleyn secretly marry.
December	Henry orders the Duke of Norfolk to break up Princess Mary's household and move her to Hatfield.

1533

25 January	Henry VIII and Anne Boleyn publicly marry at Whitehall.
March	The Statute in Restraint of Appeals, drafted by Thomas Cromwell and passed by Parliament, forbids all appeals to the pope in Rome on religious or other matters.
12 April	Thomas Cromwell is appointed chancellor of the Exchequer.
May	Archbishop Cranmer declares invalid the marriage of Catherine and Henry; the Statute in Restraint of Appeals makes it impossible for Catherine to bring her divorce case to Rome.
10–23 May	The divorce trial in Parliament meets to determine the legitimacy of Catherine and Henry's marriage; Catherine does not appear or send a proxy.
23 May	Archbishop Cranmer determines that the marriage of Henry and Catherine is invalid.
28 May	Archbishop Cranmer validates the marriage of Henry and Anne Boleyn.
1 June	Anne Boleyn is crowned Queen of England.
25 June	Mary Tudor, Henry's sister and wife of Charles Brandon, dies.
11 July	Pope Clement VII declares Cranmer's judgment on the marriage to be null and void.
Late July	Catherine is moved to Ampthill (Bedfordshire), then Buckden (Cambridgeshire).
7 September	Anne Boleyn gives birth to a daughter, Elizabeth, later Queen Elizabeth I.
Autumn	Catherine is moved to the archbishop's lodgings at Lincoln.

1534

March	First Act of Succession to the Crown declares Princess Mary to be illegitimate and elevates Princess Elizabeth as the successor to the realm of England.
March	Pope Clement VII proclaims the validity of the marriage of Catherine and Henry.
May	Catherine is moved to Kimbolton (Cambridgeshire).
3 November	The Act of Supremacy establishes the king (or queen) of England as the Supreme Head of the Church of England; the Treason Act and the Act of First Fruits and Tenths further strengthen the power and economic resources of the king.

1535

22 June	John Fisher is executed.
6 July	Thomas More is executed.
December	Catherine is gravely ill.

1536

1 January	María de Salinas, Lady Willoughby of Eresby, leaves her London home of Barbican (or Bas Court) and arrives at Kimbolton.
2–5 January	Eustace Chapuys visits Catherine at Kimbolton.
7 January	Catherine dies at Kimbolton.
29 January	Catherine's funeral is held at Peterborough Cathedral, attended by María de Salinas with her daughter Katherine, the Duchess of Suffolk, and Eleanor, daughter of Mary Tudor and Charles Brandon.
March	The First Act of Dissolution of the Monasteries is enacted, which begins the Crown seizure of church property.
April	The "Reformation Parliament" is dissolved.
19 May	Anne Boleyn is executed.
July	Princess Mary submits to Henry's will, accepts the invalidity of the marriage of her mother and father, and admits to the supremacy of the king in England; her household is reestablished; Henry and Queen Jane Seymour visit Mary, and she begins to spend more time at court.
October	Pilgrimage of Grace, a popular protest of King Henry VIII's religious reforms, begins in northern England.

CHAPTER 7

Who Was That Queen?

This book began with a pair of shoes and a question: What do Catherine's shoes tell us about her and her world? That question opened up closets full of objects and another, longer, question: Does combining shoes, gowns, headdresses, books, baby blankets, miniature portraits, rosaries, illuminated manuscripts, and liturgical garments with narrative sources such as letters, descriptions of life at courts in Castile and England, and chronicles compose a fuller portrait of Catherine of Aragon? I think it does, if by portraiture we mean an image or description that "makes companionable for you a person who is identified or unknown, perhaps remote from you in geography or time (even dead, no matter), different from you in ways big or small, a lot or only the littlest bit like you in other ways, and, all in all, another exceedingly specific inhabitant of a certain planet."[1] There can be no single portrait of a woman as complex as Catherine, so the five portrait sketches that form the substance of this book tell only fragments of her life. The places and things she saw, the objects she held dear, and the painted portraits of her reveal facets of her personality and begin to create a fuller picture of who she was—a Queen of England. And, I argue, she was a powerful queen.

To understand Catherine's power as queen we need to reconsider what we mean when we talk about power in the context of monarchy, the paramount secular political institution of early modern Europe. Catherine's personal understanding of monarchy and kingship was shaped by her father and father-in-law. Both of their realms preferred rule by a man and were governed by dynastic principles. Coronation rites authorized the king (and sometimes the queen), coronation oaths bound him to his subjects and to the law, and marriage legitimized the queen and their heirs. Locating kings at the center and pinnacle of power meant that male power was considered the norm, but queens were hardly powerless. There had been no sovereign queen in England since 1154, and the English did not like queens regent. But gender is not a binary, and because monarchy was steeped in gendered expectations, it follows logically that monarchy was not binary either. Yet generations of scholars fell into the gender trap that regarded any power exercised by queens as soft power, their advice to the king as mere pillow talk, and their management of estates and diplomacy as limited agency or influence. The gendered language of kingship, which focuses on who does the work rather than the kind of work done, demeans the work of queen. Both the king and queen derived their power from the institution of monarchy, but it was both a system of governing and a family affair. Catherine was an *infanta* and princess who became a queen when she married and derived power from her centrality at court as wife and mother, and she drew wider circles of power around her from her siblings, cousins, nephews, and in-laws. Catherine embodied this complex interplay of family and power; she understood the gendered expectations that came with the job, and so we need to trace the contours of her life through the job description to see queenship and power more clearly. The circumstances that shaped the degree to which she could wield power—a lot, a little, sometimes a lot, mostly a little—stem from wellsprings of power that changed over the course of her life: natal family, birth and upbringing, education, talents and expertise, marriage, maternity, patronage, intercession, and networks of influence at court and beyond.

Power is not simply doing something, like issuing a command. It is also a latent and potential force, inherent but not always realized (like a threat), and it is always there even when not visible from our vantage point. Power is a shape-shifter, and what often passes for powerless is not necessarily powerless. Monarchical power can be expressed as latent (as an heir), dynastic (familial), governmental (regent), diplomatic (based on bonds of family and affinity), charismatic (personal), religious (piety, devotion), potential political (as hostage), and the power of resistance. Over the course of a lifetime of power, Catherine expressed most, if not all, of these aspects of power. She did not rule in her own right; she never convened a Parliament, did not order taxes to be collected or enact laws, did not order the execution of a criminal. Yet throughout her life she clearly exercised agency, which I define as the ability to take action that has the potential to affect her destiny. She did not choose her husbands, but she could choose whom at court to favor with patronage and gifts, how to spend money earmarked for her as queen, which authors to support, how to educate her daughter, and, at times, whose advice to take and whose to ignore.

"Agency" is a tricky word, however, akin to "autonomy." It may seem neutral, but it signifies personal, not coercive power, and is often used to refer to lesser forms of power that are indirect, secondary: intimate whispers instead of direct commands. But Catherine possessed more than agency, she possessed a panoply of power that she strategically used over the course of her life. Sometimes she used it and sometimes she held it in abeyance. Her power was volatile, unstable, and Henry often usurped it. But I argue that what we see here is not the absence of power but rather the dynamics of shifting forms and expressions of queenly power, running the gamut of potential, dynastic, governmental, diplomatic, charismatic, religious, political, and defiant.

The first portrait of her, painted when she was eleven, depicts a child of late medieval Iberia with an ample storehouse of potential power. A highly intelligent girl born into one of the most powerful royal families of the age, she grew up on the road, by her mother's side with her sisters and brother, with her father in the distance, at war or in council meetings. She was a young girl who soaked up the sun on the many long travels across Castile and Aragon, who relished the food of the Mediterranean, and who took in the sophisticated art and cultures of Christianity, Judaism, and Islam. She grew up a pious Christian, but she also witnessed, from the safe distance of the royal court, the persecution and expulsion of the Jews and the conquest and expulsion of the Muslims of Granada.

To think of a young girl as powerful may seem a stretch of the imagination, but from her birth in 1485 to her second marriage in 1509 she drew power from her dynastic potential. She was a diplomatic prize: young, nubile, dutiful, well educated, cosmopolitan, sophisticated. She did not have to do anything to demonstrate her potential power, which stemmed from both her parents. Questions of gender swirled around her parents' court during Catherine's childhood, and her education empowered her tough intelligence, eloquence, and unwavering convictions, which influenced her understanding of the power of queenship. She knew that a king and queen shared a job description, and that this was affected by gender norms. She saw this every day as her parents lived out their motto, "Tanto monta, monta tanto, Isabel como Fernando" (as much Isabel as Fernando). And a royal chronicler remarked when she was born that "a son would have caused *los reyes* greater happiness, for a succession depending on only one son inspired no small fear."[2] She was taught carefully to nourish her dynastic power by her mother, Isabel, a sovereign queen regnant who ruled Castile from 1474 to 1504 with a careful balance of pious femininity and virile rulership.

A second portrait depicts Catherine as a sixteen-year-old virgin in October 1501 who had just begun the transition from *infanta* to *princessa de Gales* (Princess of Wales). When she married Arthur Tudor in a marriage that joined the royal families of Spain and England, she literally embodied dynastic power as the promise of maternity, of children and an heir. Any chance of queenship with Arthur was curtailed by his death in April 1502, which left her a young widow, struggling with the loss of both her husband and her life as Queen of England. This period of potential power continued as she remained a focal point of a marriage alliance for other powerful men, but as a widow she was vulnerable. Despite the insecurity of her status and her future, she remained highly valuable, filled with the potential power of a marital prize. During this poorly documented period in her life, we know that her father, Fernando, and her father-in-law, Henry VII, sought to use her dynastic power to secure an alliance between England and Spain. She suffered an emotional loss when both her mother-in-law and mother died (1503 and 1504, respectively) and she had to fend for herself. Private letters and diplomatic missives reveal that her finances were shaky, and she appears to be weak, pleading with her troublesome father and parsimonious father-in-law for more material resources. But to look only at the surface is to miss the main point: she was able to exercise limited diplomatic power, maintain a household, build strong and enduring relationships, and, above all, stay in England, empowered by her status as a potential royal bride for Prince Henry. She turned to her friends and new family and found her footing in her work as ambassador for her father and gradually moved on toward an uncertain future.

In the third portrait, she is a twenty-four-year-old bride to her brother-in-law Henry, whom she had known for seven years. Catherine's queenship began in 1509 when she married Henry, and over the course of their marriage her power fluctuated in type and degree. It is most evident in her powerful dynastic and charismatic role as the beloved wife of the king. At the chronological center of this period is her leadership as regent, which led England to a victory against the Scots, her in-laws, at the Battle of Flodden in 1513. This point marks a dramatic shift in her power, from latent and potential to one marked by the sorts of actions we easily recognize as powerful—managing a war—and then swung back again. At first she was her new husband's best close adviser at court, and his regent who led the government of England during a battle against the Scots. She was a strong influence on Henry in the first five years due both to her age— she was six years older than Henry—and to her experience from the years she spent in England as princess dowager and ambassador at the English court for her father. Henry routinely sought her advice, and she is present in much of the official record from 1509 to 1513. Many of the king's decisions were taken with her advice, he trusted her, and he was confident in her loyalties. He particularly valued her active work in Anglo-Iberian diplomacy as a key liaison with the Spanish diplomats at court, but he held sovereign power. This portrait shows a woman who knew well and intimately that a queen could act honorably in public and govern skillfully. She had a powerful network of family and allies that stretched across the continent, and she was a powerful patron of arts and literature, including luminaries such as Thomas More and Desiderius Erasmus. Catherine's keen awareness of the contradictions and responsibilities of queenship, taught to her by women who knew the intricacies and demands of the job, informed her regency and are clear again in the steely dignity of her intellect and demeanor during the divorce proceedings in the late 1520s.

This portrait has a more mature color and tone because for the first decade of their marriage she was pregnant at least six times. She endured pregnancies, miscarriages, stillbirths, the death of an infant, and finally the birth of a daughter who outlived her and went on to rule as queen in her own right. Catherine's maternal power grew over the course of her pregnancies, but diminished significantly because of Henry's stubborn insistence on a male heir. It is significant that she miscarried just a few weeks after the Battle of Flodden and that afterward her public influence at court was superseded by Thomas Wolsey. After 1513, Catherine appeared less and less often in the official record. Her father's death in 1516 was a significant factor in the decline in her exercise of public power. She had been the linchpin of Anglo-Iberian diplomacy, corresponding often with Fernando, working closely with Spanish ambassadors, and getting vital information in both whispers and diplomatic dispatches. She increasingly grew English in her orientation, and Flodden was a turning point in her relationship with her father, whose duplicitous tactics tested Catherine's loyalties. She supported the war with France, which was to the advantage of both Spain and England, but Fernando was not a reliable ally and often changed his mind. In 1516, Fernando was succeeded by his grandson Charles, who decisively changed politics in Europe and the Western world. Charles worked through his ambassadors and was not personally close to Catherine. As Spanish ambassadors and secretaries took her place, she was no longer the conduit for vital information. When Charles became emperor in 1519, the distance widened. They had many shared political interests, and he was, of course, her staunch ally against Henry in the divorce. But it is significant that her role as queen shifted from one of close adviser to Henry to one consumed with pregnancies and motherhood. The queen's pregnancies made a space for Wolsey to step into, and Catherine's virtual disappearance from the official records after 1516 is striking. Mary was born a month after the death of her grandfather, and Catherine was pregnant once more in 1517 and miscarried again. In the same year, she performed a public act of intercession during the Evil May Day riots, when London apprentices protested foreign workers. She appeared on the scene with her two sisters-in-law, Mary and Margaret, and they successfully begged Henry and Cardinal Wolsey to show mercy. But she makes few appearances in the official records until 1520, when she and Henry go to France for the Field of the Cloth of Gold. Even as Catherine's power waxed and waned relative to the patriarchal power held by her husband, she was never passive and hardly powerless. It was the character of her job that changed, from political to maternal and dynastic.

Regarding Catherine as Isabel of Castile's daughter and Elizabeth of York's daughter-in-law provides a richer understanding of what it meant to be a queen consort to a very difficult man. We see how she learned to be queen, how cultural and personal experiences informed decisions that affected both her family and the realm. When we adjust our sightlines and see her not exclusively through the eyes of men but also the sensibilities of women, we see her more on her own terms. We see her as essential to the public and private aspects of monarchy and governance, and we witness a complex practice of queenship that balanced duty, maternity, honor, humility, experience, and intellect with the harsh realities of factional politics and masculine notions of dynasty.

In the fourth portrait, Catherine is thirty-five, with no more pregnancies and no son. Her husband has turned his affections to other women from her household, but she remains an important figure in diplomacy and was an important patron of artists and humanist writers who enliven her intellectually and culturally. Her political, personal, and cultural capital diminished as tensions arose in her marriage and divorce loomed. Once again, she was comforted by her friends who stood by her at court and sent messages and gifts of hope and love. Her diplomatic power, as aunt of Emperor Charles V, retained its force, as did her political networks. Her marital power decreased dramatically as Henry's eyes wandered to other women: to Elizabeth Blount, who bore him a son, to Mary Boleyn, and then to Mary's sister, Anne. With a dignified show of dynastic, marital, and maternal power, she resisted Henry's actions.

During the end of this period in her life, Catherine expressed her power as queen as both mother and powerful foe as she pushed against her husband's efforts to divorce her and delegitimize the marriage and her daughter. Her resistance is best understood not as the action of a powerless women but as a countervailing form of power, in which "where there is power, there is resistance."[3] Catherine tenaciously summoned her intellect, her allies, and her body to resist Henry's actions. She used a variety of strategies, but her still considerable diplomatic power is most evident in the divorce, when the church's high estimation of her coupled with her relationship with Emperor Charles V to create a formidable wall of resistance. The fact that ultimately these efforts failed does not change the fact that she exerted considerable power.

The interplay of power and resistance in the dynamic relationship of Catherine and Henry reveals important nuances of power, even when it is more illusory than evident. The reciprocal power of push and pushback between Catherine and Henry is the defining characteristic of the 1520s. When she was ignored, first privately and then publicly, she resisted. She defied Henry, Wolsey, and Cromwell as they sought a divorce and then a break with Rome. The diplomatic records of the Spanish ambassadors can be read as pathos, if power is considered only as an active, public coercive force. But read with the power of resistance in mind, a different narrative emerges. She is neither still nor silent. She is strategic, confident, and assertive as she pushes back with the voice of a woman raised to be queen.

Thinking of Catherine's power as an expression of resistance, not submission, allows us to grasp a fuller dimension of Catherine's power. This is a departure from most political theorists and political historians of the Middle Ages, who consider coercion and dominance as the hallmarks of power, with the experience of power as its converse, powerlessness. But seeing Catherine in this way illuminates the fluctuations of power in both kind and degree and allows a better understanding of Catherine as queen and the nature of gender in monarchy in general.

Catherine's life is often narrated from the perspective of her death, but, as the fifth portrait shows, her tragic end does not mean her life was a tragedy. In the final period of her life, from 1532 to 1536, Catherine's resistance was powerful indeed, even as it ultimately failed. Henry usurped the narrative as he resisted her to keep her from spoiling his marriage to Anne. Catherine's religious power sustained her as she was shunned and banished from court, and her pious charisma served as a rallying point for Henry's disaffected Catholic subjects. For a few years, her force matches his. Instead of mustering troops, she mustered the support of the papacy. She eloquently and passionately addressed the English lords and the papal legate, and then was shoved aside and packed off to country houses, far away from Richmond. Catherine's power was embedded in the potential for damage to her husband and the threat of further damage to his reputation. The lengths to which Henry went to keep Catherine from her daughter are witness to the queen's power, even at her most vulnerable. Henry ultimately was stymied by the very real power she possessed even as she was confined at Kimbolton Castle. Like other high-value women who were held for long periods of time and kept but not killed, Catherine had economic, social, and political value, and this value signified power.[4] Her natal family ruled most of the Western world and had a tight bond with the pope, and this was an incalculably potent power. As a hostage, which Catherine was although Henry and his officials never used the term, she embodied the precarious relationship of power and vulnerability. She posed a potential threat to Henry, and he clearly sensed that she was more threatening than vulnerable, that her power was potentially damaging to him because it posed a serious threat to his reputation.

In the end, all that remained was her forceful resistance to Henry's efforts to divorce her. Catherine at this point seems weak, desperate, powerless, noisily protesting but eventually submitting to the will of a bully. But her resistance was formidable; she challenged him publicly at the divorce proceedings, and in fact Henry feared her, worried that her powerful Habsburg family and Spanish allies, supported by the pope, would attack England. Henry feared her potential to summon armed allies, to bring down the wrath of a powerful cadre of Catholic nobles enraged by his actions. He tried to limit her access to friends, who lied and pounded on doors to get to her as she was on her deathbed.

Her inability to outmaneuver Henry was a sign of his superior monarchical power, not of her powerlessness. She was simply outmatched. During the last years of her life, she was a formidable foe who used all the resources she had, but they simply were not enough. She refused to compromise her royal birthright, the legality of her marriage, and the integrity of her daughter to please her husband. But the tragic end is often the part of Catherine's life that receives the most attention, and it tends to be suffused with pathos and tinged with the inevitable—the divorce and all the political wrangling to restore some semblance of order, Henry's marriage to Anne Boleyn, and the birth of Elizabeth.

Catherine's life as a queen has much to say more broadly about power. Because of the shifts over the course of a woman's life, and because historically her power was ultimately dependent on the men in her life, we commonly associate public power with men and personal agency with women. But this muddles our understanding of both agency and power. Agency is usually, if not always, the ability to act and make choices that affect only one's self, but these choices can have a wide impact. Power is not simply a coercive force—one person making another bow down to them—it also intrinsically includes much more—potential, dynastic, maternal, political, influential, diplomatic—than simply a coercive force. And, as Catherine knew well, there is power in resistance. Such expansive and dynamic aspects of power are available to the study of all ranks of people who historically have less access to the tools that allow one to act powerfully in the traditional sense.

Catherine's composed demeanor and assertive voice have been muffled by Henry and drowned out by the narrative of her life as essentially that of a tragic, pathetic, embittered powerless victim. This explains, I think, why she has for so long been neglected as a subject of queenship. Yet the fact remains that she forced Henry to make difficult decisions. She did not retreat to a nunnery. Catherine's very real, very potent pushback, recorded through her laments about Henry's infidelities and the papal envoys who pleaded her case, reveals very real power. Over the course of her life, she was in and out of royal favor while Henry did everything he could to limit her power. Her refusal to relent is a weapon of a weakened but still powerful woman. Until the day of her death, Henry so feared Catherine that he refused to allow even her closest female friends access to her at Kimbolton Castle. They nearly had to break down the door to get to her. Henry's fear of her was his resistance to a powerful woman. In all its forms, her power waxed and waned, but it was exercised by a woman with a a deep intellect guided by a moral compass and informed by decades of experience, influence, and charisma.

When we peer beneath the surface of political events dominated by Henry's desire and actions and thicken the narrative with objects as our sources, we see that Catherine's life was rich and surprising and often filled with joy. It began with fifteen years of traveling across Spain, which fashioned her identity as a Spanish *infanta* whose marriage to an English prince was settled when she was three years old. The Spain she saw, heard, smelled, tasted, and touched shaped her intellect and her understanding of her place in the world. Her aesthetic taste matured into meaningful social practices that are evident throughout her life, not just in Spain, but in England, too. She wore hooped skirts and her *chapines* until she died. An inventory of her possessions taken on 14 February 1536, just a few weeks after her death, noted seven pairs of shoes "of the Spanysshe fashion, corked and garnysshid with golde."[5] Her Spanish cork-soled shoes, covered in a luxurious fabric and garnished with gold trim, are the visual symbols of her Spanish travels. Her personal identity and her fashion sense were shaped during her childhood in Medina del Campo and Granada, crafted in Valencia and Madrid, and brought with her to London along with Spanish blackstitch embroidery, books, and a pomegranate for an emblem. Her ideas on queenship were shaped by her Castilian mother and English mother-in-law and are reflected in everything she did after her marriage to Henry.

These five portraits reveal a dynamic queen who rolled and tumbled with the events of a tumultuous life. Some of this can be read in chronicles and official letters and papers, but the array of objects she left behind gives a glimpse of her identity. Catherine's image as queen was defined and spread through heraldic devices, literary odes and book dedications, allegorical performances at pageants, festivals, performances at court, and royal progresses through the countryside. Across England and Wales, architectural remnants of Catherine's arms and pomegranates serve as potent symbols of Catherine and pre-Reformation piety: Arthur's tomb in the chantry, Worcester Cathedral; Saint Gwenog's Church, Llanwenog (near Llanybydder, Ceredigion, Wales); prebendal choir stalls at Saint David's Cathedral (Pembrokeshire); oak wall panels from Waltham Abbey (Essex); an oak panel, perhaps from Windsor Castle; a painted roof in the Tudor Chapel at Ightham Mote; and even a modest carved-oak ceiling fragment.[6]

This constellation of objects composes her life and bridges the distance of five centuries so we can see Catherine more clearly and fully as she lived her life. They allow us to see her more directly. Embroidering with the women in her household and composing and signing a letter to her daughter allow us to see the emotional meanings of the psychological grief, terror, humiliation, and trauma of her later life. These objects are more than props for ceremonies or signifiers of status that mark betrothals, weddings, births, deaths, and diplomatic events. Shoes and shards of napkins allow us to recover a sense of who she was and who mattered to her.

ABBREVIATIONS

AGS	Archivo General de Simancas, Valladolid
CSP Milan	*Calendar of State Papers, Milan I (1385–1618)*. Edited by Allen B. Hinds. London: His Majesty's Stationery Office, London, 1912.
CSP Spain 1	*Calendar of State Papers, Spain*. Vol. 1, *1485–1509*. Edited by G. A. Bergenroth. London: Her Majesty's Stationery Office, 1862.
CSP Spain 2	*Calendar of State Papers, Spain*. Vol. 2, *1509–1525*. Edited by G. A. Bergenroth. London: Her Majesty's Stationery Office, 1866.
CSP Spain 3.2	*Calendar of State Papers, Spain*. Vol. 3, part 2, *1527–1529*. Edited by Pascual de Gayangos. London: Her Majesty's Stationery Office, 1877.
CSP Spain 4.1	*Calendar of State Papers, Spain*. Vol. 4, part 1, *Henry VIII, 1529–1530*. Edited by Pascual de Gayangos. London: Her Majesty's Stationery Office, 1879.
CSP Spain 4.2	*Calendar of State Papers, Spain*. Vol. 4, part 2, *Henry VIII, 1531–1533*. Edited by Pascual de Gayangos. London: Her Majesty's Stationery Office, 1882.
CSP Spain 5.2	*Calendar of State Papers, Spain*. Vol. 5, part 2, *1536–1538*. Edited by Pascual de Gayangos. London: Her Majesty's Stationery Office, 1888.
CSP Spain Supp 1	*Calendar of State Papers, Spanish, Supplement to Vols. 1 and 2*. Edited by G. A. Bergenroth. London: Longmans, 1868.
CSP Venice	*Calendar of State Papers, Venice*. Edited by Rawdon Brown. 38 vols. London: Longman, 1864.
L&P Henry VIII	*Letters and Papers, Foreign and Domestic of the Reign of Henry VIII, 1509–1547*. Edited by J. S. Brewer, James Gairdner, and R. H. Brodie. 21 vols. London: Her Majesty's Stationery Office, 1870.
TNA	The National Archives, Kew

CHAPTER I

The epigraph to this chapter is from
Vincent van Gogh, letter to Theo van
Gogh, July 1880. Translated by Johanna van
Gogh-Bonger, edited by Robert Harrison, #
133; http://webexhibits.org/vangogh/letter/8
/133.htm.

1. Earenfight, "Shoes of an *Infanta*."

2. Hall, *Hall's Chronicle*, 493–94,
507–13, 516–19, 539, 584, 667, 728, 782,
794–95, 814–15, 818.

3. Mattingly, *Catherine of Aragon*;
Tremlett, *Catherine of Aragon*; Williams,
Katharine of Aragon. Antonia Fraser and
David Starkey consider Catherine not on
her own, but rather as one of the six wives
of Henry VIII. Fraser, *Wives of Henry VIII*;
Starkey, *Six Wives*.

4. Luke, *Catherine, the Queen*;
Claremont, *Catherine of Aragon*; Weir,
Katherine of Aragon; Gregory, *Three Sisters,
Three Queens*.

5. Two autograph letters by Catherine
that were owned by a manuscript collector,
Alfred Morrison, recently were sold at
auction (one at Sotheby's in New York, the
other at Ader in Paris). Both autograph
letters, which regard the divorce, are written
in Spanish, in a scribal secretarial hand, and
signed by Catherine, and were sent to her
nephew, the emperor Charles V (3 October
1529, 22 February 1531). The letter sold at
Sotheby's is now in the manuscript
collection of the Morgan Library in New
York City (MA 6443).

6. Parr, *Katherine Parr: Complete Works*;
Mueller, "Tudor Queen Finds Voice"; King,
"Patronage and Piety."

7. "Horæ B. Mariæ, Virginis et
Officia," ca. 1500, London, British Library,
Add Ms 17012, ca. 1500; Carley, *Books of
Henry VIII*, 109.

8. Alphonsus de Villa Sancta, *Problema
indulgentiarum aduersus Lutherum*, 1523,
London, British Library, C.47.g.2; Carley,
Books of Henry VIII, 115.

9. Woolf, "Feminine Past"; Hall, *Hall's
Chronicle*.

10. Hillgarth, *Mirror of Spain*.

11. Travitsky, "Reprinting Tudor
History"; Appleford, "Shakespeare's
Katherine of Aragon"; Meyer, "Politics of
Queenship"; Meyer, "Richard III's
Forelives"; Hansen, "'And a Queen of
England, Too'"; Ziegler, "Re-Imagining a
Renaissance Queen."

12. Elston, "Almost the Perfect Woman";
Elston, "Transformation or Continuity";
Elston, "Widow Princess or Neglected
Queen"

13. Beer, *Queenship*; Beer, "Between
Kings and Emperors"; Beer, "Queenly
Affinity"

14. Mattingly, *Catherine of Aragon*,
441–43.

15. New York, Morgan Library and
Museum, Literary and Historical Manu-
scripts (LHMS), Rulers of England Box 02,
Henry VIII, no. 29, record ID# MA 6443.

16. *L&P Henry VIII* 5, item 112.

17. Domínguez Casas, "Artistic
Patronage of Isabel the Catholic."

18. Hand and Koppel, *Michel Sittow*.

19. Beaven and Eichberger, "Family
Members and Political Allies," 236–37.

20. Dolman, "Wishful Thinking."

21. Matthews, "Henry VIII's Favorite
Sister"

22. On 30 June 1514, Gerard de Pleine,
ambassador to Marguerite of Austria, noted
that "the painter has made a good likeness
of Mary [sister of Henry VIII]," but he does
not identify the painter. *L&P Henry VIII* 1,
item 3041.

23. For example, *Madonna and Child*,
ca. 1515–18 (Berlin); *Portrait of a Woman*,
early sixteenth century (Vienna); and
various figures in *Saint James the Great and
the Virgin and Child*, ca. 1520 (Tallinn). In
Hand and Koppel, *Michel Sittow*, 78–82,
100–101, 110–12; Hepburn, "Portraiture."

24. Dugan and Farina, "Intimate
Senses / Sensing Intimacy."

25. Howes, "Cultural Life of the Senses,"
452.

26. Weniger, "Michel Sittow," 36.

27. "Inventory of the Wardrobes," 39.

28. Johnston and Woolley, *Shoes*, 10–13.

29. For a discussion of the theoretical framework for using inventories, see Smail, *Legal Plunder*, 3–19.

30. Hamilton and Proctor-Tiffany, "Women and the Circulation"; Proctor-Tiffany, *Medieval Art in Motion*; Stanton, "Personal Geography"; Keane, *Material Culture and Queenship*; Keane, "Moving Possessions and Secure Posthumous Reputation."

31. Proctor-Tiffany, *Medieval Art in Motion*, 6–13.

32. Smail, *Legal Plunder*, 9; Jurkowlaniec, Matyjaszkiewicz, and Sarnecka, *Agency of Things*, 3–14.

33. Bedos-Rezak, "Mutually Contextual"; Smith, "Premodern Sexualities."

34. For example, a wooden trencher in the Victoria and Albert Museum, London (inv. # 702B-1891) has been dated to the sixteenth century, but it could have belonged to anyone.

35. For the Isabelline court in Spain, see Fernández de Córdova Miralles, *La Corte de Isabel I*.

36. *L&P Henry VIII* 10, item 141.

37. *Privy Purse Expenses of Elizabeth of York*; Okerlund, *Elizabeth of York*; Harris, *English Aristocratic Women*.

38. Hamling and Richardson, *Everyday Objects*; French, "Genders and Material Culture"; Gerritsen and Riello, "Introduction: Writing Material Culture History"; Adams and Bradbury, *Medieval Women and Their Objects*; Garver, "Material Culture and Social History"; Miller, *Cultural Histories*, 1–29.

39. Bedos-Rezak, "Medieval Identity."

40. Overbey, "Materiality and Place"; Wicker, "Gold in Motion"; Appudurai, *Social Life of Things*.

41. Martin, "Margin to Act."

42. Weiner, *Inalienable Possessions*, 36–38.

43. Kelly, "In the Sight of an Old Pair of Shoes."

44. De Certeau, *Practice of Everyday Life*, 21.

45. Stanton, "Personal Geography," 206.

46. Miller, *Cultural Histories of the Material World*, 1–29.

CHAPTER 2

The epigraph to this chapter is from F. Bermúdez de Pedraza (1638), quoted in Fernández de Córdova Miralles, *Corte de Isabel I*, 79.

1. Proctor-Tiffany, *Medieval Art in Motion*; Hamilton and Proctor-Tiffany, *Moving Women Moving Objects*, 1–12.

2. Fuchs, *Exotic Nation*.

3. Liss, *Isabel the Queen*, 235; Ruiz, *King Travels*, 298–304.

4. *Cuentas*, 1:115–16. A *maravedí* was originally a silver or gold coin, akin to the gold *dinar*, with a value in 1.91 grams of silver in 1303. By 1500, the *maravedí* was only a unit of account that did not circulate. Martz, *Poverty and Welfare*, xvii.

5. Pulgar, *Crónica*, 2:226.

6. Liss, *Isabel the Queen*, 236–41.

7. Rumeu de Armas, *Itinerario de los Reyes Católicos*.

8. Pulgar, *Crónica*; Valera, *Crónica de los Reyes Católicos*; Bernáldez, *Memorias*.

9. Liss, *Isabel the Queen*, 296.

10. Fernández de Córdova Miralles, *Corte de Isabel I*, 79.

11. *Cuentas*, 1:238. In 1492, it cost 206,886 *maravedíes* to move Juan, María, and Catalina, plus Juana's officials and their wives. *Cuentas*, 2:21–22.

12. Fernández de Córdova Miralles, *Corte de Isabel I*, 17–40.

13. Ibid., 160–67; *Cuentas*, 1:403–4 (30 July 1491).

14. Gómez Molleda, "Cultura feminina."

15. Weiss, "What Every Noblewoman Needs to Know."

16. Muñoz Fernández, "Notas para la definición"; Surtz, "In Search of Juana de Mendoza."

17. Fernández de Córdova Miralles, *Corte de Isabel I*, 162. The other twelve ladies at court are not known.

18. *Cuentas*, 2:457–58 (10 March 1501).

19. For example, the household accounts of Isabel note several other women who served Catalina just before she left for England. Juana de Murcia ("moça de camara de la prinçesa de Galis") received payment in clothing, and Isabel de Barboa ("guarda de las damas de la ylustrisima princesa de Galis") was paid "para unas angarillas de su mula." *Cuentas*, 2:531 (9 October 1501), 2:583 (2 May 1502).

20. *Cuentas*, 2:308.

21. Ibid., 2:400, 412 (23 March 1495); 2:585. On 20 October 1500, she received 25,000 *maravedíes* "de quitaction," but this was in fact a payment for 1498: "para ayuda de su costa del dicho año pasado, que no heran pagados, a cabsa por donde se le avian de pagar se perdio," 408. She received two payments in 1501 for prior years; see *Cuentas*, 2:457–58, 511–15; 573–75 (23 September 1502). On 2 October 1503, she was paid 44,000 *maravedíes* for eight months of 1503 and 66,000 *maravedíes* for 1502; *Cuentas*, 2:612.

22. *Cuentas*, 2:367 (20 November 1497).

23. Fernández de Córdova Miralles, *Corte de Isabel I*, 425–26 (15 January 1499).

24. *Cuentas*, 2:471 (10 February 1500).

25. Fernández de Córdova Miralles, *Corte de Isabel I*, 144–60.

26. *Cuentas*, 2:408, 457–58, 535. On 26 November 1503, Juana de Porras was paid 6,000 *maravedíes* for all of 1503 until the end of December; *Cuentas*, 2:613.

27. Fernández de Córdova Miralles, *Corte de Isabel I*, 166–67.

28. *Cuentas*, 2:630 (20 December 1504). Inés Vanegas, the mother of Teresa and Inés, had died before September 1504, and the money was designated to her heirs; *Cuentas*, 2:654–57.

29. *Cuentas*, 1:157–58.

30. Liss, *Isabel the Queen*, 248–50.

31. Pulgar, *Crónica*, 341–60, quote on 359; *Cuentas*, 1:203–6 and 256–58; Liss, *Isabel the Queen*, 241–47. For detailed descriptions of the garments, see Anderson, *Hispanic Costume*, 200–203.

32. Cahill Marrón, "Alianza castellano-inglesa"; Cahill Marrón, "Catalina, la esperada Princesa de Gales."

33. One of the English emissaries estimated that the jewels displayed by Isabel on that occasion were worth 200,000 gold crowns. Machado, *Journals of Roger Machado*, 170–84; Cahill Marrón, "Influencia de la joyería"; Anderson, *Hispanic Costume*, 135.

34. *CSP Spain 1*, item 34.

35. Rubin, *Isabella of Castile*, 262.

36. Liss, *Isabel the Queen*, 249.

37. Pulgar, *Crónica*, 363, 418; Ruiz, *King Travels*, 305–7; Liss, *Isabel the Queen*, 247–53, 321.

38. Ruggles, "Alcázar of Seville."

39. Val Valdivieso, "Educación en la corte"; Val Valdivieso, "Isabel la Católica y la educación"; Surtz, "In Search of Juana de Mendoza."

40. *Cuentas*, 2:120, 125, 206, 263, 340, 378, 420–22, 455, 653. See also Earenfight, "Regarding Catherine of Aragon"; Val Valdivieso, "Isabel la Católica y la educación"; Val Valdivieso, "Educación en la corte."

41. *Cuentas*, 2:332–33.

42. Museo del Prado, Madrid (inventory nos. P000618, P000609).

43. Domínguez Casas, "Casas de las Reinas hispano-portuguesas"; Knighton, "Isabel of Castile and Her Music Books"; Ros-Fábregas, "Melodies for Private Devotion."

44. Dronzek, "Gendered Theories of Education"; Cadden, *Meanings of Sex Difference*, 21–26.

45. Elston, "Transformation or Continuity"; Elston, "Almost the Perfect Woman," 40; Aram, *Juana the Mad*, 23; Silleras Fernández, *Chariots of Ladies*; Viera, "Francesc Eiximenis on Women."

46. Francomano, *Three Spanish "Querelle" Texts*, 51.

47. *CSP Spain 1*, item 185.

48. Aram, *Juana the Mad*, 24–27; Liss, *Isabel the Queen*, 286.

49. Earenfight, "Raising *Infanta* Catalina de Aragón."

50. Bernáldez, *Memorias*, 215–15; *Cuentas*, 1:381–83.

51. Pulgar, *Crónica*, 437–44; Liss, *Isabel the Queen*, 253–55.

52. Münzer, *Viaje por España y Portugal*, 93–97, 103, 127.

53. Ruggles, *Gardens, Landscape, and Vision.*

54. Johnston, "Catherine of Aragon's Pomegranate."

55. Bernáldez, *Memorias*, 223; Liss, *Isabel the Queen*, 255–63, 282–86, 324–27, 353.

56. Earenfight, "Raising *Infanta* Catalina"; Bernáldez, *Memorias*, 659–62; Liss, *Isabel the Queen*, 256–58.

57. Museo del Prado, Madrid (inventory nos. P007135, P002693).

58. Nickson, *Toledo Cathedral.*

59. Museo Arqueológico Nacional, Madrid, inventory nos. 663, 52340, 52092.

60. Fernando and Isabel played an important role in the development of Hispano-Flemish art, particularly portraiture. As patrons to both Juan de Flandes and Michel Sittow they were astutely aware of the importance of their image. They had their portraits included in religious works such as the celebrated "Virgin of the Catholic Kings" (Madrid), and in others such as the panels of Fernando the Catholic (Vienna) and Isabel the Catholic (Madrid). Domínguez Casas, "Artistic Patronage of Isabel the Catholic"; Ishikawa, "*Llave de palo*"; Brans, *Isabel la Católica*; Sánchez Cantón, *Libros, Tapices y Cuadros.*

61. Liss, *Isabel the Queen*, 354–62.

62. Museo Arqueológico Nacional, Madrid, inventory no. 51717.

63. Caballero Escamilla, "*Virgen de los Reyes Católicos.*"

64. Ishikawa, *Retablo de Isabel la Católica*, 46–48; Silva Maroto, *Juan de Flandes*; Weiss, "Juan de Flandes"; Weiss, "Isabel of Castile, Flemish Aesthetics."

65. Hand and Koppel, *Michel Sittow*; Knighton, "Northern Influence."

66. *CSP Spain 1*, item 127; Gairdner, *Memorials of King Henry the Seventh*, 349–51.

67. Anderson, *Hispanic Costume*, 201; Bernis Madrazo, *Indumentaria medieval Española*, 35–53.

68. Ruiz, *King Travels*, 19.

69. *CSP Spain 1*, item 202.

70. Eichenberger, "Margareta of Austria."

71. Fernández de Córdova Miralles, *Corte de Isabel I*, 307, 321; Bernáldez, *Memorias*, 393; Liss, *Isabel the Queen*, 365–75.

72. *Rymer's Foedera* 12:721–36, 756–62 (July–December 1499); *CSP Spain 1*, items 241–48.

73. British Library, Egerton MS 626, fol. 10, 5 October 1499; transcribed in Wood, *Letters*, 1:121–22.

74. *Receyt.*

75. Hamilton and Proctor-Tiffany, "Women and the Circulation," 12.

CHAPTER 3

1. *CSP Spain 1*, items 296–302, 304–6 (1501).

2. Liss, *Isabel the Queen*, 381.

3. Museo Arqueológico Nacional, Madrid (inventory no. 1968/36/1; 1968/51/1); both dated to the fifteenth century.

4. Museo Arqueológico Nacional, Madrid (inventory no. 52207, fifteenth century, 16 × 12 inches).

5. See, for example, in the Museo Arqueológico Nacional, Madrid: a large fifteenth-century *arca* (inventory no. 57882) and a sixteenth-century Florentine *arca de esponsales* (inventory no. 51936).

6. Victoria and Albert Museum, London (inventory nos. 7224–1860 and 7223–1860).

7. *Cuentas*, 2:449; see, for example, Museo Arqueológico Nacional, Madrid (inventory no. 1968/29/1, fifteenth century, 49 × 31.5 × 31.5 inches).

8. Victoria and Albert Museum, London. Unknown potter, lustreware bowl,

Manises (Spain), before 1458, height, 11.2 cm, diameter: 50.9 cm (inventory no. 243–1853).

9. *Cuentas*, 2:535 (22 January 1501).

10. Anderson, *Hispanic Costume*, 114, 200, 208–9; Marino, "How Portuguese Damas Scandalized."

11. *Cuentas*, 2:425–26, 465–66, 470, 480, 487, 498, 520, 525.

12. Colomer, "Black and the Royal Image"; Lambert and Wilson, *Europe's Rich Fabric*; Monnas, *Merchants, Princes, and Painters*; Monnas, *Renaissance Velvets*.

13. Wunder, "Women's Fashions and Politics"; Anderson, *Hispanic Costume*, 34.

14. *Cuentas*, 1:368–80; 2:506, 527.

15. See fig. 1. See also Semmelhack, "Above the Rest"; Semmelhack, "Reveal or Conceal"; Anderson, "Chapín."

16. Anderson, *Hispanic Costume*, 225–29; Semmelhack, *On a Pedestal*, 26.

17. Semmelhack, "Above the Rest," 139.

18. Anderson, *Hispanic Costume*, 229–35; Carrión, "Balcony of the Chapín"; Cristo González Marrero, "Calzado y su manufactura"; Cristo González Marrero, "Vestido."

19. Anderson, "Chapín," 36–37.

20. *Cuentas*, 1:368–70, 506 (for 1497 and 1501); Cristo González Marrero, "Calzado y su manufactura," 104–5.

21. Fernández de Oviedo, *Libro de la cámara*, 60.

22. Men wore a cork-soled shoe that had a much lower platform than those of women. Anderson, "Chapín," 35–38; Anderson, *Hispanic Costume*, 81.

23. Fernández de Oviedo, *Libro de la cámara*, 60; Hayward, "Gift Giving at the Court."

24. Anderson, *Hispanic Costume*, 225, 263.

25. Riello and MacNeil, *Shoes*, 3.

26. Barthes, *Fashion System*, x–xii; Bourdieu, *Distinction*.

27. Bernáldez, *Memorias*, 394–95; Liss, *Isabel the Queen*, 381. Baeza recorded expenses for moving Catalina from Madrid to Segovia; see *Cuentas*, 2:535, 623.

28. *Receyt*, 45–46, 59.

29. Elvira Manuel de Villena Suárez de Figueroa was the daughter of Juan Manuel, lord of Belmonte de Campos, and Aldonza Suárez de Figueroa. *Receyt*, 46, 59. On 10 March 1501, she was paid 100,000 *maravedíes* for her service. *Cuentas*, 2:457–58.

30. Their salaries for 1501 are noted in *Cuentas*, 2:545–47, 513–15, 585.

31. In 1508, Francesca de Caceres married Francesco Grimaldi, who was one of the two Italian bankers who handled the payment of Catherine's dowry; see González Arévalo, "Francesco Grimaldi." Cecile Goff speculated that María de Rojas, daughter of Francesco de Rojas, count de Salinas, and María de Salinas were related and that when María de Rojas returned to Spain ca. 1504, María de Salinas replaced her at Catherine's court; see *Woman of the Tudor Age*, 3–4. María de Salinas was the daughter of Martín de Salinas and Josefa Gonzales de Salas. Portilla, "Vitoriano." For what little is known of María de Salazar, see Wood, *Letters*, 1:126.

32. Wood, *Letters*, 1:160, 203, note b; *Cuentas*, 2:535.

33. *CSP Spain 1*, items 246, 258, 261–62, 304.

34. Bernáldez, *Memorias*, 394.

35. *CSP Spain 1*, items 304–5; *Receyt*, 4–5.

36. *Receyt*, 6–7.

37. *CSP Spain 1*, item 293 (1501).

38. Letter to John Paston, in *Paston Letters*, 6:161.

39. TNA E 101/415/3; *Receyt*, 31.

40. *Receyt*, 49.

41. Coldstream, "Roles of Women."

42. Okerlund, *Elizabeth of York*, 154.

43. *Receyt*, 8. The exact sources of the author of *The Receyt* are not known, but his detailed description of the events suggest that he was a Londoner of elite status with a close knowledge of the topography of the city, the people in power, the inhabitants, and both local and royal customs.

44. Jones and Underwood, *King's Mother*, 161, 166.

45. *Receyt*, 38.

46. Coldstream, "Roles of Women," 179.

47. Hentschell, "Question of Nation." On the influence of Islamicate fashion on Castilian royal fashion, see Fuchs, *Exotic Nation*, 60–72, 94–99; More, *Correspondence of Sir Thomas More*, 4.

48. Heng, *Invention of Race*, 75–96.

49. *Receyt*; Kipling, *Enter the King*, 209–21; Anglo, "London Pageants."

50. Heal, *Power of Gifts*, 107; Lancashire, *London Civic Theatre*, 132.

51. *Receyt*, 12–33.

52. Ibid., 32.

53. Hayward, *Dress at the Court*, 158–67, 170–74; Hayward, "Spanish Princess or Queen of England," 18–20.

54. *Receyt*, 33; Classen, "Spain and Germany," 395–406.

55. *Receyt*, 33–38.

56. Pierce, *Margaret Pole*.

57. *Receyt*, 41–44; Haywood, "Princess and the Unicorn."

58. *Receyt*, 43.

59. *Cuentas*, 2:487; Bernis Madrazo, *Indumentaria medieval Española*, 35–53; Bernis Madrazo, "Modas moriscas."

60. Hayward, *Dress at the Court*, 165.

61. The fabric for her dress may be the "3.5 varas [roughly one yard] of white sateen" paid for on 24 March 1501 in the *Cuentas*, 2:520.

62. Marino, "How Portuguese Damas Scandalized," 208–9.

63. Hayward, "Spanish Princess or Queen of England," 19.

64. *Receyt*, 47.

65. Ibid.

66. *CSP Spain 1*, items 246 and 4, item 572; Tremlett, *Catherine of Aragon*, 89, citing Real Academia de Historia, MS 9-4674 (Veruela); Tremlett's transcript and Spanish translation.

67. Kane, *Popular Memory and Gender*.

68. *L&P Henry VIII 4*, item 5774, citing British Library MS Cotton Vitelius B. XII, fols. 70, 80, and 85. Hall, *Hall's Chronicle*, 494.

69. *CSP Spain 1*, item 210, Ambassador Pedro de Ayala, to Ferdinand and Isabella (25 July 1498).

70. Cunningham, *Prince Arthur*, 148–60; Arthurson, "'King of Spain's Daughter.'"

71. *Receyt*, 49.

72. Ibid., 60–79.

73. Carley, *Books of King Henry VIII*, 109.

74. *Receyt*, 60–79.

75. Heal, *Power of Gifts*, 87–97.

76. Carley, *Libraries of King Henry VIII*, 50, 53, 59, 68, 94, 97, 110–11, 163, 204.

77. *CSP Spain Supp 1*, item 1.

78. For payments to carters, see *Chamber Books*, fol. 73; Pierce, *Margaret Pole*, 28–34.

79. Burton, *History of Bewdely*, 31–35.

80. There are scattered references to food imported from Spain in *Privy Purse Expenses of King Henry the Eighth*, 71, 80, 92, 95, 105, 108–10, 117, 141, 152, 171–72, 181, 193, 203, 258, 279; *Chamber Books*, BL Add MS 7099 fol. 73 and E101/415/3 fol. 83v.

81. Woolgar, Serjeantson, and Waldron, *Food in Medieval England*; Wilson, "Evolution of the Banquet Course"; Lloyd, "Dietary Advice and Fruit-Eating."

82. Liss, *Isabel the Queen*, 381–82.

83. Okerlund, *Elizabeth of York*, 185.

84. *L&P Henry VIII 7*, item 128, record of the testimony of Margaret Clorke, 31 January 1534. British Library Yelverton, MS. 12, fol. 81.

85. The ambassadors reported that they "have heard that the Princess of Wales is suffering. She must be removed, without loss of time, from the unhealthy place where she now is" (12 May). *CSP Spain 1*, items 317–20 (10–21 May 1502); Simancas, Archivo General, Estado, Tratados con Inglaterra, caja 1, legajo 4, fol 24.

86. *CSP Spain 4.1*, items 573, 577.

87. Hall, *Hall's Chronicle*, 497.

88. *Receyt*, 87.

89. *Cuentas*, 2:545–47.

90. Laynesmith, *Last Medieval Queens*, 211; Cunningham, *Prince Arthur*, 178–92.

91. For the archaeology of Durham House, see Schofield, *London, 1100–1600*; Schofield, *Medieval London Houses*; Wheatley, "Original Plan of Durham House."

92. *Privy Purse Expenses of Elizabeth of York*, 10, 14, 43, 48, 54, 60–61, 66, 69, 74, 89, 93, 94, 103; Okerlund, *Elizabeth of York*, 113, 194.

93. Earenfight, "Precarious Household."

94. Wood, *Letters*, 1:126–54.

95. *Chamber Books*, E36/210 fol. 52; Okerlund, *Elizabeth of York*, 113, 194.

96. *Cuentas*, 2:630, 652, 655; Fernández de Córdova Miralles, *Corte de Isabel I*, 164–67.

97. *Cuentas*, 2:655.

98. Liss, *Isabel the Queen*, 383.

99. Stevens, *Music and Poetry*, 233–63.

100. Hayward, *Dress at the Court*, 168–69.

101. Jones and Stallybrass, *Renaissance Clothing*, 136, 171; Synge, *Art of Embroidery*; Mazzola, "Schooling Shrews and Grooming Queens," 12.

102. Jones and Stallybrass, *Renaissance Clothing*, 116–21.

103. James, *Feminine Dynamic in English Art*, 88; Frye, *Pens and Needles*, 1–29, 77, 116–21.

104. Harris, "View from My Lady's Chamber."

105. Unknown embroiderer, orphrey, ca. 1450–1500, embroidered with devices of Isabel of Castile, London, Victoria and Albert Museum, ID# 271-1880. Isabel paid Fernando de la Cuevas Rubias and Juan de la Vega for embroidery. It is unlikely that they did the needlework themselves; rather, they would have employed female embroiderers. See *Cuentas*, 2:309, 312.

106. Hans Holbein, portrait of Jane Seymour, ca. 1536, oil on wood, Vienna Kunsthistorisches Museum, inv. no. GG 881; Hayward, *Dress at the Court*, 160.

107. Cabrera Lafuente, "Tejidos como patrimonio"; Cabrera Lafuente, "Proyecto Marie S.-Curie *Interwoven*." She examined textiles in the collection of the Victoria and Albert Museum that were originally labeled

as Sicilian, and argues that they were in fact made in Spain, such as two cushion covers (inv. # 586-1884 and inv. #230-1880).

108. Vives, *Education of a Christian Woman*, 61.

109. *CSP Spain 4.1*, item no. 354.

110. Vives, *Education of a Christian Woman*, 58.

111. Frye, *Pens and Needles*; Frye, "Sewing Connections."

112. Okerlund, *Elizabeth of York*, 113, 194, 215; *CSP Spain 1*, items 300, 398.

113. Bernáldez, *Memorias*, 695.

114. Okerlund, *Elizabeth of York*, 215ff.

115. Gairdner, *Memorials of King Henry the Seventh*, 415–16.

116. *Testamentaria de Isabel la Católica*, 73, 86.

117. Goff, *Woman of the Tudor Age*, 3–4.

118. *CSP Spain 1*, items 403–5, 407, 408.

119. Sadlack, *French Queen's Letters*, 12–13; Pierce, *Margaret Pole*, 31.

120. Wood, *Letters*, 126–54.

121. Eichenberger, "Margareta of Austria."

122. *Chronicle of the Grey Friars*, 29–53, esp. 28–29.

123. Aram, *Juana the Mad*, 82–83.

124. William Makefyrr to Roger Darcy and Giles Alyngton, 17 January 1506, in Gairdner, *Paston Letters*, 6:172–74; Monnas, *Merchants, Princes, and Painter*, 307.

125. Aram, *Juana the Mad*, 97.

126. Wood, *Letters*, 1:143–54.

127. Ibid., 1:132–33.

128. Beer, "Between Kings and Emperors."

129. *L&P Henry VIII 1*, items 38, 39.

CHAPTER 4

The epigraph to this chapter is from Diego Fernández, chancellor to King Fernando of Aragon, 25 May 1510. *CSP Spain Supp 1*, items 7, 34–36.

1. *CSP Spain 2*, items 9–10, 12–18.

2. Loades, *Mary Tudor*, 11–12.

3. Hall, *Hall's Chronicle*, 507–12; Hunt, *Drama of Coronation*, 12–39; Blair, *Crown*

Jewels, 304–6; Hayward, *Dress at the Court*, 41–45.

4. Wood, *Letters*, 1:120–64, 207, 238–39. For letters to her father, see AGS Estado, Legajo 1365.35 (6 November 1532) and Patronato, Legajo 54, Document 51 (3 November 1509). See also an autograph letter signed by her, writing from Richmond to her nephew, the emperor Charles V, on 22 February 1531 at the Morgan Library and Museum (New York), record ID# 79926, accession # MA6443.

5. Stevens, *Music and Poetry*, 238; Anglo, *Spectacle, Pageantry*, 111.

6. Stephen Hawes, *A Joyfull Medytacyon*, 1509, Cambridge, Cambridge University Library, Rare Book Sel. 5.55.

7. Carley, *Books of King Henry VIII*, 111–12.

8. For the Latin text, see Thomas More, Epigram 19, in volume 3, part 2, *Latin Poems*, 100–13.

9. Carley, *Books of Henry VIII*, 112. For another example of the twinned emblems, see British Library, Royal MS 15.D.iv, fol, 219; Hayward, "Spanish Princess or Queen of England," 17.

10. *L&P Henry VIII* 1, items 82, 128; Jones and Stallybrass, *Renaissance Clothing*, 18.

11. Pierce, *Margaret Pole*, 32.

12. Jones and Underwood, *King's Mother*, 232–49.

13. Hayward, *Dress at the Court*, 177–78.

14. Anglo, *Spectacle, Pageantry*, 116–23.

15. Trollope, "King Henry's Jewel Book."

16. Hayward, *Dress at the Court*, 276, 388, 414–16 for items A309, A762, B50, B64, B91, B107, B139, B345, B347, B394. See also Hentschell, "Question of Nation"; Hayward, "Fashion, Finance, Foreign Politics," 167, 173.

17. *L&P Henry VIII* 1, item 1549.

18. Hayward, *Dress at the Court*, 376, 382, 386, 388, 391, 414, and items A497, A498, A691, A762, A884, A885, B50.

19. Hayward, *Dress at the Court*, 376, 414–15, and items A309, B64, B91.

20. Thurley, *Royal Palaces of Tudor England*, 36, 139–41.

21. Hall, *Hall's Chronicle*, 513.

22. For other holiday revels and a record of New Year's gifts in 1519, see *L&P Henry VIII* 3, 1548–59 (Revels Miscellaneous for 1519, 1520, and 1522).

23. Gunn, *Charles Brandon*, 95.

24. The dowry was 1,100 marks. *L&P Henry VIII* 2, item 2172.

25. Goff, *Woman of the Tudor Age*, 3–8.

26. Hayward, *Dress at the Court*, 157.

27. Gunn, *Charles Brandon*, 95–96, 130, 132–33, 142.

28. Kisby, "Kingship and the Royal Itinerary"; Samman, "Progresses of Henry VIII"; Heal, *Power of Gifts*, 102–3.

29. Hayward, *Dress at the Court*, 129–33.

30. Heal, "Food Gifts"; Samman, "Progresses of Henry VIII," 65.

31. Hayward, "Spanish Princess," 25; Samman, "Progresses of Henry VIII," 61.

32. Hayward, *Dress at the Court*, 177–80; Hayward, "Spanish Princess," 20–26.

33. Cahill Marrón, "Primera aproximación," 274.

34. Only one set of accounts of her estates has survived, from 1524 to 1529, and they reveal receipts from rents, and payments for repairs on the properties, salaries to her household staff, expenses for clothing, and gifts. Beer, "Queenly Affinity," 430–31.

35. Mattingly, *Catherine of Aragon*, 139–46.

36. *CSP Venice* 2, items 86–88.

37. Buchanan, *Margaret Tudor*, 68; Goodwin, *Fatal Rivalry*; Mattingly, *Catherine of Aragon*, 147–61.

38. David-Chapy, "Political, Symbolic"; Shears, "Like Father, Like Daughter"

39. Holinshed, *Chronicles*, 1479 (pagination per Early English Books Online).

40. TNA C 82/393.

41. TNA C 54/381, m. 2d; Cunningham, "Katherine of Aragon."

42. Mattingly, *Catherine of Aragon*, 137–45.

43. TNA E 36/215, p. 267; E 101/517/23, no. 36; Cunningham, "Katherine of Aragon."

44. Hall, *Hall's Chronicle*, 545–48, 555–64.

45. *Chronicle of the Grey Friars*, 29–53.

46. *Original Letters*, 1: no. 89.

47. Finn, *Last Plantagenet Consorts*.

48. Holinshed, *Chronicles*, 1493–94.

49. Patterson, *Reading Holinshed's "Chronicles,"* 22–31.

50. *CSP Milan* 1, item 396.

51. Pietro Martire d'Anghiera, *Opus Epistolarum Petri Martyris Anglerii*, cited in *CSP Spain 2*, item 2299.

52. Cahill Marrón, "Tras la pista," 718.

53. Buchanan, *Margaret Tudor*, 83.

54. Beer, *Queenship*, 85–96.

55. Ibid., 95–96; Heal, *Hospitality*, 21.

56. Sadlack, *French Queen's Letters*, 12–13.

57. Starkey, "Court and Government"; Guy, "Wolsey and the Tudor Policy"; Mattingly, *Catherine of Aragon*, 166–69.

58. Hurren, "Cultures of the Body"; Furdell, *Royal Doctors*, 21–43.

59. Green, "From 'Diseases of Women' to 'Secrets of Women.'"

60. Scarisbrick, *Henry VIII*, 150; Chapman, *Anne Boleyn*, 41–42; Williams, *Henry VIII and His Court*, 47; Pollard, *Henry VIII*, 12; Bowle, *Henry VIII*, 159; Chamberlin, *Private Character*, 120–26.

61. Early pregnancy loss is "a nonviable, intrauterine pregnancy with either an empty gestational sac or a gestational sac containing an embryo or fetus without fetal heart activity within the first 12 6/7 weeks of gestation." American College of Obstetrics and Gynecology, "Early Pregnancy Loss," https://www.acog.org /Clinical-Guidance-and-Publications /Practice-Bulletins/Committee-on-Practice -Bulletins-Gynecology/Early-Pregnancy -Loss, accessed 29 August 2020. A stillbirth is defined as "no signs of life at or after 28 weeks' gestation." World Health Organization, "Stillbirth," https://www.who.int /maternal_child_adolescent/epidemiology

/stillbirth/en, accessed 29 August 2020. Dewhurst, "Alleged Miscarriages."

62. *L&P Henry VIII* 2, item 3802; Hayward, *Dress at the Court*, 199.

63. French, "Material Culture of Childbirth"; Brodie, "Marking and Memory," 197–99.

64. Hayward, *Dress at the Court*, 167–68.

65. "Inventory of the Wardrobes," 40.

66. L'Estrange, *Holy Motherhood*, 25–75.

67. Morrison, *Women Pilgrims*, 27–28; Beer, "Queenly Affinity."

68. Dickinson, *Shrine of Our Lady at Walsingham*, 42–44, 55–56, 141.

69. "This famous Image, however, upon the change of belief was taken from Walsingham to Chelsea, near London, and there burnt in the 30th of Henry VIII [1539]." Dugdale, *Monasticon anglicanum*, vol. 6, pt. 1, 71. See also Erasmus, *Pilgrimages to Saint Mary of Walsingham*, 11–39.

70. French, "Material Culture of Childbirth," 130.

71. *CSP Spain 2*, item 23.

72. Hayward, *Great Wardrobe Accounts*, 100, 111–13.

73. *CSP Spain 2*, item 43.

74. "Red say for covering the steps of a font, fine holland for the bottom of the same, two ells of 'sipres or lawne' [lightweight silk or linen] for a 'straynor,' and 4 ells to cover the font." *L&P Henry VIII* 1, item 394; Hayward, *Dress at the Court*, 198.

75. *CSP Spain Supp 1*, item 7.

76. *CSP Spain 2*, item 43.

77. Cohen-Hanegbi, "Postpartum Mental Distress."

78. *L&P Henry VIII* 1, item 578.

79. Hall, *Hall's Chronicle*, 516.

80. Hayward, *Great Wardrobe*, 58, citing *L&P Henry VIII* 1, 673.

81. Hall, *Hall's Chronicle*, 517.

82. Rieder, *Purification of Women*, 1–3; Lee, "Purification of Women."

83. Hayward, "Reflections on Gender and Status Distinctions"; Hayward, *Great Wardrobe*, 59; L'Estrange, *Holy Motherhood*, 94–98, 101–2.

84. Anglo, *Spectacle, Pageantry*, 111–12; Hayward, *Dress at the Court*, 236.

85. Walker, "Westminster Tournament Challenge."

86. Hall, *Hall's Chronicle*, 519.

87. *L&P Henry VIII* 1, item 707; Hayward, *Great Wardrobe*, 68.

88. Barnes, "Diagnosis in Retrospect."

89. Dewhurst, "Alleged Miscarriages," 52.

90. *Original Letters*, 1: no. 89.

91. *L&P Henry VIII* 1, item 2287.

92. Ibid., item 3041.

93. *CSP Venice* 2, item 505.

94. "To deliver Henry Rooper, yeoman of the Beds with the Queen, blue saye, &c. for the Queen's beds" and "to deliver Wm. Lambert, 'for the use of our nursery, God willing'; a cradle covered with scarlet 'without a frame,' a couch, &c." *L&P Henry VIII* 1, items 3332, 3333; Hayward, *Dress at the Court*, 198.

95. *L&P Henry VIII* 1, item 3581.

96. Ibid., item 3500.

97. *L&P Henry VIII* 2, item 1563. On 20 February, Sebastian Giustinian, in his announcement of the birth of Mary, wrote that Fernando's death was "kept secret, because of the most serene Queen's being on the eve of her delivery." In Giustinian, *Four Years*, 181.

98. *L&P Henry VIII* 2, items 1551, 1556, 1573; *Chamber Books*, fol. 215r (27 February 1516).

99. Richards, *Mary Tudor*, 33–34.

100. Carley, *Books of King Henry VIII*, 117–18.

101. "Inventory of the Wardrobes," 30, 36, 40.

102. McIntosh, *From Heads of Household*, 10–20; Loades, *Mary Tudor*, 28–30; Hayward, *Dress at the Court*, 311–12.

103. *L&P Henry VIII* 2, item 3018.

104. Ibid., item 4279.

105. Giustinian, *Four Years*, 240.

106. Wabuda, "Receiving the King," 178.

107. Furdell, *Royal Doctors*, 21.

108. Okerlund, *Elizabeth of York*, 202.

109. Ives, *Life and Death*, 343–48.

110. Barnes, "Diagnosis in Retrospect."

111. Whitley and Kramer, "New Explanation."

112. Beer, "Queenly Affinity."

113. *CSP Venice* 2, item 887; Beer, *Queenship*, 74–75.

114. *L&P Henry VIII* 3, item 728.

115. Beer, *Queenship*, 60–69.

116. Currin, "England's International Relations;" Beer, "Between Kings and Emperors," 35–38.

117. *L&P Henry VIII* 3, item 728.

118. Ibid., item 689; *CSP Spain Supp 1*, items 6–7 (10 March 1520).

119. Attreed, "Gender, Patronage, and Diplomacy."

120. *L&P Henry VIII* 3, item 776.

121. Hayward, *Dress at the Court*, 227.

122. *CSP Venice* 3, item 50.

123. Richardson, *Field of the Cloth of Gold*; Richardson, "'As Presence Did Present Them,'" 55–56.

124. For a visual depiction of this emblem, see figure 9; and orphrey, ca. 1450–1500, embroidered with devices of Isabel of Castile, London, Victoria and Albert Museum, ID# 271-1880.

125. *CSP Venice* 3, item 50; Hayward, "Spanish Princess," 25.

126. Beer, *Queenship*, 60–69; Hayward, *Dress at the Court*, 227.

127. Beer, *Queenship*, 63–69. For contemporary comments on the opulence, see *CSP Venice*, 3, items 44, 45; Richardson, *Field of the Cloth of Gold*, 61–65.

128. *CSP Venice* 3, items 50, 68, 81.

129. Ibid., item 85; Hayward, "Spanish Princess," 24.

130. Richardson, *Field of the Cloth of Gold*, 165.

131. Ives, *Life and Death*, 34–35.

CHAPTER 5

The epigraph to this chapter is from Catherine's speech at the papal legatine court at Blackfriars in 1529, reported by George Cavendish, *Life and Death of Cardinal Wolsey*. The holograph manuscript is at the British Library, Egerton MS 2402, fols. 72–78. The portrait of Catherine, from the collection of the Archbishop of Canterbury at Lambeth Palace, London, is on loan to the National Portrait Gallery.

1. Scott and Ablett, "Henry and Katherine Reunited."

2. Evans, *English Jewellery*, 68–69; Scarisbrick, *Rings*, 10–14.

3. *CSP Spain Supp 1*, 248–54, 375, 441 (3 July 1523).

4. Harris, "Trial of the Third Duke of Buckingham."

5. Lehfeldt, "Ruling Sexuality."

6. Weissberger, *Isabel Rules*, 28–68; Earenfight, "Two Bodies, One Spirit."

7. Harris, "Marriage, Sixteenth-Century Style"; Beer, *Queenship*, 39–44; Loades, *Tudor Court*, 49.

8. Harris, *Edward Stafford*.

9. Harris, *English Aristocratic Women*, 210–40; Streitberger, *Court Revels*, 65–120.

10. Hall, *Hall's Chronicle*, 580.

11. Ives, *Life and Death*.

12. Shears, "Like Father, Like Daughter," 5.

13. Blockmans and Prevenier, *Promised Lands*, 213, 229; Anne de France, *Anne of France: Lessons*.

14. Eichenberger, "Margareta of Austria"; Liss, *Isabel the Queen*, 362–66.

15. Heal, *Power of Gifts*, 87–97.

16. Bordes, "Materiality of Art," 43.

17. Scholten, *Small Wonders*, 68; Romanelli, "South Netherlandish Boxwood Devotional Sculpture," 1–3, 107–22.

18. Suda and Boehm, "Handpicked," 351.

19. Dillon, "Praying by Number." The Victoria and Albert Museum, London, has a similar paternoster bead that may be from the same workshop (accession # A. 535 & A-1910).

20. Anglo, *Spectacle, Pageantry*, 180–206.

21. Winston-Allen, *Stories of the Rose*, 13–26, 111–32; Hirsh, "Twenty-Five Joys of Our Lady."

22. Ringbom, "Devotional Images."

23. Dillon, "Praying by Number," 459.

24. Beer, *Queenship*, 111.

25. Duffy, *Stripping of the Altars*, 256–65; Dillon, "Praying by Number," 451–53; Romanelli, "South Netherlandish Boxwood Devotional Sculpture," 107–22.

26. Petrus Alamire, "Book of 28 Motets"; Petti, "Music Manuscripts"; Blockmans and Kellman, *Treasury of Petrus Alamire*; Carley, *Books of King Henry VIII*, 119.

27. Thomas, "Patronage and Personal Narrative," 338, n3.

28. London, British Library Royal 8 G.vii, Motet 31, "Dulces exuviae," translation in Thomas, "Patronage and Personal Narrative," 360.

29. Thomas, "Patronage and Personal Narrative," 349.

30. Ibid., 352.

31. Val Valdivieso, "Educación, en la corte" 255–73; Val Valdivieso, "Isabel la Católica y la educación"; Surtz, "In Search of Juana de Mendoza."

32. Unknown artist, *Catherine of Aragon Kneeling Before St. Catherine*, ca. 1518–28, detail of stained-glass window in the chapel at the Vyne, Sherborne Saint John, Hampshire.

33. *Receyt*, 77.

34. *L&P Henry VIII* 4, item 6121; 217–18.

35. Cahill Marrón, "Serenissimae Anglie Reginae"; Cahill Marrón, "Lucrecia"; Attreed and Winkler, "Faith and Forgiveness," 976; Mattingly, *Catherine of Aragon*, 181–90.

36. *L&P Henry VIII* 4, item 6121.

37. The manuscript contains two matched texts, one concerning the care of the body, *De salute corporis*, by Willelmus de Saliceto, and one concerning the salvation of the soul, *De salute anime*, by Johannes de Turrecremata. London, British Library, C .J7, fol. 1v; Carley, *Books of King Henry VIII*, 112.

38. Cahill Marrón, "Tras la pista," 714.

39. The Hague, Koninklijke Bibliotheek, KB, ms 76, F7; Cahill Marrón, "Tras la pista," 714.

40. Cahill Marrón, "Tras la pista," 708; Fraser, *Wives of Henry VIII*, 77.

41. Carley, *Libraries of King Henry VIII*, 50, 52, 53, 59, 68, 94, 97, 110, 163. The Morgan Library in New York City owns several devotional, medical, and political texts and autograph manuscripts associated with both Catherine and Henry. See, for example, Aegineta Paulus, *Praecepta salubria* (1512, accession # 77703.1); Marsilio Ficino, *Consiglio contro la pestilenza* (accession # PML 77703.4); *Hore beate Marie virginis ad usum insignis ac preclare ecclesie Sarum* (1528, accession # PML 1034), and three other books of hours.

42. Dowling, *Humanism*, 243; King, "Patronage and Piety," 59; Mueller, "Tudor Queen."

43. London, British Library, STC 24856.

44. Cahill Marrón, "Tras la pista," 717.

45. Wieck, Voelkle, and Hearne, *Hours of Henry VIII*; Schutte, "'To the Illustrious Queen,'" 17–18.

46. The titles are not recorded, however. "Inventory of the Wardrobe," 37, 40. For Castilian sources that James Carley did not include in his study, see Cahill Marrón, "Tras la pista," 712–14.

47. Schutte, "'To the Illustrious Queen,'" 24.

48. Vives personally gave a copy of the *De ratione studii puerilis* to Catherine on a visit to Oxford. Elston, "Transformation or Continuity," 14.

49. Vives, *Education of a Christian Woman*; Loades, *Mary Tudor*, 31.

50. Cambridge University, Emmanuel College MSS 3.2.30, 1526. In 1526, a deluxe presentation copy of the manuscript with a handwritten dedication was given to Catherine. Carley, *Books of King Henry VIII*, 119.

51. Elston, "Transformation or Continuity," 19–23; Richards, *Mary Tudor*, 48.

52. Richards, *Mary Tudor*, 31–44.

53. Hall, *Hall's Chronicle*, 692; *CSP Spain Supp 1*, 71; Anglo, *Spectacle, Pageantry*, 170–206.

54. Backhouse, "Illuminated Manuscripts," 91.

55. Now in the Alte Pinakothek, Munich, Inv. # WAF 1190.

56. Frye, *Pens and Needles*, 78–79; Strong, *English Renaissance Miniature*, 12–44.

57. Bordes, "Materiality of Art," 42–43.

58. Orlin, "Empty Vessels."

59. James, *Feminine Dynamic in English Art*, 25–27, 57–58, 62, 82, 149, 245. There are double portraits of Catherine and Henry after 1529 (in the collection of Maud Parr in 1529, in the 1536 inventory at Baynard's, in the 1542 and 1546 inventories of Princess Mary). Dolman, "Wishful Thinking," 118; "Inventory of the Wardrobes."

60. Mattingly, *Catherine of Aragon*, 226–29; Hayward, *Dress at the Court*, 310–12.

61. Transcription in *Original Letters*, 3, letter 107, 19–20; original in London, British Library, MS Cotton Vespasian F, XIII, fol. 72.

62. Thanks to María Bullon-Fernández for sharing their expertise in decoding the nuances of Middle English. See Williams, "'O! When Degree Is Shak'd,'" 90–94.

63. Watson, *Vives*, 148.

64. "Inventory of the Wardrobes," 40. The velvet-covered desk was delivered to Henry, and the coffer covered in crimson velvet went to Anne Boleyn.

65. *L&P Henry VIII* 3, item 1.

66. Strong, *English Renaissance Miniature*, 40–42.

67. Starkey, *Inventory of King Henry VIII*.

68. For the perspective from imperial ambassadors at the English court, see Froude, *Divorce of Catherine of Aragon*.

69. Ives, *Life and Death*, 37–52.

70. *CSP Spain 3.2*, item 586 (18 November 1528).

71. Kelly, *Matrimonial Trials of Henry VIII*; Scarisbrick, *Henry VIII*, 198–240; Mattingly, *Catherine of Aragon*, 263–94.

72. Cavendish, *Life and Death of Cardinal Wolsey*.

73. Ibid., 72–78; Anderson, *Biographical Truth*, 27–39.

74. Cavendish, *Life and Death of Cardinal Wolsey*, 100; Walker, "'To Speak Before the King,'" 74–75.

75. Beer, "Queenly Affinity"; Rhodes, "Count Lodovico Nogarola."

76. Rummel, *Erasmus on Women*, 189–229.

77. Walker-Meikle, "Late Medieval Pet Keeping," 22–23, 101.

78. Grosvenor, "Henry VIII's Queens," 56–57; Grosvenor, "Happy Birthday Katherine of Aragon."

79. Dolman, "Wishful Thinking," 117.

80. Dillon, "Powerful Obedience," 119–20; Mattingly, *Catherine of Aragon*, 307.

81. Dillon, "Powerful Obedience," 129.

82. Ibid., 128.

83. Ibid.

84. Walker, "'To Speak Before the King,'" 71–73.

CHAPTER 6

The epigraph to this chapter is from Thomas Cromwell, reported by Eustace Chapuys, *CSP Spain 4.2*, item 1100 (11 July 1533).

1. Earenfight, "Lifetime of Power."

2. Beer, "Queenly Affinity," 427.

3. Elston, "'Widow Princess or Neglected Queen.'"

4. *CSP Venice* 4, item 871 (15 April 1533).

5. *L&P Henry VIII* 8, item 196 (11 February 1535).

6. *L&P Henry VIII* 9, item 136 (20 August 1535).

7. *CSP Spain 4.1*, item 548.

8. The making of the king's shirts was the responsibility of the groom of the stool, but shirts were usually given by women and would have provided a good vehicle for them to display their embroidery skills. Hayward, *Dress at the Court*, 111; Hayward, "Gift Giving," 140.

9. Catherine to Emperor Charles V. 22 February 1531, New York, Morgan Library and Museum, record ID# 79926, accession # MA6443.

10. *L&P Henry VIII* 5, item 1377.

11. *CSP Spain 4.2*, item 860.

12. *CSP Spain 2*, item 238.

13. *L&P Henry VIII* 5, item 70; 6, item 585; Harris, "View from My Lady's Chamber," 244.

14. Gunn, *Charles Brandon*, 38.

15. *L & P Henry VIII* 6, item 1252 (10 October 1533).

16. Guy, *Public Career*, 138, 142, 147, 178; Dowling, "Humanist Support."

17. Gunn, *Charles Brandon*, 95–96, 118, 130, 132–33, 142, 154, 156, 158, 199.

18. *L&P Henry VIII* 6, items 1161 and 1164; Gunn, *Charles Brandon*, 109–10, 118.

19. Warnicke, *Elizabeth of York*, 100; Loades, *Mary Tudor*, 72; Mattingly, *Catherine of Aragon*, 365–65, 374–75.

20. "She thinks that she would be irredeemably damned if she took any path that led to war," Chapuys reported. *CSP Spain 4.2*, item 1063.

21. Hayward, *Dress at the Court*, 310–12.

22. 25 Hen 8 c 22 in *Statutes of the Realm*, 3:471–74.

23. For Castile, see Phillips, *Enrique IV*; Suárez-Fernández, *Trastámaras*. For challengers to Henry VII, see Arthurson, *Perkin Warbeck Conspiracy*.

24. Beer, "Queenly Affinity"; Dillon, "Powerful Obedience"; Hansen, "'And a Queen of England, Too.'"

25. Mattingly argues that it was sent in April 1534, after the Act of Supremacy, but Loades thinks it was sent much earlier, when her household was diminished. Mattingly, *Catherine of Aragon*, 406–8; Loades, *Mary Tudor*, 77–79.

26. I am grateful to Talia Zajac for her suggestions on how to interpret this passage.

27. Villena, *Portraits of Holy Women*.

28. Beer, *Queenship*, 17, 20, 26, 60–69, 110, 149–53.

29. Attreed and Winkler, "Faith and Forgiveness"; Schutte, "'To the Illustrious Queen,'" 24; Richards, "'To Promote a

Woman to Beare Rule'"; Matheson-Pollock, Paul, and Fletcher, introduction to *Queenship and Counsel.*

30. Anne de France, *Lessons*; Adams, "Appearing Virtuous"; Rohr, "Lessons for My Daughter."

31. *L&P Henry VIII* 7, item 1126; 8, item 328.

32. The title to this section is from London, British Library Royal 8 G.vii, Motet 31, "Dulces exuviae," in Thomas, "Patronage and Personal Narrative," 360.

33. *CSP Spain 5.1*, item 134.

34. *L&P Henry VIII* 9, item 1040; Wood, *Letters*, 2:207–8.

35. Carley, *Books of King Henry VIII*, 119.

36. Illingworth, "Copy of an Original Minute of Council," 23–25.

37. *L&P Henry VIII* 10, item 284; Hayward, *Dress at the Court*, 66.

38. *L&P Henry VIII* 10, item 141.

39. Wayment, "East Window of St. Margaret's"; Wayment, "Stained Glass in Henry VIII's Palaces"; Wayment, "Twenty-Four Videmuses."

40. *L&P Henry VIII* 10, item 128.

41. She left small sums for women of her household: Emma Browne, Elizabeth Darrell, Elizabeth Fynes, Elizabeth Lawrence, Elizabeth Otwell, Marjorie Otwell (had a daughter named Isabel; she was left £40 by Catherine in 1536), Blanche Twyforde (left £100 by Catherine in 1536), and Dorothy Wheler (or Whiller; left £40 by Catherine in 1536). *L&P Henry VIII* 10, item 40.

42. Attreed and Winkler, "Faith and Forgiveness," 980–89.

43. Earenfight, "Two Bodies, One Spirit," 8–14, 17–18.

44. Carley, *Books of King Henry VIII*, 120.

45. Glanville, "Howard Grace Cup."

46. "Horæ B. Mariæ, Virginis et Officia," ca. 1500, London, British Library, Add Ms 17012. Other, later owners were Sir John Poynz; Thomas Manners, first Earl of Rutland; Philibert II, Duke of Savoy, and

his wife, Yolande. Carley, *Books of Henry VIII*, 109.

47. Alphonsus de Villa Sancta, *Problema indulgentiarum aduersus Lutherum*, 1523, London, British Library, C.47.g.2; Carley, *Books of Henry VIII*, 115.

48. Weiner, *Inalienable Possessions*, 40–42.

49. Cahill Marrón, "Tras la pista," 721.

50. Harris, *Ancient, Curious, and Famous Wills*, 39; *CSP Spain 5.2*, items 30–39.

51. Coughton Court, Warwickshire, National Trust inventory no. NT 135701.

52. French, "'I Leave My Best Gown.'"

53. Hayward, "Reflections on Gender"; Lowe, "Women's Devotional Bequests."

54. D'Elboux, "Pre-Reformation Vestments," 23, 25–28.

55. *CSP Spain 5.2*, items 30–39.

56. I am indebted to Laura Gathagan for her research into the donations of liturgical garments by Anglo-Norman queens and the theological implications for these gifts, and for sharing with me the draft of chapter 7 of her forthcoming book *Embodying Conquest*.

57. Duffy, *Stripping of the Altars*, 474, 492–93, 567.

58. Hayward, "Reflections," 405–6, 412–13, 421.

59. Duffy, *Stripping of the Altars*, 389.

60. *CSP Spain 4.2*, item 1077 (29 May 1533).

61. Hansen, "'And a Queen of England, Too.'"

62. Cahill Marrón, "Tras la pista," 718.

63. Hans Kels (circle of), gamespiece bearing portrait of Catherine of Aragon. ca. 1530–40, boxwood, London, Victoria and Albert Museum. ID# A.35-1934. Eichenberger, "Playing Games."

64. "Inventory of the Wardrobe," 39.

65. Marshall, *Religious Identities*; Orlin, *Private Matters and Public Culture.*

66. Dillon, "Powerful Obedience"; Walker, "'To Speak Before the King.'"

67. Parr, *Complete Works.*

68. Elston, "Transformation or Continuity"; Elston, "'Widow Princess or Neglected Queen.'"

69. Hansen, "'And a Queen of England, Too'"; Meyer, "Politics of Queenship"; Meyer, "*Richard III*'s Forelives"; Marlow and Moss, "Six."

70. "Inventarios reales (Juan II a Juana la Loca)," 233.

71. "Inventory of the Wardrobe."

72. Elston, "Widow Princess or Neglected Queen," 25–26.

73. Cahill Marrón, "Primera aproximación," 272–73.

CHAPTER 7

1. Schjeldahl, "Beheld," 68.

2. Earenfight, "Two Bodies, One Spirit"; Weissberger, *Isabel Rules*; Liss, *Isabel the Queen*, 233–34.

3. Foucault, *History of Sexuality*, 1:95–96.

4. Parks, "Rescuing the Maidens"; Seabourne, *Imprisoning Medieval Women*.

5. "Inventory of the Wardrobes," 39.

6. London, Victoria and Albert Museum, inventory nos. 2011 to Q-1899, W.76-1911, and 116&A-1908; The National Trust, NTPL Ref. No. 8853.

MANUSCRIPTS

Alamire, Petrus. "Book of 28 motets, 6 Latin secular pieces, and 1 canon (a later addition)." London, British Library Royal 8 G VII, ca. 1513–44.

Anonymous. "Horæ B. Mariæ, Virginis et Officia." London, British Library, Add Ms 17012, ca. 1500.

Catherine of Aragon. Letter to Emperor Charles V. 22 February 1531. New York, Morgan Library and Museum, record ID# 79926, accession # MA6443.

Hawes, Stephen. *A Joyfull Medytacyon.* 1509. Cambridge, Cambridge University Library, Rare Book Sel. 5.55.

More, Thomas. "Coronation Suite." London, British Library Cotton Titus D iv.

Villa Sancta, Alphonsus de. *Problema indulgentiarum aduersus Lutherum.* 1523. London, British Library, C.47.g.2.

PRINTED PRIMARY SOURCES

Anne de France. *Anne of France: Lessons for My Daughter.* Edited and translated by Sharon L. Jansen. Rochester, NY: Boydell and Brewer, 2004.

Bernáldez, Andrés. *Memorias del reinado de los Reyes Católicos.* Edited by Manuel Gómez-Moreno and Juan de Mata Carriazo. Madrid: RAH, 1962.

Burnet, Gilbert. *The History of the Reformation of the Church of England.* Edited by Nicholas Pocock. 7 vols. Oxford: Clarendon Press, 1865.

Carley, James, P., ed. *The Libraries of King Henry VIII.* London: British Library, 2000.

Cavendish, George. *The Life and Death of Cardinal Wolsey.* Boston: Houghton Mifflin, 1905.

The Chamber Books of Henry VII and Henry VIII, 1485–1521. Edited by M. M. Condon, S. P. Harper, L. Liddy, S. Cunningham, and J. Ross. http://www.tudorchamberbooks.org.

Chronicle of the Grey Friars of London. Edited by John Gough Nichols. Camden Society Old Series 53. London: Camden Society, 1852.

Cuentas de Gonzalo Baeza, tesorero de Isabel la Católica. Edited by Antonio de la Torre and E. A. de la Torre. 2 vols. Madrid: Consejo Superior de Investigaciones Científicas, 1955.

Dugdale, William. *Monasticon anglicanum.* 6 vols. London: Longman, Hurst, Rees, Orme and Brown, 1817–30.

Erasmus, Desiderius. *Pilgrimages to Saint Mary of Walsingham and Saint Thomas of Canterbury with the*

Colloquy on Rash Vows, and the Characters of Archbishop Warham and Dean Colet. Edited by John Gough Nichols. London: John Murray, 1875.

Fernández de Oviedo, Gonzalo. *Libro de la cámara real del Principe Don Juan e ofiçios de su casa e serviçio ordinario.* Madrid: Sociedad de Bibliófilos Españoles, 1870.

Francomano, Emily, ed. and trans. *Three Spanish "Querelle" Texts: "Grisel and Mirabella," "The Slander Against Women," and "The Defense of Ladies Against Slanderers."* Toronto: University of Toronto Press, 2013.

Gairdner, James, ed. *Memorials of King Henry the Seventh.* London: Longman, Brown, Green, Longmans and Roberts, 1858.

Giustinian, Sebastian. *Four Years at the Court of Henry VIII: January 12, 1515 to July 26, 1519.* Translated by Rawdon Brown. 2 vols. London: Smith, Elder, 1854.

Hall, Edward. *Hall's Chronicle.* 1548. New York: AMS Press, 1965.

Harris, Virgil M., ed. *Ancient, Curious, and Famous Wills.* Boston: Little, Brown, 1911.

Hayward, Maria, ed. *The Great Wardrobe Accounts of Henry VII and Henry VIII.* London: London Record Society, 2012.

A History of the County of Lincoln. Vol. 2. Edited by William Page. London, 1906.

Holinshed, Raphael. *Holinshed's Chronicles of England, Scotland, and Ireland.* Edited by Abraham Fleming. 6 vols. London, 1807–8.

Illingworth, W. "Copy of an Original Minute of Council for Preparations for the Ceremonial for the Funeral of Queen Catherine, the Divorced Wife of King Henry the Eighth." *Archaeologia* 16 (1812): 22–28.

"Inventarios reales (Juan II a Juana la Loca)." In *Datos Documentales para la Historia del Arte Español*, edited and translated by José Ferrandis, 3:171–375. Madrid: Instituto Diego Velazquez, Consejo Superior de Investigaciones Científicas, 1943.

"An Inventory of the Wardrobes, Plate, Chapel Stuff, etc. of Henry Fitzroy, Duke of Richmond, and of the Wardrobe Stuff at Baynard Castle of Katherine, Princess Dowager." Edited by John Gough Nichols. In *The Camden Miscellany*, 3:23–41. London: Camden Society, 1855.

Machado, Roger. *Journals of Roger Machado, Rerum britannicarum medii aevi scriptore.* London: Great Britain Public Record Office, 1858.

More, Thomas. *The Complete Works of St. Thomas More.* Vol. 3, part 2, *Latin Poems.* Edited by Clarence H. Miller, Leicester Bradner, Charles A. Lynch, and Revilo P. Oliver. New Haven: Yale University Press, 1984.

———. *The Correspondence of Sir Thomas More.* Edited by Elizabeth Frances Rogers. Princeton: Princeton University Press, 1947.

Münzer, Jeronimo. *Viaje por España y Portugal: 1494–1495.* Madrid: Polifemo, 1991.

Original Letters, Illustrative of English History: Including Numerous Royal Letters, from Autographs in the British Museum, the State Paper Office, and One or Two Other Collections. Edited by Henry Ellis. 11 vols. London: Dawsons, 1969.

Parr, Katherine. *Katherine Parr: Complete Works and Correspondence.* Edited by Janel Muller. Chicago: University of Chicago Press, 2011.

The Paston Letters. Edited by James Gairdner. 6 vols. London: Chatto and Windus, 1904.

Privy Purse Expenses of Elizabeth of York; Wardrobe Accounts of Edward IV, with a Memoir of Elizabeth of York, and Notes. Edited by Nicholas Harris Nicolas. London: Pickering, 1830.

Facsimile ed., New York: Barnes and Noble, 1972.

The Privy Purse Expenses of King Henry the Eighth: November 1529–End of December 1532. Edited by Nicholas Harris Nichols. London: William Pickering, 1827.

Pulgar, Fernando de. *Crónica del los Señores Reyes Católicos.* Edited by Juan de Mata Carriazo. 2 vols. Granada: Universidad de Granada, 2008.

The Receyt of the Ladie Kateryne. Edited by Gordon Kipling. Oxford: Oxford University Press, 1990.

Rummel, Erika, ed. *Erasmus on Women.* Toronto: University of Toronto Press, 1996.

Rymer's Foedera with Syllabus. Edited by Thomas Rymer. London, 1739–45. *British History Online,* http://www .british-history.ac.uk/rymer-foedera.

Starkey, David, ed. *The Inventory of King Henry VIII.* London: Harvey Miller, 1998.

Statutes of the Realm. 11 vols. London: Dawsons, 1810–28.

Testamentaria de Isabel la Católica. Edited by Antonio de la Torre and Engracia Alsina. Barcelona, 1974.

Trollope, Edward, ed. "King Henry's Jewel Book." *Associated Architectural Societies* 17, no. 2 (1883–84): 155–229.

Valera, Diego de. *Crónica de los Reyes Católicos.* Madrid, 1927.

Van Gogh, Vincent. Letter to Theo van Gogh, July 1880. Translated by Johanna van Gogh-Bonger. Edited by Robert Harrison. # 133. http:// webexhibits.org/vangogh/letter/8 /133.htm.

Villena, Isabel de. *Portraits of Holy Women: Selections from the "Vita Christi."* Edited by Joan Cubert. Translated by Robert D. Hughes. Barcelona: Barcino, 2013.

Vives, Juan Luis. *The Education of a Christian Woman: A Sixteenth-Century Manual.*

Translated by Charles Fantazzi. Chicago: University of Chicago Press, 2000.

Wood, Mary Anne Everett, ed. *Letters of Royal and Illustrious Ladies of Great Britain.* 3 vols. London: Henry Colburn, 1846.

SECONDARY SOURCES

Adams, Jenny, and Nancy Mason Bradbury, eds. *Medieval Women and Their Objects.* Ann Arbor: University of Michigan Press, 2017.

Adams, Tracy. "Appearing Virtuous: Christine de Pizan's *Le livre des trois vertus* and Anne de France's *Les Enseignements d'Anne de France.*" In *Virtue Ethics for Women, 1250–1500,* edited by Karen Green and Constant Mews, 115–31. Dordrecht: Springer, 2011.

American College of Obstetrics and Gynecology. "Early Pregnancy Loss." https://www.acog.org/Clinical -Guidance-and-Publications/Practice -Bulletins/Committee-on-Practice -Bulletins-Gynecology/Early -Pregnancy-Loss. Accessed 29 August 2020.

Anderson, Judith H. *Biographical Truth: The Representation of Historical Persons in Tudor-Stuart Writing.* New Haven: Yale University Press, 1984.

Anderson, Ruth Matilda. "El chapín y otros zapatos afines." *Cuadernos de la Alhambra* 5 (1969): 17–43.

———. *Hispanic Costume, 1480–1530.* New York: Hispanic Society of America, 1979.

Anglo, Sydney. "The London Pageants for the Reception of Katharine of Aragon: November 1501." *Journal of the Warburg and Courtauld Institutes* 26, no. 1 (1963): 53–89.

———. *Spectacle, Pageantry, and Early Tudor Policy.* Oxford: Clarendon Press, 1969.

Appleford, Amy. "Shakespeare's Katherine of Aragon: Last Medieval Queen, First Recusant Martyr." *Journal of Medieval and Early Modern Studies* 40, no. 1 (2010): 149–72.

Appudurai, Arjun, ed. *The Social Life of Things: Commodities in Cultural Perspective.* Cambridge: Cambridge University Press, 1986.

Aram, Bethany. *Juana the Mad: Sovereignty and Dynasty in Renaissance Europe.* Baltimore: Johns Hopkins University Press, 2001.

Arthurson, Ian. "'The King of Spain's Daughter Came to Visit Me': Marriage, Princes, and Politics." In *Arthur Tudor, Prince of Wales: Life, Death, and Commemoration*, edited by Linda Monckton and Steve J. Gunn, 20–30. Woodbridge: Boydell Press, 2009.

———. *The Perkin Warbeck Conspiracy, 1491–1499.* Stroud: History Press, 2009.

Attreed, Lorraine. "Gender, Patronage, and Diplomacy in the Early Career of Margaret of Austria (1480–1530)." *Mediterranean Studies* 20 (2012): 3–27.

Attreed, Lorraine, and Alexandra Winkler. "Faith and Forgiveness: Lessons in Statecraft for Queen Mary Tudor." *Sixteenth Century Journal* 36, no. 4 (2005): 971–89.

Backhouse, Janet. "Illuminated Manuscripts and the Development of the Portrait Miniature." In *Henry VIII: A European Court in England*, edited by David Starkey, 88–93. London: Collins and Brown, 1991.

Barnes, Allen C. "Diagnosis in Retrospect: Mary Tudor." *Obstetrics and Gynecology* 1, no. 5 (1953): 585–90.

Barthes, Roland. *The Fashion System.* London: Jonathan Cape, 1985.

Beaven, Lisa, and Dagmar Eichberger. "Family Members and Political Allies: The Portrait Collection of Margaret of Austria." *Art Bulletin* 77, no. 2 (1995): 225–48.

Bedos-Rezak, Brigitte Miriam. "Medieval Identity: A Sign and a Concept." *American Historical Review* 105 (2000): 1489–1533.

———. "Mutually Contextual: Materials, Bodies, and Objects." In *Cultural Histories of the Material World*, edited by Peter N. Miller, 47–58. Ann Arbor: University of Michigan Press, 2013.

Beer, Michelle L. "Between Kings and Emperors: Catherine of Aragon as Counsellor and Mediator." In *Queenship and Counsel in Early Modern Europe*, edited by Helen Matheson-Pollock, Joanne Paul, and Catherine Fletcher, 35–58. Basingstoke: Palgrave Macmillan, 2018.

———. "A Queenly Affinity? Catherine of Aragon's Estates and Henry VIII's Great Matter." *Historical Research* 91, no. 253 (2018): 426–45.

———. *Queenship at the Renaissance Courts of Britain: Catherine of Aragon and Margaret Tudor, 1503–1533.* Woodbridge: Boydell Press, 2018.

Bernis Madrazo, Carmen. *Indumentaria medieval Española.* Madrid: Consejo Superior de Investigaciones Científicas, 1956.

———. "Modas moriscas en la sociedad cristiana Española del siglo XV y principios del XVI." *Boletín de la Real Academia de la Historia* 144 (1959): 199–228.

Blair, Claude. *The Crown Jewels: The History of the Coronation Regalia in the Jewel House of the Tower of London.* 2 vols. London: Her Majesty's Stationery Office, 1998.

Blockmans, Wim, and Herbert Kellman, eds. *The Treasury of Petrus Alamire: Music and Art in Flemish Court Manuscripts, 1500–1535.* Chicago: University of Chicago Press, 1999.

Blockmans, Wim, Herbert Kellman, and Walter Prevenier. *The Promised Lands: The Low Countries Under Burgundian Rule, 1369–1530.* Translated by Elizabeth Fackelman; revised translation by Edward Peters. Philadelphia: University of Pennsylvania Press, 1999.

Bordes, Philippe. "The Materiality of Art." In *Cultural Histories of the Material World*, edited by Peter N. Miller, 39–44. Ann Arbor: University of Michigan Press, 2013.

Bourdieu, Pierre. *Distinction: A Social Critique of the Judgment of Taste.* Translated by Richard Nice. Cambridge, MA: Harvard University Press, 1984.

Bowle, John. *Henry VIII.* Newton Abbot: David and Charles, 1964.

Brans, J. V. L. *Isabel la Católica y el Arte Hispano-Flamenco.* Madrid: Ediciones Cultura Hispánica, 1952.

Brodie, Antonia. "Marking and Memory: An Embroidered Sheet in the Collection of the Victoria and Albert Museum." *Textile: Cloth and Culture* 14, no. 2 (2016): 160–75.

Buchanan, Patricia Hill. *Margaret Tudor, Queen of Scots.* Edinburgh: Scottish Academic Press, 1985.

Burton, John. *A History of Bewdely.* London: William Reeves, 1883.

Caballero Escamilla, Sonia. "*La Virgen de los Reyes Católicos*: Escaparate de un poder personal e institucional." *Revista Reales Sitios* (2007): 20–41.

Cabrera Lafuente, Ana. "Proyecto Marie S.-Curie *Interwoven*: Investigación sobre el coleccionismo y exposición de tejidos relacionados con España en el Victoria and Albert Museum de Londres." In *1 Coloquio de Investigadores en Textil y Moda, 17 y 18 noviembre de 2017*, 71–76. Libro de Actas. Barcelona: Centre de Documentació i Museu Tèxtil, 2018.

———. "Los tejidos como patrimonio: investigación y exposición." *Bienes culturales: Revista del Instituto del Patrimonio Histórico Español* 5 (2005): 5–19.

Cadden, Joan. *The Meanings of Sex Difference in the Middle Ages: Medicine, Science, and Culture.* Cambridge: Cambridge University Press, 1993.

Cahill Marrón, Emma Luisa. "La alianza castellano-inglesa en la Baja Edad Media a través de sus matrimonios regios." In *Reinas e infantas en los reinos medievales ibéricos: Contribuciones para su estudio*, edited by Miguel García-Fernández and Silvia Cernadas Martínez, 415–26. Santiago de Compostela: Universidade de Santiago de Compostela, 2018.

———. "Catalina, la esperada Princesa de Gales: Arte y ceremonia en los festejos nupciales de 1501." In *Las artes y la arquitectura del poder*, 2597–614. Castelló de la Plana: Servei de Comunicació i Publicacions, 2013.

———. "La influencia de la joyería y orfebrería tardogótica de la corte de los Reyes Católicos en la Inglaterra Tudor." *Anales de Historia del Arte* 24 (2014): 39–52.

———. "Una Lucrecia del siglo XVI: Los libros de Catalina de Aragón." In *El imperio y las Hispanias de Trajano a Carlos V: Clasicismo y poder en el arte español*, 419–28. Bologna: Bononia University Press, 2014.

———. "Una primera approximación al patrocinio arquitectónico de Catalina de Aragón en la Inglaterra Tudor." *Arquitectura Tardogótica en la Corona de Castilla: Trayectorias e intercambios* 5 (2014): 265–84.

———. "*Serenissimae Anglie Reginae Erasmus Roterdami dono misit*: Catalina de Aragón y la comisión de obras humanistas." *Titivillus—International Journal of Rare Books: Revista Internacional sobre Libro Antiguo* (2015): 227–36.

———. "Tras la pista de Catalina de Aragón: La granada en los manuscritos de la época Tudor." In *Líneas recientes de investigación en Historia Moderna*, edited by Felix Labrador Arroyo, 707–25. Madrid: Universidad Rey Juan Carlos, 2015.

Carley, James P. *The Books of King Henry VIII and His Wives.* London: British Library, 2005.

Carrión, María M. "The Balcony of the Chapín, or the Vain Architecture of Shoes in Early Modern Spain." *Journal of Spanish Cultural Studies* 14, no. 2 (2013): 143–58.

Chamberlin, F. *The Private Character of Henry VIII.* London: Bodley Head, 1932.

Chapman, Hester W. *Anne Boleyn.* London: Jonathan Cape, 1974.

Claremont, Francesca. *Catherine of Aragon.* London: Robert Hale, 1939.

Classen, Albrecht. "Spain and Germany in the Late Middle Ages: Christoph Weiditz Paints Spain (1529); A German Artist Traveler Discovers the Spanish Peninsula." *Neuphilologische Mitteilungen* 105, no. 4 (2004): 395–406.

Cohen-Hanegbi, Naama. "Postpartum Mental Distress in Late Medieval Europe." *Mediæval Journal* 9, no. 1 (2019): 109–41.

Coldstream, Nicola. "The Roles of Women in Late Medieval Civic Pageantry in England." In *Reassessing the Roles of Women as "Makers" of Medieval Art and Architecture*, edited by Therese Martin, 1:175–94. Leiden: Brill, 2012.

Colomer, José Luis. "Black and the Royal Image." In *Spanish Fashion at the Courts of Early Modern Europe*, edited by José Luis Colomer and Amalia Descalzo, 1:77–112. Madrid: Centro de Estudios Europa Hispánica, 2014.

Cristo González Marrero, María del. "El calzado y su manufactura en Tenerife en la primera mitad del siglo XVI." *Revista de historia canaria* (1996): 93–105.

———. "El vestido, su tipología, y su significación social y económica: El caso de Tenerife tras su incorporación a la Corona de Castilla." In *IX Coloquio de Historia Canario-Americana*, edited by Francisco Morales Padrón, 291–308. Las Palmas de Gran Canaria: Cabildo Insular de Gran Canaria, 1994.

Cunningham, Sean. "Katherine of Aragon and an Army for the North in 1513." London: The National Archives blog: https://blog.nationalarchives.gov.uk/katherine-of-aragon-and-an-army-for-the-north-in-1513/

———. *Prince Arthur: The Tudor King Who Never Was.* Stroud: Amberley, 2016.

Currin, John. "England's International Relations, 1485–1509: Continuities Amidst Change." In *Tudor England and Its Neighbours*, edited by Susan Doran and Glenn Richardson, 14–43. New York: Palgrave Macmillan, 2005.

David-Chapy, Aubrée. "The Political, Symbolic, and Courtly Power of Anne de France and Louise de Savoie." In *Women and Power at the French Court, 1483–1563*, edited by Susan Broomhall, 43–64. Amsterdam: Amsterdam University Press, 2018.

De Certeau, Michel. *The Practice of Everyday Life.* Translated by Steven F. Rendall. Berkeley: University of California Press, 1984.

D'Elboux, R. H. "Pre-Reformation Vestments in Catholic Churches in Monmouthshire." *Archaeological Journal* 81 (1924): 21–30.

Dewhurst, John. "The Alleged Miscarriages of Catherine of Aragon and Anne Boleyn." *Medical History* 28 (1984): 49–56.

Dickinson, J. C. *The Shrine of Our Lady at Walsingham*. Cambridge: Cambridge University Press, 1956.

Dillon, Anne. "Praying by Number: The Confraternity of the Rosary and the English Catholic Community, c. 1580–1700." *History* 88, no. 3 (2003): 451–71.

Dillon, Janette. "Powerful Obedience: Godly Queen Hester and Katherine of Aragon." In *Interludes and Early Modern Society*, edited by Peter Happé and Wim Hüsken, 117–39. Leiden: Brill, 2007.

Dolman, Brett. "Wishful Thinking: Reading the Portraits of Henry VIII's Queens." In *Henry VIII and the Court: Art, Politics, Performance*, edited by Thomas Betteridge and Suzannah Lipscomb, 115–29. Aldershot: Ashgate, 2013.

Domínguez Casas, Rafael. "The Artistic Patronage of Isabel the Catholic: Medieval or Modern?" In *Queen Isabel I of Castile: Power, Patronage, Persona*, edited by Barbara Weissberger, 123–48. Woodbridge: Tamesis, 2008.

———. "Las Casas de las Reinas hispano-portuguesas de Juan II a los Reyes Católicos." In *Las relaciones discretas entre las Monarquías Hispana y Portuguesa: Las Casas de las Reinas (siglos XV–XIX)*, edited by José Martínez Millán and Maria Paula Marçal Lourenço, 233–74. Madrid: Ediciones Polifemo 1, 2008.

Dowling, Maria. *Humanism in the Age of Henry VIII*. London: Croom Helm, 1986.

———. "Humanist Support for Katherine of Aragon." *Bulletin of the Institute for Historical Research* 56 (1982): 46–55.

Dronzek, Anna. "Gendered Theories of Education in Fifteenth-Century Conduct Books." *Medieval Cultures* 29 (2001): 135–59.

Duffy, Eamon. *The Stripping of the Altars: Traditional Religion in England, 1400–1580*. New Haven: Yale University Press, 1992.

Dugan, Holly, and Lara Farina. "Intimate Senses / Sensing Intimacy." *Postmedieval: A Journal of Medieval Cultural Studies* 3, no. 4 (2012): 373–79.

Earenfight, Theresa. "A Lifetime of Power: Beyond Binaries of Gender." In *Medieval Elite Women and the Exercise of Power, 1100–1400: Moving Beyond the Exceptionalist Debate*, edited by Heather Tanner, 271–93. Cham, Switzerland: Palgrave Macmillan, 2019.

———. "A Precarious Household: Catherine of Aragon in England, 1501–1504." In *Royal and Elite Households in Medieval and Early Modern Europe*, edited by Theresa Earenfight, 338–56. Leiden: Brill, 2018.

———. "Raising *Infanta* Catalina de Aragón to Be Catherine, Queen of England." *Anuario de Estudios Medievales* 46, no. 1 (2016): 417–43.

———. "Regarding Catherine of Aragon." In *Scholars and Poets Talk About Queens*, edited by Carole Levin and Christine Stewart-Nuñez, 137–57. Basingstoke: Palgrave Macmillan, 2015.

———. "The Shoes of an *Infanta*: Bringing the Sensuous, Not Sensible, 'Spanish Style' of Catherine of Aragon to Tudor England." In *Moving Women Moving Objects*, edited by Tracy Chapman Hamilton and Mariah Proctor-Tiffany, 293–317. Leiden: Brill, 2019.

———. "Two Bodies, One Spirit: Isabel and Fernando's Construction of Monarchical Partnership." In *Queen Isabel I of Castile: Power, Patronage, Persona,* edited by Barbara Weissberger, 3–18. Woodbridge: Boydell and Brewer, 2008.

Eichenberger, Dagmar. "Margareta of Austria, A Princess with Ambition and Political Insight." In *Women of Distinction: Margaret of York, Margaret of Austria*, edited by Dagmar Eichenberger, 49–55. Turnhout: Brepols, 2005.

———. "Playing Games: Men, Women, and Beasts on the Backgammon Board for King Ferdinand I and Queen Anna of Bohemia and Hungary." In *Women at the Burgundian Court: Presence and Influence*, edited by Dagmar Eichenberger, Anne-Marie Legaré, and Wim Hüsken, 123–39. Turnhout: Brepols. 2010.

Elston, Timothy. "Almost the Perfect Woman: Public and Private Expectations of Catherine of Aragon, 1501–1536." PhD diss., University of Nebraska–Lincoln, 2004.

———. "Transformation or Continuity? Sixteenth-Century Education and the Legacy of Catherine of Aragon, Mary I and Juan Luis Vives." In *"High and Mighty Queens" of Early Modern England: Realities and Representations*, edited by Carole Levin, Jo Eldridge Carney, and Debra Barrett-Graves, 11–26. New York: Palgrave Macmillan, 2003.

———. "'Widow Princess or Neglected Queen?' Catherine of Aragon, Henry VIII, and English Public Opinion, 1533–1536." In *Queens and Power in Medieval and Early Modern England*, edited by Carol Levin and Robert O. Bucholz, 16–30. Lincoln: University of Nebraska Press, 2009.

Evans, Joan. *English Jewellery from the Fifth Century A.D. to 1800*. London: Metheun, 1921.

Fernández de Córdova Miralles, Álvaro. *La Corte de Isabel I: Ritos y ceremonias de una reina 1474–1504*. Madrid: Dykinson, 2002.

Finn, Kavita Mudan. *The Last Plantagenet Consorts*. Basingstoke: Palgrave Macmillan, 2012.

Foucault, Michel. *The History of Sexuality*. Vol. 1. Trans. Robert Hurley. New York: Random House, 1978.

Fraser, Antonia. *The Wives of Henry VIII*. New York: Random House, 1994.

French, Katherine L. "Genders and Material Culture." In *The Oxford Handbook of Women and Gender in Medieval Europe*, edited by Judith Bennett and Ruth Mazo Karras, 197–212. Oxford: Oxford University Press, 2013.

———. "'I Leave My Best Gown as a Vestment': Women's Spiritual Interests in the Late Medieval English Parish." *Magistra* 4, no. 1 (1998): 57–77.

———. "The Material Culture of Childbirth in Late Medieval London and Its Suburbs." *Journal of Women's History* 28, no. 2 (2016): 126–48.

Froude, James Anthony. *The Divorce of Catherine of Aragon: The Story as Told by the Imperial Ambassadors Resident at the Court of Henry VIII*. London: Longmans Green, 1891.

Frye, Susan. *Pens and Needles: Women's Textualities in Early Modern England*. Philadelphia: University of Pennsylvania Press, 2010.

———. "Sewing Connections: Elizabeth Tudor, Mary Stuart, Elizabeth Talbot, and Seventeenth-Century Anonymous Needleworkers." In *Maids and Mistresses, Cousins and Queens: Women's Alliances in Early Modern England*, edited by Susan Frye and Karen Robertson, 165–82. Oxford: Oxford University Press, 1999.

Fuchs, Barbara. *Exotic Nation: Maurophilia and the Construction of Early Modern Spain*. Philadelphia: University of Pennsylvania Press, 2011.

Furdell, Elizabeth Lane. *The Royal Doctors, 1485–1714: Medical Personnel at the*

Tudor and Stuart Courts. Rochester: University of Rochester Press, 2001.

Garver, Valerie L. "Material Culture and Social History in Early Medieval Western Europe." *History Compass* 12 (2014): 784–93.

Gerritsen, Anne, and Giorgio Riello. "Introduction: Writing Material Culture History." In *Writing Material Culture History*, edited by Anne Gerritsen and Giorgio Riello, 1–13. London: Bloomsbury, 2014.

Glanville, Philippa. "The Howard Grace Cup." *History Today* 44, no. 10 (1994): 41–45.

Goff, Cecilie. *A Woman of the Tudor Age*. London: John Murray, 1930.

Gómez Molleda, María Dolores. "La cultura feminina en la época de Isabel la Católica." *Revista de Archivos, Bbibliotecas y Museos* 61 (1955): 137–91.

González Arévalo, Raúl. "Francesco Grimaldi, un mercader-banquero genovés entre Granada, la Corte e Inglaterra (siglos XV–XVI)." *En la España Medieval* 39 (2016): 97–126.

Goodwin, George. *Fatal Rivalry: Flodden 1513, Henry VIII, James IV, and the Battle for Renaissance Britain*. New York: W. W. Norton, 2013.

Green, Monica. "From 'Diseases of Women' to 'Secrets of Women': The Transformation of Gynecological Literature in the Later Middle Ages." *Journal of Medieval and Early Modern Studies* 30, no. 1 (2000): 5–39.

Gregory, Philippa. *Three Sisters, Three Queens*. New York: Simon and Schuster, 2017.

Grosvenor, Bendor. "Happy Birthday Katherine of Aragon." *Art History News*, 16 December 2011. https://arthistorynews.com/articles/897_Happy_birthday_Katherine_of_Aragon. Accessed 2 September 2020.

———. "Henry VIII's Queens." In *Lost Faces: Identity and Discovery in Tudor Royal Portraiture*, edited by David Starkey, Bendor Grosvenor, and Alasdair Hawkyard, 70–75, 109–24. London: Philip Mould, 2007.

Gunn, Steven J. *Charles Brandon, Duke of Suffolk, 1484–1545*. Oxford: Oxford University Press, 1988.

Guy, John. *The Public Career of Sir Thomas More*. Brighton: Harvester Press, 1980.

———. "Wolsey and the Tudor Policy." In *The Tudor Monarchy*, edited by John Guy, 308–29. London: Arnold, 1997.

Hamilton, Tracy Chapman, and Mariah Proctor-Tiffany, eds. *Moving Women Moving Objects (400–1500)*. Leiden: Brill, 2019.

———. "Women and the Circulation of Material Culture: Crossing Boundaries and Connecting Spaces." In *Moving Women Moving Objects (400–1500)*, edited by Tracy Chapman Hamilton and Mariah Proctor-Tiffany, 1–12. Leiden: Brill, 2019.

Hamling, Tara, and Catherine Richardson, eds. *Everyday Objects: Medieval and Early Modern Material Culture and Its Meanings*. Farnham: Palgrave, 2010.

Hand, John Oliver, and Greta Koppel with Till-Holger Borchert, Anu Mänd, Ariane van Suchtelen, and Matthias Weniger. *Michel Sittow: Estonian Painter at the Courts of Renaissance Europe*. Washington, DC: National Gallery of Art, 2018.

Hansen, Matthew C. "'And a Queen of England, Too'": The 'Englishing' of Catherine of Aragon in Sixteenth-Century English Literary and Chronicle History." In *"High and Mighty Queens" of Early Modern England: Realities and Representations*, edited by Carole Levin, Jo Eldridge Carney, and Debra Barrett-Graves, 79–99. New York: Palgrave Macmillan, 2003.

Harris, Barbara. *Edward Stafford, Third Duke of Buckingham, 1478–1521.* Stanford: Stanford University Press, 1986.

———. *English Aristocratic Women, 1450–1550: Marriage and Family, Property and Careers.* Oxford: Oxford University Press, 2002.

———. "Marriage, Sixteenth-Century Style: Elizabeth Stafford and the Third Duke of Norfolk." *Journal of Social History* 15 (1982): 371–82.

———. "The Trial of the Third Duke of Buckingham—A Revisionist View." *American Journal of Legal History* 20, no. 1 (1976): 15–26.

———. "The View from My Lady's Chamber: New Perspectives on Early Tudor Monarchy." *Huntington Library Quarterly* 60, no. 3 (1997): 215–47.

Hayward, Maria, ed. *Dress at the Court of King Henry VIII.* Leeds: Maney, 2007.

———. "Fashion, Finance, Foreign Politics, and the Wardrobe of Henry VIII." In *Clothing Culture, 1350–1650,* edited by Catherine Richardson, 165–78. London: Routledge, 2017.

———. "Gift Giving at the Court of Henry VIII: The 1539 New Year's Gift Roll in Context." *Antiquaries Journal* 85 (2005): 125–75.

———. "Reflections on Gender and Status Distinctions: An Analysis of the Liturgical Textiles Recorded in Mid-Sixteenth-Century London." *Gender and History* 14, no. 3 (2002): 403–25.

———. "Spanish Princess or Queen of England? The Image, Identity and Influence of Catherine of Aragon at the Courts of Henry VII and Henry VIII." In *Dressing the Spanish in the European Courts (XVI and XVII centuries),* edited by José Luis Colomer and Amalia Descalzo, 2:11–36. Madrid: Centro de Estudios Europa Hispánica, 2014.

Haywood, Louise M. "The Princess and the Unicorn: Arthur, Prince of Wales, and Catherine of Aragon?" In *The Medieval Mind: Hispanic Studies in Honour of Alan Deyermond,* edited by Alan David Deyermond, Ian Richard Mac Pherson, and Ralph John Penny, 189–204. Woodbridge: Tamesis, 1997.

Heal, Felicity. "Food Gifts, the Household, and the Politics of Exchange in Early Modern England." *Past and Present* 199 (2008): 41–70.

———. *Hospitality in Early Modern England.* Oxford: Clarendon Press, 1990.

———. *The Power of Gifts: Gift Exchange in Early Modern England.* Oxford: Oxford University Press, 2014.

Heng, Geraldine. *The Invention of Race in the European Middle Ages.* Cambridge: Cambridge University Press, 2018.

Hentschell, Rose. "A Question of Nation: Foreign Clothes on the English Subject." In *Clothing Culture, 1350–1650,* edited by Catherine Richardson, 49–62. London: Routledge, 2017.

Hepburn, Frederick. "The Portraiture of Prince Arthur and Katharine of Aragon." In *Arthur Tudor, Prince of Wales,* edited by Steven Gunn and Linda Monckton, 31–49. Woodbridge: Boydell, 2009.

Hillgarth, J. N. *The Mirror of Spain, 1500–1700: The Formation of a Myth.* Ann Arbor: University of Michigan Press, 2000.

Hirsh, John C. "The Twenty-Five Joys of Our Lady: An English Marian Rosary of the Fifteenth Century from the Bodleian Library MS Don. d. 85." *Traditio* 71 (2016): 333–42.

Howes, David. "The Cultural Life of the Senses." *Postmedieval* 3, no. 4 (2012): 450–54.

Hunt, Alice. *The Drama of Coronation: Medieval Ceremony in Early Modern*

England. Cambridge: Cambridge University Press, 2008.

Hurren, Elizabeth T. "Cultures of the Body, Medical Regimen, and Physic at the Tudor Court." In *Henry VIII and the Court: Art, Politics, Performance*, edited by Thomas Betteridge and Suzannah Lipscomb, 65–89. Aldershot: Ashgate, 2013.

Ishikawa, Chiyo. "*La llave de palo*: Isabel la Católica as Patron of Religious Literature and Painting." In *Isabel la Católica, Queen of Castile: Critical Essays*, edited by David A. Boruchoff, 103–19. New York: Palgrave Macmillan, 2003.

———. *The Retablo de Isabel la Católica by Juan de Flandes and Michel Sittow*. Turnhout: Brepols, 2004.

Ives, Eric W. *The Life and Death of Anne Boleyn*. Oxford: Blackwell, 2004.

James, Susan E. *The Feminine Dynamic in English Art, 1485–1603*. Farnham: Ashgate, 2009.

Johnston, Hope. "Catherine of Aragon's Pomegranate Revisited." *Transactions of the Cambridge Bibliographic Society* 13, no. 2 (2005): 153–73.

Johnston, Lucy, and Linda Woolley. *Shoes: A Brief History*. London: V&A, 1999.

Jones, Ann R., and Peter Stallybrass, *Renaissance Clothing and the Materials of Memory*. Cambridge: Cambridge University Press, 2000.

Jones, Michael K., and Malcolm G. Underwood. *The King's Mother: Lady Margaret Beaufort, Countess of Richmond and Derby*. Cambridge: Cambridge University Press, 1992.

Jurkowlaniec, Grażyna, Ika Matyjaszkiewicz, and Zuzanna Sarnecka, eds. *The Agency of Things in Medieval and Early Modern Art: Materials Power, and Manipulation*. New York: Routledge, 2017.

Kane, Bronach C. *Popular Memory and Gender in Medieval England: Men, Women, and Testimony in the Church Courts, c. 1200–1500*. Woodbridge: Boydell and Brewer, 2019.

Keane, Marguerite. *Material Culture and Queenship in Fourteenth-Century France: The Testament of Blanche of Navarre (1331–1398)*. Leiden: Brill, 2016.

———. "Moving Possessions and Secure Posthumous Reputation: The Gifts of Jeanne of Burgundy (ca. 1293–1349). In *Moving Women Moving Objects (400–1500)*, edited by Tracy Chapman Hamilton and Mariah Proctor-Tiffany, 228–46. Leiden: Brill, 2019.

Kelly, Henry Ansgar. *The Matrimonial Trials of Henry VIII*. Stanford: Stanford University Press, 1976.

Kelly, Stephen. "In the Sight of an Old Pair of Shoes." In *Everyday Objects: Medieval and Early Modern Material Culture and Its Meanings*, edited by Tara Hamling and Catherine Richardson, 57–70. Farnham: Palgrave, 2010.

King, John. "Patronage and Piety: The Influence of Catherine Parr." In *Silent but for the Word: Tudor Women as Patrons, Translators, and Writers of Religious Works*, edited by Margaret P. Hannay, 43–60. Kent: Kent State University Press, 1985.

Kipling, Gordon. *Enter the King: Theatre, Liturgy, and Ritual in the Medieval Civic Triumph*. Oxford: Clarendon Press, 1998.

Kisby, Fiona. "Kingship and the Royal Itinerary: A Study of the Peripatetic Household of the Early Tudor Kings, 1485–1547." *Court Historian* 4 (1999): 29–39.

Knighton, Tess. "Isabel of Castile and Her Music Books: Franco-Flemish Song in Fifteenth-Century Spain." In *Queen Isabel I of Castile: Power, Patronage, Persona*, edited by Barbara F. Weissberger, 29–52. Woodbridge: Tamesis, 2008.

———. "Northern Influence on Cultural Developments in the Iberian Peninsula During the Fifteenth Century." *Renaissance Studies* 1, no. 2 (June 1987): 221–37.

Lambert, Bart, and Katherine Wilson, eds. *Europe's Rich Fabric: The Consumption, Commercialization, and Production of Luxury Textiles in Italy, the Low Countries, and Neighboring Territories (Fourteenth–Sixteenth Centuries)*. Farnham: Ashgate, 2016.

Lancashire, Anne. *London Civic Theatre: City Drama and Pageantry from Roman Times to 1558*. Cambridge: Cambridge University Press, 2002.

Laynesmith, J. L. *The Last Medieval Queens: English Queenship, 1445–1503*. Oxford: Oxford University Press, 2004.

Lee, Becky R. "The Purification of Women After Childbirth: A Window onto Medieval Perceptions of Women." *Florilegium* 14 (1995–96): 43–55.

Lehfeldt, Elizabeth. "Ruling Sexuality: The Political Legitimacy of Isabel of Castile." *Renaissance Quarterly* 53 (2000): 31–56.

L'Estrange, Elizabeth. *Holy Motherhood: Gender, Dynasty, and Visual Culture in the Later Middle Ages*. Manchester: Manchester University Press, 2008.

Liss, Peggy. *Isabel the Queen: Life and Times*. 2nd ed. Philadelphia: University of Pennsylvania Press, 2004.

Lloyd, Paul S. "Dietary Advice and Fruit-Eating in Late Tudor and Early Stuart England." *Journal of the History of Medicine and Allied Sciences* 67, no. 4 (2012): 553–86.

Loades, David M. *Mary Tudor: A Life*. Oxford: Blackwell, 1989.

———. *The Tudor Court*. London: Batsford, 1986.

Lowe, Nicola. "Women's Devotional Bequests of Textiles in the Late Medieval English Parish Church,

c. 1350–1550." *Gender and History* 22, no. 2 (2010): 407–29.

Luke, Mary. *Catherine, the Queen*. New York: Coward-McCann, 1967.

Marino, Nancy. "How Portuguese Damas Scandalized the Court of Enrique IV of Castile." *Essays in Medieval Studies* 18 (2001): 43–52.

Marlow, Toby and Lucy Moss. *Six: The Musical*. Edinburgh: Edinburgh Fringe, 2017.

Marshall, Peter. *Religious Identities in Henry VIII's England*. London: Routledge, 2006.

Martin, Therese. "The Margin to Act: A Framework of Investigation for Women's (and Men's) Medieval Art-Making." In "'Me fecit': Making Medieval Art (History)," special issue, *Journal of Medieval History* 42 (2016): 1–25.

Martz, Linda. *Poverty and Welfare in Habsburg Spain*. Cambridge: Cambridge University Press, 1983.

Matheson-Pollock, Helen, Joanne Paul, and Catherine Fletcher, eds. *Queenship and Counsel in Early Modern Europe*. Basingstoke: Palgrave Macmillan, 2018.

Matthews, Paul G. "Henry VIII's Favorite Sister? Michel Sittow's Portrait of a Lady in Vienna." *Jahrbuch des Kunsthistorischen Museums Wein* 10 (2008): 140–49.

Mattingly, Garrett. *Catherine of Aragon*. Boston: Little, Brown, 1941.

Mazzola, Elizabeth. "Schooling Shrews and Grooming Queens in the Tudor Classroom." *Critical Survey* 22, no. 1 (2010): 1–25.

McIntosh, Jeri. *From Heads of Household to Heads of State: The Preaccession Households of Mary and Elizabeth Tudor, 1516–1558*. New York: Columbia University Press, 2009.

Mecham, June L. *Sacred Communities, Shared Devotions: Gender, Material Culture, and Monasticism in Late

Medieval Germany. Edited by Alison I. Beach, Constance Berman, and Lisa Bitel. Turnhout: Brepols, 2014.

Meyer, Allison Machlis. "The Politics of Queenship in Francis Bacon's *The History of the Reign of King Henry VII* and John Ford's *Perkin Warbeck*." *Studies in Philology* 111, no. 2 (2014): 312–45.

———. "*Richard III*'s Forelives: Rewriting Elizabeth(s) in Tudor Historiography." *Medieval and Renaissance Drama in England* 26 (2013): 156–83.

Miller, Peter N., ed. *Cultural Histories of the Material World*. Ann Arbor: University of Michigan Press, 2013.

Monnas, Lisa. *Merchants, Princes, and Painters: Silk Fabrics in Italian and Northern Paintings, 1300–1550*. New Haven: Yale University Press, 2008.

———. *Renaissance Velvets*. London: V&A, 2012.

Morrison, Susan Signe. *Women Pilgrims in Late Medieval England: Private Piety as Public Performance*. London: Routledge, 2000.

Mueller, Janel. "A Tudor Queen Finds Voice: Katherine Parr's Lamentation of a Sinner." In *The Historical Renaissance: New Essays on Tudor and Stuart Literature and Culture*, edited by Heather Dubrow and Richard Strier, 15–47. Chicago: University of Chicago Press, 1988.

Muñoz Fernández, Ángela. "Notas para la definición de un modelo sociorreligioso femenino: Isabel de Castilla." In *Las Mujeres en el cristianismo medieval: Imágenes teóricas y cauces de actuación religiosa*, edited by Angela Muñoz Fernandez, 415–34. Madrid: Marcial Pons, 1989.

Nickson, Tom. *Toledo Cathedral: Building Histories in Medieval Castile*. University Park: Penn State University Press, 2015.

Okerlund, Arlene Naylor. *Elizabeth of York*. Basingstoke: Palgrave Macmillan, 2009.

Orlin, Leah Cowen. "Empty Vessels." In *Everyday Objects: Medieval and Early Modern Material Culture and Its Meanings*, edited by Tara Hamling and Catherine Richardson, 299–308. Farnham: Palgrave, 2010.

———. *Private Matters and Public Culture in Post-Reformation England*. Ithaca: Cornell University Press, 1994.

Overbey, Karen. "Materiality and Place in a Medieval Scottish Pendant Reliquary." *RES: Anthropology and Aesthetics* 65/66 (2014/15): 242–58.

Parks, Annette P. "Rescuing the Maidens from the Tower: Recovering the Stories of Female Political Hostages." In *Feud, Violence and Practice: Essays in Medieval Studies in Honor of Stephen D. White*, edited by Belle S. Tuten and Tracey L. Billado, 279–92. Burlington, VT: Ashgate, 2010.

Patterson, Annabel. *Reading Holinshed's "Chronicles."* Chicago: University of Chicago Press, 1994.

Petti, Erin. "Music Manuscripts at the Court of Henry VIII." MA thesis, Newcastle University, 2020.

Phillips, William D. *Enrique IV and the Crisis of Fifteenth-Century Castile (1425–1480)*. Cambridge: Medieval Academy of America, 1978.

Pierce, Hazel. *Margaret Pole, Countess of Salisbury, 1473–1541*. Cardiff: University of Wales Press, 2003.

Pollard, A. F. *Henry VIII*. London: Longman Green, 1925.

Portilla, M. J. "Un vitoriano en la corte de Carlos V." *Boletín de la Institución Sancho el Sabio* 8, nos. 1–2 (1964): 121–60.

Proctor-Tiffany, Mariah. *Medieval Art in Motion: The Inventory and Gift Giving of Queen Clémence de Hongrie*. University Park: Penn State University Press, 2019.

Rhodes, Dennis E. "Count Lodovico Nogarola and the Divorce of Catherine of Aragon." *British Library Journal* 16, no. 1 (1990): 100–2.

Richards, Judith. *Mary Tudor*. London: Routledge, 2008.
———. "'To Promote a Woman to Beare Rule': Talking of Queens in Mid-Tudor England." *Sixteenth Century Journal* 28 (1997): 101–21.
Richardson, Glenn. "'As Presence Did Present Them': Personal Gift-Giving at the Field of the Cloth of Gold." In *Henry VIII and the Court: Art, Politics, Performance*, edited by Thomas Betteridge and Suzannah Lipscomb, 47–63. Aldershot: Ashgate, 2013.
———. *The Field of the Cloth of Gold*. New Haven: Yale University Press, 2014.
Rieder, Paula. *On the Purification of Women: Churching in Northern France, 1100–1500*. New York: Palgrave, 2006.
Riello, Giorgio, and Peter MacNeil, eds. *Shoes: A History from Sandals to Sneakers*. Oxford: Oxford University Press, 2006.
Ringbom, Sixten. "Devotional Images and Imaginative Devotions: Notes on the Place of Art in Late Medieval Private Piety." *Gazette des beaux-arts* 73, no. 6 (1969): 159–70.
Rohr, Zita. "Lessons for My Daughter: Self-Fashioning Stateswomanship in the Late Medieval Crown of Aragon." In *Self-Fashioning and Assumptions of Identity in Medieval and Early Modern Iberia*, edited by Laura Delbrugge, 46–78. Leiden: Brill, 2015.
Romanelli, Susan J. "South Netherlandish Boxwood Devotional Sculpture, 1475–1530." PhD diss., Columbia University, 1992.
Ros-Fábregas, Emilio. "Melodies for Private Devotion at the Court of Queen Isabel." In *Queen Isabel I of Castile: Power, Patronage, Persona*, edited by Barbara F. Weissberger, 83–107. Woodbridge, Tamesis, 2008.
Rubin, Nancy. *Isabella of Castile: The First Renaissance Queen*. New York: St. Martin's Press, 1992.

Ruggles, D. Fairchild. "The Alcázar of Seville and Mudejar Architecture." *Gesta* 43, no. 2 (2004): 87–98.
———. *Gardens, Landscape, and Vision in the Palaces of Islamic Spain*. University Park: Penn State University Press, 2000.
Ruiz, Teofilo. *A King Travels: Festive Traditions in Late Medieval and Early Modern Spain*. Princeton: Princeton University Press, 2012.
Rumeu de Armas, Antonio. *Itinerario de los Reyes Católicos, 1474–1516*. Madrid: Consejo Superior de Investigaciones Científicas, 1974.
Sadlack, Erin A. *The French Queen's Letters: Mary Tudor Brandon and the Politics of Marriage in Sixteenth-Century Europe*. New York: Palgrave Macmillan, 2011.
Samman, Neil. "The Progresses of Henry VIII, 1509–1529." In *The Reign of Henry VIII: Politics, Policy, and Piety*, edited by Diarmadd MacCullough, 59–73, 259–62. Basingstoke: Palgrave Macmillan, 1995.
Sánchez Cantón, Francisco Javier. *Libros, Tapices y Cuadros que Coleccionó Isabel la Católica*. Madrid: Consejo Superior de Investigaciones Científicas, 1950.
Scarisbrick, Diana. *Rings: Symbols of Wealth, Power, and Affection*. New York: Harry N. Abrams, 1993.
Scarisbrick, J. J. *Henry VIII*. Berkeley: University of California Press, 1968; rev. ed., 1997.
Schjeldahl, Peter. "Beheld." *The New Yorker*, 23 September 2019, 69. Published online as "The Amy Sherald Effect," *The New Yorker*, 16 September 2019, https://www.newyorker.com/magazine/2019/09/23/the-amy-sherald-effect.
Schofield, John. *London, 1100–1600: The Archaeology of a Capital City*. Sheffield: Equinox, 2011.

———. *Medieval London Houses*. 2nd ed. New Haven: Yale University Press, 2003.

Scholten, Frits, ed. *Small Wonders: Late-Gothic Boxwood Micro-Carving from the Low Countries*. Amsterdam: Rijksmuseum, 2017.

Schutte, Valerie. "'To the Illustrious Queen': Katherine of Aragon and Early Modern Book Dedications." In *Women During the English Reformations: Renegotiating Gender and Religious Identity*, edited by Julie A. Chappell and Kaely A. Kramer, 15–28. Basingstoke: Palgrave Macmillan, 2014.

Scott, Rachel, and Annie Ablett. "Henry and Katherine Reunited: Conserving the Portrait of Katherine of Aragon." National Portrait Gallery, London. https://www.npg.org.uk/research /conservation/henry-and-katherine -reunited-conserving-the-portrait -of-katherine-of-aragon#back ground.

Seabourne, Gwen. *Imprisoning Medieval Women: The Non-Judicial Confinement and Abduction of Women in England, c.1170–1509*. London: Routledge, 2016.

Semmelhack, Elizabeth. "Above the Rest: Chopines as Trans-Mediterranean Fashion." *Journal of Spanish Cultural Studies* 14, no. 2 (2013): 120–42.

———. *On a Pedestal: From Renaissance Chopines to Baroque Heels*. Toronto: Bata Shoe Museum, 2009.

———. "Reveal or Conceal: Chopines and the Display of Material Wealth in Early Modern Valencia and Venice." In *The Matter of Art: Materials, Practices, Cultural Logics, c. 1250–1750*, edited by Christy Anderson, Anne Dunlop, and Pamela H. Smith, 283–308. Manchester: Manchester University Press, 2015.

Shears, Helen. "Like Father, Like Daughter? Redefining Regency in Margaret of Austria's Correspondence with Emperor Maximilian I, 1506–1519." MA thesis, University of Chicago, 2013.

Silleras Fernández, Núria. *Chariots of Ladies: Francesc Eiximenis and the Court Culture of Medieval and Early Modern Iberia*. Ithaca: Cornell University Press, 2015.

Silva Maroto, Pilar. *Juan de Flandes*. Madrid: Caja Duero, 2006.

Smail, Daniel Lord. *Legal Plunder: Households and Debt Collection in Late Medieval Europe*. Cambridge, MA: Harvard University Press, 2016.

Smith, Bruce. "Premodern Sexualities." *PMLA* 115 (2000): 318–29.

Stanton, Anne Rudloff. "The Personal Geography of a Dowager Queen: Isabella of France and Her Inventory." In *Moving Women Moving Objects (400–1500)*, edited by Tracy Chapman Hamilton and Mariah Proctor-Tiffany, 205–27. Leiden: Brill, 2019.

Starkey, David. "Court and Government." In *The Tudor Monarchy*, edited by John Guy, 189–213. London: Arnold, 1997.

———. *Six Wives: The Queens of Henry VIII*. New York: HarperCollins, 2003.

Stevens, John. *Music and Poetry in the Early Tudor Court*. Lincoln: University of Nebraska Press, 1961.

Streitberger, W. R. *Court Revels, 1485–1559*. Toronto: University of Toronto Press, 1994.

Strong, Roy. *The English Renaissance Miniature*. London: Thames and Hudson, 1983.

———. *Splendour at Court: Renaissance Spectacle and Illusion*. London: Weidenfeld and Nicholson, 1973.

Suárez-Fernández, Luis. *Los Trastámaras y los Reyes Católicos*. Madrid: Gredos, 1985.

Suda, Alexandra, and Barbara Drake Boehm. "Handpicked: Collecting Boxwood Carvings from the

Sixteenth to the Twenty-First Centuries." In *Small Wonders: Late-Gothic Boxwood Micro-Carving from the Low Countries*, edited by Frits Scholten, 340–51. Amsterdam: Rijksmuseum, 2017.

Surtz, Ronald E. "In Search of Juana de Mendoza." In *Power and Gender in Renaissance Spain*, edited by Helen Nader, 48–70. Urbana: University of Illinois Press, 2008.

Synge, Lanto. *Art of Embroidery: History of Style and Technique*. London: Antique Collectors Club, 2005.

Thomas, Jennifer. "Patronage and Personal Narrative in a Music Manuscript: Marguerite of Austria, Katherine of Aragon, and London Royal 8 G.vii." In *Musical Voices of Early Modern Women: Many-Headed Melodies*, edited by Thomasin LaMay, 337–64. Aldershot: Ashgate, 2005.

Thurley, Simon. *The Royal Palaces of Tudor England*. New Haven: Yale University Press, 1993.

Travitsky, Betty S. "Reprinting Tudor History: The Case of Catherine of Aragon." *Renaissance Quarterly* 50, no. 1 (1997): 164–74.

Tremlett, Giles. *Catherine of Aragon: Henry's Spanish Queen*. London: Faber and Faber, 2010.

Val Valdivieso, María Isabel del. "La educación en la corte de la Reina Católica." *Miscelánea Comillas: Revista de Ciencias Humanas y Sociales* 69, no. 134 (2011): 255–73.

———. "Isabel la Católica y la educación." *Aragón en la Edad Media* 19 (2006): 555–62.

Viera, David J. "Francesc Eiximenis on Women: Complementary or Conflicting Views?" *Catalan Review* 17, no. 2 (2003): 193–204.

Wabuda, Susan. "Receiving the King: Henry VIII at Cambridge." In *Henry VIII and the Court: Art, Politics, Performance*, edited by Thomas

Betteridge and Suzannah Lipscomb, 163–78. Aldershot: Ashgate, 2013.

Walker, Alison Tara. "The Westminster Tournament Challenge (Harley 83 H 1) and Thomas Wriothesley's Workshop." *British Library Journal* (2011). https://www.bl.uk/eblj/2011articles/pdf/ebljarticle92011.pdf. Accessed 29 August 2020.

Walker, Greg. "'To Speak Before the King, It Is No Child's Play': Godly Queen Hester in 1529." *Theta* 10 (2013): 69–96.

Walker-Meikle, Kathleen. "Late Medieval Pet Keeping: Gender, Status, and Emotions." PhD diss., University of London, 2008.

Warnicke, Retha M. *Elizabeth of York and Her Six Daughters-in-Law: Fashioning Tudor Queenship, 1485–1547*. Basingstoke: Palgrave Macmillan, 2017.

Watson, Foster, ed. *Vives and the Renascence Education of Women*. New York: Longmans, Green, 1912.

Wayment, Hilary. "The East Window of St. Margaret's, Westminster." *Antiquaries Journal* 61 (1981): 292–301.

———. "Stained Glass in Henry VIII's Palaces." In *Henry VIII: A European Court in England*, edited by David Starkey, 28–31. London: Collins and Brown, 1991.

———. "Twenty-Four Videmuses from Cardinal Wolsey." *Master Drawings* 23 (1985–86): 503–7.

Weiner, Annette B. *Inalienable Possessions: The Paradox of Keeping-while-giving*. Berkeley: University of California Press, 1992.

Weir, Alison. *Katherine of Aragon, the True Queen*. New York: Ballantine, 2016.

Weiss, Jessica. "Isabel of Castile, Flemish Aesthetics, and Identity Construction in the Works of Juan de Flandes." PhD diss., University of Texas at Austin, 2014.

———. "Juan de Flandes and His Financial Success in Castile." *Journal of*

Historians of Netherlandish Art 11, no. 1 (2019). DOI: 10.5092/jhna .2019.11.1.2.

Weiss, Julian. "What Every Noblewoman Needs to Know: Cultural Literacy in Late-Medieval Spain." *Speculum* 81, no. 4 (2006): 1118–49.

Weissberger, Barbara. *Isabel Rules: Constructing Queenship, Wielding Power.* Minneapolis: University of Minnesota Press, 2004.

Weniger, Mattias. "Michel Sittow: An Artist's Career Between the Hanseatic City of Tallinn and the Princely Courts of Europe." In John Oliver Hand and Greta Koppel with Till-Holger Borchert, Anu Mänd, Ariane van Suchtelen, and Matthias Weniger, *Michel Sittow: Estonian Painter at the Courts of Renaissance Europe*, 27–37. Washington, DC: National Gallery of Art, 2018.

Wheatley, H. B. "Original Plan of Durham House, 1612." *London Topographical Record* 10 (1916): 150–62.

Whitley, Catrina Banks, and Kyra Kramer. "A New Explanation for the Reproductive Woes and Midlife Decline of Henry VIII." *Historical Journal* 53, no. 4 (2010): 827–48.

Wicker, Nancy. "Gold in Motion: Women and Jewelry from Early Medieval Scandinavia." In *Moving Women Moving Objects, 300–1500*, edited by Tracy Chapman Hamilton and Mariah Proctor-Tiffany, 13–32. Leiden: Brill, 2019.

Wieck, Roger S., William M. Voelkle, K. Michelle Hearne, eds. *The Hours of Henry VIII: A Renaissance Masterpiece by Jean Poyet.* New York: George Braziller, in association with the Pierpont Morgan Library, 2000.

Williams, Joseph M. "'O! When Degree Is Shak'd': Sixteenth-Century Anticipations of Some Modern Attitudes Toward Usage." In *English in Its Social Contexts: Essays in Historical Sociolinguistics*, edited by Tim William Machan and Charles T.

Scott, 69–101. Oxford: Oxford University Press, 1992.

Williams, Neville. *Henry VIII and His Court.* London: Weidenfeld and Nicholson, 1971.

Williams, Patrick. *Katharine of Aragon: The Tragic Story of Henry VIII's First Unfortunate Wife.* Stroud, UK: Amberley, 2013.

Wilson, C. Anne. "The Evolution of the Banquet Course: Some Medicinal, Culinary and Social Aspects." In *Banquetting Stuffe: The Fare and Social Background of the Tudor and Stuart Banquet*, edited by C. Anne Wilson, 9–35. Edinburgh: Edinburgh University Press, 1991.

Winston-Allen, Anne. *Stories of the Rose: The Making of the Rosary in the Middle Ages.* University Park: Penn State University Press, 1997.

Woolf, D. R. "A Feminine Past? Gender, Genre, and Historical Knowledge in England, 1500–1800." *American Historical Review* 102 (1997): 645–79.

Woolgar, Christopher M., Dale Serjeantson, and Tony Waldron, eds. *Food in Medieval England: Diet and Nutrition.* Oxford: Oxford University Press, 2006.

World Health Organization. "Stillbirth." https://www.who.int/maternal _child_adolescent/epidemiology /stillbirth/en. Accessed 29 August 2020.

Wunder, Amanda. "Women's Fashions and Politics in Seventeenth-Century Spain: The Rise and Fall of the *Guardainfante.*" *Renaissance Quarterly* 68, no. 1 (2015): 133–86.

Ziegler, Georgianna. "Re-Imagining a Renaissance Queen: Catherine of Aragon Among the Victorians." In *"High and Mighty Queens" of Early Modern England: Realities and Representations*, edited by Carole Levin, Jo Eldridge Carney, and Debra Barrett-Graves, 203–22. New York: Palgrave Macmillan, 2003.